BTEC

HNC HND *Business*

Core module five:

Organisational Structures and Processes

PUBLISHING

BTEC HNC & HND BUSINESS

First edition September 1996

ISBN 0 7517 7014 0

British Library Cataloguing-in Publication Data

A catalogue record for this book
is available from the British Library

Published by

BPP Publishing Limited
Aldine House, Aldine Place
London W12 8AW

Printed and bound by Progressive Printing (U.K.) Limited, Leigh-on-Sea, Essex.

Our thanks are due to:

Genesys Editorial for additional editorial and
production work

Contents

Preface

The HNC and HND qualifications in Business are very demanding. The suggested content, set out by BTEC in guidelines for each module, includes sophisticated topics which are normally only covered at degree level. Students therefore need books which get straight to the heart of these topics, and which relate them clearly to existing knowledge derived from school, college or work experience. BPP's series of textbooks is designed to meet that need.

The second edition of this book has been written specifically for Core Module 5: *Organisational structures and processes*. It covers the BTEC guidelines and suggested content in full, and includes the following features.

(a) The BTEC guidelines.

(b) A study guide, which explains the features of the book and how to get the most out of it.

(c) A glossary and index.

Each chapter contains:

(a) an introduction and study objectives;

(b) summary diagrams and signposts, to guide you through;

(c) numerous activities, topics for discussion and definitions;

(d) a chapter roundup, a quick quiz, answer guidelines to activities and an assignment (with answer guidelines at the end of the book).

BPP Publishing have for many years been the leading providers of targeted texts for professional qualifications. We know that our customers need to study effectively, and that they cannot afford to waste time. They expect clear, concise and highly-focused study material. With this new series, we are bringing the same high standards to the HNC and HND qualifications.

BPP Publishing
September 1996

Other titles in this series:

Core Module 1	Market Relations
Core Module 2	Operating Environment
Core Module 3	Managing People and Activities
Core Module 4	Managing Finance and Information
Core Module 6	Planning and Decision Making
Option Module 1	Financial Accounting Framework
Option Module 5	Marketing
Option Module 9	Personnel Management in the Organisation

For more information, or to place an order, please call 0181 740 2222

If you would like to send in your comments on this book,
please turn to the review form on the last page.

BTEC GUIDELINES FOR CORE MODULE 5

Organisational Structures and Processes

DESCRIPTION OF MODULE

This module will contribute towards students' analysis of, and effectiveness within, a range of work organisations. The module examines approaches to enhancing personal and organisational effectiveness through focusing on the internal nature of organisations, identifying alternative structures and common patterns of behaviour.

This module provides a framework for students to examine the varied and dynamic nature of organisations' structures and internal relations.

*This module has **four** sections.*

Section One: Identifying Structures

On completion of this section students will be able to:

- identify and describe different organisational structures
- evaluate the appropriateness of different organisational structures
- participate in the design of different structures to meet identified needs.

Suggested content

Types of organisation and associated structures: classifications of organisations; organisation charts; levels, span of control, formal and informal, line and staff, project teams and matrix; scale, purposes, interests, the influence of technology and organisational size.

Structural factors which influence success and failure of organisations: configuration; symptoms of efficient/deficient organisation; manifest functions, latent functions, dysfunctions; synergies and contradictions.

Establishing and designing organisations: the development of organisation theory and relevance to the modern context, questioning management paradigms; centralisation, decentralisation; structural integration and business functions.

Section Two: Changing Structures

On completion of this section students will be able to:

- identify different organisational environments
- analyse the relationship between different structures and an organisation's performance and development
- participate in the management of organisational change.

Suggested content

Different environments: placid-random, placid-clustered, disturbed-reactive and turbulent; influence of technological change and stability; configuration; contingency

Different structures: bureaucratic, functional, divisional, mechanistic, organic, matrix; stages of development; phases of growth and decline: evolution, revolution; expansion, consolidation, contraction; influence of technology; power; chaos theory and organisations; trends and development: franchising, flexible structures, home working.

Responding to change: sources of innovation; classification of control systems; driving and restraining forces; the management of organisational change through structures; contingency approach; technology and change.

Section Three: Communicating in Organisations

On completion of this section students will be able to:

● evaluate the effectiveness of different communication systems
● identify and evaluate relationships between organisation type and communication systems
● examine and evaluate the impact and implications of technology on communication and administrative systems
● communicate through formal and informal organisation channels using a variety of appropriate media
● make recommendations for improved organisational communication.

Suggested content

The media of communication: models of communication; formal and informal; advantages and disadvantages; communication channels and networks, formal and informal; controlling communication systems; the communication process and information and communication technology; criteria of efficiency/deficiency in communications; the relationship between organisation type and communication systems; type; structure, size, culture, stage of development.

Section Four: Identifying and Changing Organisational Culture

On completion of this section students will be able to:

● identify organisational cultures, rules and norms
● identify and analyse the factors which influence changing organisational cultures, rules and norms
● identify and evaluate the relationship between organisational cultures, structures and performance
● influence and adapt to organisational change.

Suggested content

Culture: formal, informal; positive, negative; backward-facing, forward-looking; autocratic, democratic; profit-driven, social responsibility; public image; tribal features; rules and codes of behaviour, sub-cultures; winning teams, winning departments; power, influence, tasks, working practices, co-operation, competition.

Influencing factors: history, ownership, size, technology, goals and objectives, external cultural environment; organisational ethics: product ethics, business practice, trading policies.

Influencing and adapting: managerial styles; authority and hierarchy; responsibility and freedom; group needs, task needs, individual needs; reactions to change: acceptance, resistance and conflict; force field analysis; quality circles, monitoring change, review and feedback, communication strategies, barriers to change, business sub-units, approaches and development of corporate culture, mission statement, charter approach.

Study Guide

As well as giving comprehensive coverage of the BTEC guidelines, this book includes several features which are designed specifically to make learning efficient. The features are these.

(a) At the start of each chapter, there is a summary diagram which maps out the ground covered by the chapter. There are more detailed summary diagrams at the start of each main section of each chapter, giving more detail on the contents of the section.

(b) After the summary diagram there is an introduction, which sets the chapter in context. This is followed by learning objectives, which show you what you will have achieved by the time you reach the end of the chapter.

(c) Throughout the text, there are special aids to learning. These are indicated by symbols in the margin as follows.

Signposts guide you through the text, showing how each section is connected with the next one.

Definitions give the meanings of key terms. The *glossary* at the end of the text consolidates these.

Activities allow you to consolidate and test your learning. An indication of the time required for each is given. Answers are given at the ends of the chapters.

For discussion points are for use in seminars. They give you a chance to share your views with your fellow students.

(d) The wide margin at the outside edge of each page is for your notes. You will get the best out of this book if you engage in a dialogue with it. Put in your own ideas. Many things in business are matters of opinion, so do not be afraid to disagree with what you read.

(e) At the end of each chapter, there is a chapter roundup and a quiz with answers. Use both of these to consolidate your knowledge. The chapter roundup summarises the chapter. The quiz tests what you have learnt (the answers often refer you back to the chapter so you can look over subjects again).

(f) There is an assignment at the end of each chapter, which will normally take you 1 – 3 hours to prepare. Answer guidelines are provided at the end of the text.

(g) The text ends with a glossary of key terms and an index.

Chapter 1

BUSINESS ORGANISATIONS

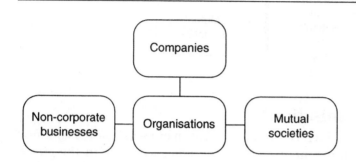

Introduction

We are surrounded by organisations. Even if you are curled up in bed reading this book several organisations are involved in making it possible for you to do so: the publishing company which produced it, the electricity company that lights your room, the firms that manufactured the bed, bed covers and other furnishings, the firms that built the house and decorated it, and the college and course that are causing you to read this book at all. You may have brought a drink to bed with you, courtesy of British Gas. You may regret not going to your sports club or the student union before you settled down to read – perhaps you didn't have the money to go because your grant cheque was late.

Organisations take many different forms: they may be in the *private* sector, in the *public sector*, or may operate on a *not-for profit basis. All* types of organisation have to communicate. They communicate with *external* agents such as suppliers, customers, shareholders and regulators, and, equally importantly, they communicate *internally* with staff or members. Communications pass through *formal* and *informal* channels; both these channels are equally important.

Your objectives

After completing this chapter you should:

(a) understand why organisations are necessary;

(b) be able to describe the various types of organisation in the private business sector;

(c) understand why different types of organisation have developed;

(d) appreciate the reasons for internal and external communication by businesses;

(e) recognise the difference between formal and informal communication channels.

First we shall look at what organisations are and why they exist.

1 ORGANISATIONS

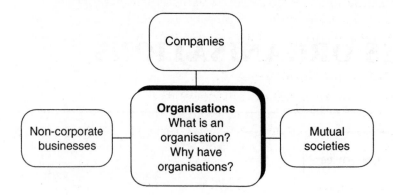

1.1 What is an organisation?

All sorts of organisation exist. Each is formed by a group of people with a common aim. Many of the organisations mentioned in the *Introduction* are in the *private sector*; that is, they are privately owned and exist primarily to make profits. Some private-sector organisations are *privatised* and *regulated* firms that used to be in the *public sector* (for example, British Gas and possibly your college). Organisations that are still in the public sector include local authorities. Still other organisations operate on a *not-for-profit* basis; these include clubs and charities.

Not all members of an organisation necessarily ever meet. For example, shareholders in a large public company may never attend the annual general meeting yet are bound together by their membership of the group. Many large charities such as Greenpeace have a common sense of identity and yet recruit contributors by post. Other groups may meet regularly; for example, football teams, aerobics clubs, staff in a supermarket, Post Office workers and Members of Parliament. All these are clearly recognisable as organisation groupings and you would be able to identify them.

Definition

Organisation: a clearly definable group of people who act together to achieve a common goal or set of objectives.

Membership of an organisation is defined by setting clear boundaries. Such boundaries may be paid employment, owning shares, paying a subscription or turning up at meetings.

Activity 1 [15 minutes]

(a) List all the organisations you have come across in the past two days. You may have:

- participated in them;
- used their services or products;
- heard or read about them.

(b) Now write down what kind of organisation you think each one is: profit making, voluntary, public service, subscription and so on.

You have seen how prevalent organisations are. We now look at why they are created.

1.2   Why have organisations?

We have seen that organisations exist to achieve a purpose. This overall purpose, or mission, is achieved by meeting a series of objectives. The mission is stated in broad, general terms and a hierarchy of objectives sets out specific actions.

Formal and informal organisations

People join in organisations because they can achieve more by co-operating with others than they can on their own. Informal groupings have to develop into a formal organisation if they are to be effective. Chester Barnard said that people had to accept a group purpose to co-ordinate their activities. A formal organisation comes into being when:

(a) people are willing to contribute to a common purpose;

(b) they communicate with each other.

People are prepared to co-operate because they accept the common purpose. Communication is essential to translate this purpose into action. The common purpose is achieved in practice through specific actions carried out by small subgroups of people called units. The size of a unit in an organisation depends on the complexity of its purpose and the technology it uses. Larger organisations consist of greater numbers of units.

EXAMPLE: BPP PUBLISHING

The employees of the publisher of this book accept that their common purpose is to publish books which will provide a return on the investment of the owners of BPP Publishing. To achieve that common purpose the company is divided into two large units: sales/marketing and production. The two units communicate at director, management and executive levels, both formally and informally. Within those large units there are small units whose purpose is specifically to market and produce this text. These are the people who commission, edit, typeset, proof and organise the printing of the book (the production unit) and who disseminate information, take orders, store, pack and distribute the book (the sales/marketing unit).

In organisations, people interact on a personal level in systematic ways that become organised into an informal organisation existing alongside the formal one; the informal organisation provides an individual with an essential communication channel and an escape from the routine and rigidity of the formal organisation.

Mission and objectives

Many organisations, especially those in the public sector, have a mission statement that sets out their purpose. For any organisation to survive, its members must continue to accept its purpose, so the mission is usually general and acceptable to all.

For discussion

What is your college's (or your work organisation's) mission statement?
Do the staff and students find it acceptable or unacceptable?

Most organisations exist for the long term. Many objectives have a time horizon (of a year, say) so new objectives have to be set regularly so that the organisation can continue to fulfil its mission.

Forming an organisation can be as simple a process as people getting together to form a darts team because their objective is to play in the local league. Alternatively, it can be a complex process involving many people and procedures – for example, forming a public company with the objective of providing courier services world wide. The darts team achieves its general purpose by playing specific matches. The courier company's units may aim to open a new route, deliver faster to Paris, carry more parcels to Dallas or buy a new plane; all fit into the mission of providing a global service.

Activity 2 [10 minutes]

Could your college achieve its purpose without establishing a formal organisation? Write down brief reasons for your answer.

The rest of this chapter examines private-sector business organisations. We start by looking at two kinds of organisations that are not incorporated: sole traders and partnerships.

2 NON-CORPORATE BUSINESSES

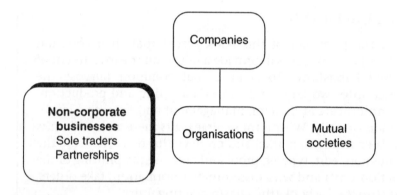

Definition

Private sector: that sector of the economy comprising all activities that are not government owned. Business organisations in the private sector that exist to make a profit include sole traders, partnerships, mutual societies and private and public companies.

We start by looking at sole traders.

2.1 Sole traders

Also known as sole proprietors, a sole trader may be just that: a one person business. On the other hand, in theory a sole tradership can employ many people and even have a fairly complicated management structure.

In a sole trader organisation, one person has ownership and control of the business and the ultimate power to make decisions. Management and decision making may be delegated, but the owner remains in control. The owner provides the finance and remains responsible for the success or failure of the business.

A sole trader business is not a legal entity separate from the owner. This means that the proprietor has unlimited liability and legally all contracts with the business are in fact made with the individual proprietor. If the firm fails, the proprietor could lose everything; all personal assets as well as the business assets could go to satisfy creditors.

Despite this risk, thousands of people start up new sole traderships every year. Anyone can set up as a sole trader without any formal procedures, except where a licence is required to operate (for example to retail wines and spirits or for consumer credit). Around eighty per cent of UK businesses are sole traderships. They flourish in business sectors where:

(a) personal expertise is important;

(b) there are no great economies of scale;

(c) little capital is required.

Sole traders tend to serve a local market, where they are often important to the community.

Definition

Economies of scale: economies that arise within a firm as output increases and average total cost falls. The economies arise from technical factors (such as employing larger, more efficient machines) and from such managerial factors as specialisation, bulk buying and mass marketing.

Activity 3 [30 minutes]

Look at six different local sole proprietor businesses. List the factors necessary for them to start up.

Some individuals set up in business as sole traders, perhaps under a different name (for example, 'Joe Bloggs trading as *Excelsior*') and with a separate bank account, invoices and premises. Although legally speaking the affairs of Joe Bloggs and *Excelsior* are the same, there are a number of advantages in treating the business as a separate entity including:

(a) the need to create an identifiable presence in the market;

(b) the need to satisfy regulations on tax and employment;

(c) the need for a business entity to deal with bankers, suppliers and customers;

(d) the informality of establishing the business;

(e) the informality of running the business – there is no requirement to publish accounts or to keep records except for tax purposes;

(f) the desire to be one's own boss.

Sole traders and communication

Even this simplest form of business still has quite a complex network of communications. External communications are with:

(a) customers and potential customers;

(b) suppliers;

(c) service providers such as plumbers and local newspaper advertising departments;

(d) trade associations, professional bodies and chambers of commerce;

(e) various authorities and official bodies, including VAT inspectors, local planning officers and weights and measures inspectors.

Internal communications could be between proprietor and staff or, in larger sole traderships, between proprietor, managers and staff.

NOTES

Activity 4 [15 minutes]

For each of the external and internal communication relationships listed above, write down whether communication is likely to be official and formal or unofficial and informal, and give an example.

When two or more people join in a business venture, they often create a partnership. Partnerships are the preferred form of organisation for professional practices, such as lawyers.

2.2 Partnerships

Forming a partnership increases the financial resources and widens the range of expertise available to a business. Each new partner may bring in new capital and new skills. However, every new partner has a say in running the business and can take decisions binding on the others whether or not they agree or even know of it.

The Companies Act 1985, and later amendments, limits the number of partners to twenty, but exempts from the limit qualified and practising accountants and solicitors and the business members of a recognised stock exchange.

A partnership, like a sole proprietorship, is not a separate legal entity. Two or more persons carrying on a business together constitute a partnership. It does not require any formal written agreement: a verbal arrangement is sufficient. Any partner can bind the partnership to a contract with third parties. The partnership is automatically dissolved by the withdrawal, bankruptcy or death of a partner.

Informality can be dangerous. Unless there are procedures set down for operating and dissolving the partnership, the individual members can be suddenly faced by all the financial difficulties caused by unlimited liability for all the debts of the partnership. In fact, partnerships are usually regulated by a formal agreement that covers the terms for subscribing capital, the division of profits and losses, duties, salaries and the procedures for dissolving the partnership. It is very unwise to carry on business without such an agreement. Partnerships do not have to publish accounts so they can maintain secrecy over their profitability, or lack of it.

In rare cases, because limited companies are more attractive, there can be a limited partnership where:

(a) limited (or sleeping) partners' liabilities are limited to the capital contributed by them;

(b) limited partners take no part in running the business;

(c) there must be at least one general partner.

The partnership form of organisation has particular attraction for accountants because the partners, in even the largest firm like Deloitte & Touche, can keep their own clients, have a say in running the business and enjoy the advantages of large scale. However, recent very large judgements against the top firms for negligence in auditing accounts and for bad advice have caused them to query the advantages of being a partnership and consider incorporation or moving to Jersey where large limited partnerships are possible.

Partnerships flourish in the same areas as sole traders. They appeal especially to professional people who can retain a lot of individual freedom of action and maintain their personal relationship with clients while gaining the advantages of larger capital and more expertise. They appeal to clients because the principle of professional responsibility and accountability is retained.

Partnerships and communication

Partnerships have to communicate internally and externally just like sole traders. They also have to communicate amongst themselves, especially because of the need to agree policies and make joint decisions. The fact that there is more than one 'boss' makes internal communications more complex. Decision making can be slow.

Activity 5 [20 minutes]

Identify four local partnerships.

For each, suggest three advantages to them of being a partnership as opposed to a sole trader.

We will next look at the principle of limited liability, which makes it possible to have very large business organisations.

3 COMPANIES

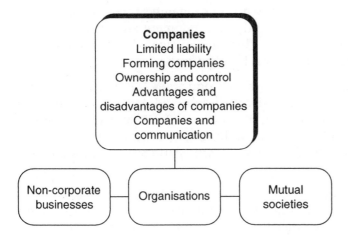

3.1 Limited liability

The principle of joint stock companies brought together venturers for centuries – people risked their capital jointly with others in the stock of the company. But joint ownership brought all the risks of a big partnership until the principle of limited liability was recognised in 1855. The Companies Acts introduced general limited liability for shareholders in companies and made it possible for firms to raise large amounts of capital with only limited risk to their owners. It took many years for people to trust companies, but by the end of the last century the structure of businesses had been transformed as limited liability companies made the risk of forming large firms acceptable to investors.

Definition

Limited liability: an arrangement by which the owners of a business that fails have their individual responsibility for its debts limited in some way. The most common situation is where the shareholders in a company are responsible for the unpaid debts only to the extent of any unpaid amount for their shares. For example, they may have paid up only 50 pence of a one pound share. Should the firm fail they would be called upon for only 50 pence for each share owned, no matter how large the size of the company's outstanding debt. The liability to pay has no relation to the ability to pay.

Corporations can be established in various ways and are of different types:

(a) Royal Charter, once the only method, now used for special cases;

(b) Act of Parliament, used for public corporations;

(c) registration under the Companies Acts (by far the most common).

Let us see how a company is formed.

3.2   Forming companies

The Companies Act 1985 differentiated between:

(a) *private limited companies* required to have 'Limited' or 'Ltd' as part of their names ('cyf' can be used in Wales); and

(b) *public limited companies* which must have 'Plc' as part of their names ('ccc' in Wales).

The owners of both types of company are the owners of the ordinary shares, also known as equities, which represent the 'equity', or capital, of the company. At a company general meeting the ordinary shareholders, known as members, normally have one vote for each share owned.

Anyone can form a company. You could set one up for about £50. It then becomes a separate legal person from the persons who are its members. The corporate legal person 'is invisible, immortal, and rests only in intendment and consideration of the law'. (Case of Sutton's Hospital 1612) The company would still exist even if all its human members were dead, until it was legally dissolved.

A company is formed by registration under the Companies Acts by its promoter or promoters. Documents, including the Memorandum and Articles of Association which set out the objectives and rules, are filed with the Registrar of Companies (an official of the Department of Trade and Industry), who issues a certificate of incorporation. The promoter can then proceed with setting up the company and raising capital.

Over 90% of companies are private. Most are small, but a few, like Littlewoods with the eightieth largest sales of UK firms in 1995 (just above W H Smith), are as large as the bigger Plcs. A small firm is officially classified as a 'small or medium sized enterprise' (SME), a category used by governments and the European Union.

Activity 6   [5 minutes]

How many employees do you think that there are in a SME?

(a) 20

(b) 50

(c) 100

(d) 200

Now we look at ownership and control within the different types of companies.

3.3   Ownership and control

The advantage of forming a private company is to be able to raise more capital with limited liability while still retaining control. Although a private company can raise capital in all the same ways as a public one, it cannot offer shares to the general public.

Public companies are able to raise large sums from wider sources of capital by:

(a) selling shares direct to the public; or

(b) issuing shares through the Stock Exchange; or

(c) placing shares with investing institutions such as insurance companies, pension funds and investment trusts, which are themselves public companies formed specifically to invest in the shares of other companies.

Unit trusts also invest in shares. In 1995 there were about ten million individual shareholders owning around 17% of UK shares. The rest were mainly held by pension and insurance firms. This split is important for the governance of public companies.

The main differences between private limited companies and Plcs are as follows.

(a) Shares in private companies can only be traded with the agreement of the shareholders, they cannot be offered to the general public; so shares in public companies can be offered to the general public and are often, though not always, traded on the Stock Exchange. (Plc stands for Public *Limited* company, not *listed*.)

(b) A private company can have a few shareholders or one shareholder, while a public company must have at least seven.

(c) A private company must have at least one director (two if the Company Secretary is a director), while a public company must have at least two directors.

Companies are controlled by their shareholders, who, at general meetings, can appoint and dismiss the directors who manage the company. Each share has one vote so that anyone or any group with more than 50% of the ordinary shares can control the firm.

Holding companies

This makes it easy to establish holding companies which control subsidiaries set up as separate companies. These are often used to maintain the separate identity of a business that has been taken over, and for joint ventures. For example, a construction and a generator company may join forces to build a hydroelectric scheme by setting up a subsidiary to do the work. Unilever and Shell, both in the top three largest UK companies, are Anglo-Dutch firms. The ownership of a company is important for its structure, culture and communications.

Holding company organisation

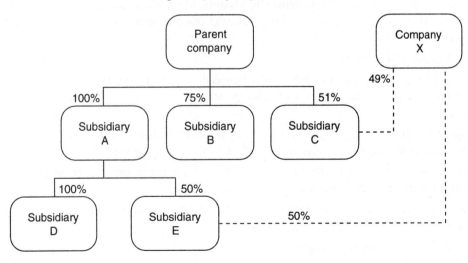

Notes:
(a) The percentage figures refer to ownership of the ordinary shares
(b) These are joint ventures with Company X in cases of subsidiaries C and E

Figure 1.1 Holding company organisation

Activity 7 [20 minutes]

Turn to the business pages of a quality paper and look through them to gain a picture of the range of public companies. (You may find that more information on capital appears in weekend and Monday editions, especially in the *Financial Times*.)

(a) Find the listings of Plcs quoted on the Stock Exchange and of Unit Trusts. Try to spot those companies that are obviously overseas owned (for example, Vauxhall – a subsidiary of General Motors of the US, Kodak and Norsk Hydro UK).

(b) Compare some of the capital amounts in different sectors to gain an idea of the size of firms, and compare the current share price with the usual nominal £1 share.

(c) If you can, look at some of the company information in any Annual Reports, where you will find lists of subsidiary companies and details of operations by product and country.

Notes:

1   You will find 'ordinary', 'deferred' and 'preference' shares and debentures listed and terms such as 'price/earnings ratio' (P/E ratio). All these terms are explained in the glossary.

2   As well as a full Stock Exchange listing, which requires a lengthy record of profitable trading, smaller and newer companies can seek a listing on the Alternative Investment Market (AIM), or their shares can be traded off-market on Ofex, which gives them liquidity. For example, Manchester United has a full listing on the Stock Exchange for its value of £231 million, Chelsea (£58 million) on AIM and Manchester City (£9 million) on Ofex.

Company directors

Directors may be executive, responsible for specific functions, or non-executive, representing the general interest of the shareholders. The voluntary code of corporate governance set out by the Cadbury Committee requires all Plcs to have non-executive directors who can take an independent view of the company management.

At this point it is useful to summarise the advantages and disadvantages of forming a company.

3.4   Advantages and disadvantages of companies

The advantages of forming a company include the following.

(a) It has a separate legal entity from the shareholders who, therefore, cannot be sued for the actions of the company beyond the amount outstanding on their shares.

(b) There is limited liability.

(c) Ownership and management of the business are separated so that investors can put money into shares without taking any responsibility for running the company.

(d) Large amounts of capital can be raised from large numbers of investors (private companies can approach only a limited number of members).

(e) Stocks and shares can easily be transferred so that investors can recover their capital (there are restrictions in private companies).

(f) The continuation and legal standing of a company are not affected by the death of a member or withdrawal of a director.

There are also some disadvantages.

(a) The procedures for setting up a company are costly and complicated compared to starting as a sole trader or partnership.

(b) Detailed annual accounts have to be prepared, audited and submitted to the Registrar, an Annual Report, made to shareholders and a register of shareholdings has to be maintained; these can all be inspected by the public (smaller companies, in terms of turnover, have a lesser burden in this respect).

(c) Shareholders have little control of Plcs in practice as individual shareholdings tend to be small and most shares are held by the pension funds and insurance companies etc. (investing institutions), which have rarely taken an interest in the management of the firms where they have holdings.

(d) Public companies are vulnerable to take-over bids.

(e) Managers are unlikely to put in as much effort as the sole trader or partners.

(f) Incentive schemes for directors and senior managers have been severely criticised as being too generous to the extent that, in 1996, there were moves by groups of investing institutions to join in voting against the proposals at AGMs.

(g) Small and new companies may have difficulty in getting credit because their limited liability makes suppliers and lenders wary (directors of private companies often have to give personal guarantees or security for loans).

For discussion

Given that a private limited company can be formed for as little as £50 plus the Registrar's fees and a bit of paperwork, why do people continue to set up as sole traders and partnerships? What are the benefits and disadvantages of the different types of business in different fields?

Companies limited by guarantee

A special type of company is often set up by charities. The liability of members is limited to the extent to which they individually guarantee the debts of the company, not through any shareholding. Most of them set the maximum amount of the guarantee at £1. The institution gets all the benefits of the company type of organisation without the costs and disadvantages of issuing shares.

3.5 Companies and communication

Companies have extensive communications networks both internally and externally. While there is the direct line from directors to managers to staff, the links can become very complicated when there are many subsidiaries at home and overseas. The Board has to communicate with shareholders, both as required by law in Annual Reports and at AGMs, and to retain their interest in and loyalty to the company. External communications include the official bodies like the Registrar and Stock Exchange and information provided to investment analysts and the financial press. You should look out for comment on firms in the press – perhaps news about a new venture, an acquisition or a warning of a slump in profits. The sensitivity of share prices to information, whether official or a rumour, has led the Stock Exchange to ban off-the-record briefings and make companies announce officially any changes in their trading conditions. Using price-sensitive information to make a profit is a criminal offence (insider dealing).

Next we look at businesses which are owned by their members, the mutual societies.

4 MUTUAL SOCIETIES

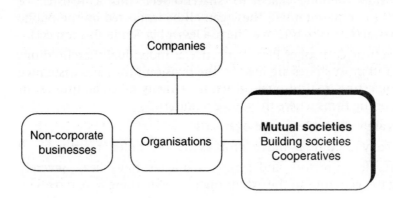

A mutual society is owned by its members. Building societies and mutual insurance societies are both types of mutual society.

(a) A building society's members are those depositors who subscribe money into a share account, which pays interest like any other deposit account.

(b) Mutual insurance companies are owned by their policy holders.

A mutual society is managed by a Board of Directors, elected by the members who each have a vote. Like a public company, a mutual society is incorporated and its members have limited liability.

We start by considering building societies.

4.1 Building societies

The building societies have about 60% of UK mortgage loans, total assets exceeding £280 billion and over 22 million personal sector customers. Over-capacity in a shrinking mortgage market, which has halved the annual number of new loans since the mid-eighties, competition from the banks and the advantages of a large branch network have combined to reduce the number of societies from 273 in 1980 to 90 in 1994. Since 1988 rationalisation has seen more branches closed than have been opened.

Deregulation of building societies

The Building Societies Act 1986 greatly increased the types of business open to the societies. They could continue to provide mortgage loans secured on property and could enter the new businesses of making unsecured personal loans up to £10,000, issuing cheque books and credit cards, providing pension services, insurance and financial advice and acting as estate agents.

In 1994 the government reviewed the 1986 Act and, as a first step, removed some further restrictions on the societies.

(a) They can raise up to 50% of funds on the money markets. (Before the 1986 Act, they could only raise money from deposits made by individual members).

(b) They can make loans to companies.

(c) They can own a general insurance company which can write housing related policies covering buildings, contents and mortgage protection.

The second stage of the review concentrates on the relationship between societies and their members. The government intends to introduce a package of measures designed to increase the accountability of boards to members, provide members with more and better information and remove the distinction between retail depositors and shareholders. (The distinction is important when a society converts to a bank and loses its mutual status or is taken over by a bank.) In future all members will have the rights and obligations of shareholding members. Borrowing members will get voting rights. A society will be able to have a maximum of 25% of its lending in areas other than mortgages. They will continue to be regulated by the Building Societies Commission. The government has made it clear that it does not intend to make it any easier for societies to give up their mutual status.

After the 1986 Act made it possible, the Abbey National quickly converted to a bank as a Plc. Contrary to expectations, others did not follow. Since 1994 the situation has changed. Lloyds Bank and the Cheltenham and Gloucester Building Society merged and then merged with the TSB. Some societies have proposed converting from their mutual status to become banks; these include the Halifax, the biggest building society in the world. Conversion brings a cash windfall of around £1,000 to the members and has some advantages, including:

(a) an end to any restrictions on types of business in the UK and abroad;

(b) the ability to raise money through the Stock Exchange and on the other capital markets. This makes it possible to expand faster than by waiting for deposits to grow.

Some large societies (such as Nationwide) have opted to remain mutual organisations, as they believe that they can be more competitive, offering higher deposit and lower lending rates while continuing to provide high quality service to members.

Activity 8 [30 minutes]

Look at the building societies and banks in your local High Street. Do you think that the average person would find any significant differences between them?

If possible, ask a few other people what they think and see if you all agree.

The advantages of economies of scale and the cost of large-scale computerisation will mean more mergers between societies. Smaller ones will continue to flourish by serving a local market with a restricted range of services.

Some mutual insurance societies have also chosen to convert for the same reasons as building societies. Competition from direct sales organisations (such as Direct Line's telephone operation), banks and building societies has caused some insurance companies to merge.

Building societies and communications

There are likely to be more mergers among these businesses as a result of recent technological changes that make it easier to communicate with customers. Such developments tend to lead away from structures involving large numbers of local branches supported by area and regional offices. Technological change is just as important a factor as the ability to raise more finance when mutual societies consider merging. As we will see later, the legal and technical changes that are reshaping the mutual societies will have profound effects on their structures and communications.

Now we look at co-operative societies.

4.2 Co-operative societies

The first successful co-operative society was founded in 1844 by the Rochdale Pioneers. Twenty-eight members joined together, each subscribing £1, to buy foodstuffs at wholesale prices and sell them to members with any profits being shared according to the value of their purchases. The same principles of one member one vote and a dividend based on profits, or profits returned to members, still apply to co-operatives today.

There are now co-operative movements in over 70 countries with over 500 million members worldwide. There are eight million members in the UK. The Co-operative Retail Society (CRS), with its regional branches operating supermarkets, department stores, local food stores and funeral parlours has a presence in most towns. The Co-operative Bank, with High Street branches and a presence in every CRS shop, makes a particular point of its ethical stance, refusing to invest in firms that pollute the environment or operate in repressive countries. There is a youth movement and an extensive programme of educational activities. Although co-operative manufacturing enterprise has been successful in other countries, notably Spain, it never made much headway in the UK. There are several marketing and purchasing co-operatives formed by farmers to get the advantages of sharing costs and the economies of buying in bulk.

Management of the local CRS is by a committee of management elected by the members. This tends to make decision making slow, and change can be difficult to implement. The same applies at the national level. For the last forty years the number of societies and their membership has been falling and the CRS has lost market share to the more aggressive supermarket groups such as Safeway and Sainsbury's.

For discussion

From the points of view of customers, employees and the owners of businesses, what are the advantages and disadvantages of public companies and mutual societies?

Chapter roundup

- An organisation is a defined group of people with a common purpose.
- Organisations exist because of the advantages of co-operation to achieve a common purpose.
- Private sector businesses exist to make profits and include sole proprietors, partnerships, private and public companies and mutual societies.
- Private and public companies have the advantage of limited liability and can raise money from people who take no part in the running of the business.
- Businesses all have to communicate externally and internally in order to be effective.

Quick Quiz

1   What procedures are necessary to establish a sole proprietorship?
2   Give three reasons for setting up in business as a sole trader.
3   What two advantages does a partnership have over a sole proprietor?
4   Give three disadvantages of a partnership.
5   Why are communications likely to be more complex in a partnership than in the case of a sole proprietor?
6   What is the main difference between a private limited company and a public limited company?
7   What is a holding company?
8   Who owns a company and who manages it?

9   Who owns a mutual society?

10 Who receives the profits in (i) a company and (ii) a co-operative society?

Answers to Quick Quiz

1   None unless a licence is required.

2   (i) The business can be established without any formal requirements, (ii) it does not have to keep (except for tax) or publish any special accounts and (iii) people want to be their own boss. You might have also added that there is the need to have a business identity recognised by customers, the public, suppliers, bankers, official bodies and others.

3   More partners can mean more finance and more expertise.

4   (I) The partners have unlimited liability,(ii) any one of them can enter an agreement on behalf of them all, and (iii) the partnership is dissolved if one leaves or dies.

5   There has to be communication between the partners, who are all at the same authority level, whereas the sole trader alone has ultimate responsibility for decisions.

6   A public company can sell its securities to the general public, a private company cannot.

7   A holding company holds shares in subsidiaries which can be controlled if 51% of the ordinary shares are owned. They can be run as separate businesses.

8   A company is owned by the ordinary shareholders and managed by the Board of Directors they appoint at an Annual General Meeting.

9   A mutual society is owned by its members.

10 (I) The shareholders receive the profits made by a company in the form of dividends or of additional share value from reinvestment. (ii) A co-operative's profits are returned to members through a dividend on purchases or lower prices.

Answers to Activities

1   Your list might include some of the following: your college – a corporation that provides a service and tries, at least, to avoid a loss; supermarkets, newsagents or other shops – profit making businesses: a sports club – an organisation based on subscription members; street lighting – a profit-making electricity company and public service local authority. You may easily have listed 50 or more organisations.

2   Your college would be unlikely to achieve much without a formal organisation. Individual teachers could hold classes, but there would be timetabling clashes and problems about paying for resources, among other disadvantages.

3   You might have chosen, for example, your local newsagent, hairdresser, plumber, dentist, car mechanic and window cleaner. They all require personal qualities, such as the desire to be their own boss and willingness to work on their own and make decisions. They need varying amounts of capital depending on the premises, equipment and stock they must have. They require certain skills and training. Dentists must be qualified and registered. It is desirable for hairdressers, plumbers and car mechanics to be qualified and trained and to belong to recognised bodies. Shop keepers need expertise to run the business. Window cleaners need skill and knowledge to handle long ladders, for example.

4   All the cases could be either official and formal or unofficial and informal. For example, customers can be sent formal letters about late payment or greeted verbally with chat about the weather. Suppliers can be sent official orders or 'phoned about a query on a delivery. Trade associations can be sent formal reports when they send out questionnaires on trading conditions or there can be informal social gatherings at meetings, which can be formal. Most communication with official bodies will be formal, but there can be informal unofficial contacts with officers to get information.

Internal communication can also be both: written procedures, reports and verbal instructions can all be official and formal, social occasions like tea breaks informal.

5   Accountants, doctors, solicitors and dentists are the most likely partnerships. They benefit from more capital and shared expertise, premises and support services.

6   You are correct if you said (d), 200, which you might not think very small.

7   You should have found quite big differences between firms within a sector in terms of their size, stocks and shares and share price. Remember that a firm which is largely financed by borrowing (highly geared) will pay out a lot of interest to debenture holders before paying dividends on its equities. However, there will be no dilution of shareholdings by raising more money by selling shares, thus keeping control with the original ordinary shareholders.

8   The average person is unlikely to notice much difference as the services are much the same. Businesses and individuals with special requirements, such as the need to make large investments, would use banks.

Assignment 1 [1 hour]

Complete the table below giving any relevant information on each feature for each type of organisation. Find any information not in this chapter from books in any library.

Comparison of business organisations

Features	Sole trader	Partnership	Private company	Public company	Mutual society
Creation					
Legal status					
Liability					
Publicity					
Audit					
Reporting of results					
Ownership					
Control					
Management					
Transfer of membership					
Duration					
Ownership of assets					

Chapter 2

ORGANISATIONS AND COMMUNICATION

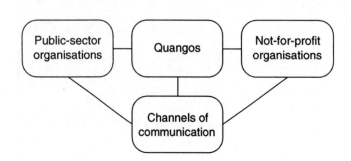

Introduction

Chapter 1 introduced the different types of *private-sector* business organisations. This chapter focuses on the *public sector, not-for-profit* organisations and *quangos*.

Central and local government spend over forty per cent of the national income. Much of this spending goes to quangos and private corporations (such as colleges) which spend public money to carry out government policy and provide public services. If you add to this the not-for-profit sector of charities and voluntary bodies, you have thousands of organisations of all sizes and types which are a major source of employment.

As stated in Chapter 1, all organisations must communicate with people and bodies outside them. There is also a need for information flows *inside* the organisation. Communication is essential for the organisation to function. At the end of this chapter, we explore why communication is necessary and look at two main types of communication channels: formal channels, which exist to transmit correct information; and informal channels, which *may* be used to send misleading messages.

Your objectives

After completing this chapter you should be able to:

(a) describe public-sector, mixed and not-for-profit organisations;

(b) appreciate their diversity of mission and type;

(c) appreciate why organisations need to communicate;

(d) be aware of the difference between formal and informal channels of communication.

We start by looking at organisations in the public sector, including those in central and local government.

1   PUBLIC-SECTOR ORGANISATIONS

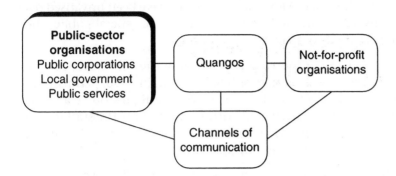

Today you may have received some post, walked down a street swept by the local council's contractor, watched a BBC TV programme or listened to its radio station and heard some Minister talk about what a government department is doing. Your life is constantly affected by public-sector organisations.

Definition

Public sector: that sector of the economy that includes all central and local government and public corporations that are government owned.

The public sector includes various types of public enterprise bodies that are expected to run on commercial lines; these are:

(a) nationalised industries;

(b) local government bodies;

(c) government agencies.

There are also many public service organisations that do not aim to earn income and make profits, including:

(a) the armed forces, police and coast guard;

(b) social services;

(c) central and local government administration;

(d) government agencies.

(Government agencies come into both lists because some have been established with the aim that they should make some profit and others are not expected to cover their costs, being supported by grants.)

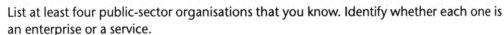

Activity 1   [10 minutes]

List at least four public-sector organisations that you know. Identify whether each one is an enterprise or a service.

First we will look at public corporations.

1.1   Public corporations

Public corporations are effectively public companies set up by Act of Parliament. A nationalised industry is one where the firms have been taken into public ownership in a public corporation. For example, the BBC became a public corporation in 1926 when the British Broadcasting Company was taken over by the government.

After World War II several industries were nationalised and the firms reorganised by Act of Parliament into corporations. Examples include: British Steel, British Airways, British Gas and British Rail. Most such industries have been privatised over the years from 1979 onwards: shares in them were sold to the general public when they turned into public limited companies.

Parliament did not approve the proposed privatisation of the Post Office in 1995, but the Post Office did gain more commercial freedom and, in 1996, permission to introduce new services. (Watch out for changes in your local post office and look for changes in the way it is run, in particular with regard to how the staff interact with the public. Any differences that you notice could well be down to a change in 'culture'; we will return to this subject later in this text.)

The Act that establishes a public corporation sets out its objectives. Any capital is held by the Treasury. There are no shareholders. The relevant Minister appoints the Board of Directors that manages the corporation. The Minister and the Treasury agree on borrowing limits. A corporation is a legal entity which can sue and be sued. The Minister is responsible to Parliament for the running of the industry.

Privatised industries where there is little competition are overseen by a government appointed regulator – for example, Ofwat for the water industry and Oftel for telecommunications. The regulator has to agree pricing in accordance with a formula laid down by Parliament. Competition is encouraged. The structures of privatised organisations have changed drastically as they have responded to private-sector commercial pressures and sought efficiency and profitability.

We now consider a second type of public-sector organisation: those in local government.

1.2 Local government

Municipal enterprises are businesses run by local authorities. Trading activities exist to earn a profit. Many are operated to provide a service also.

EXAMPLE: A SPORTS CENTRE

A local sports centre may be expected to make a profit on its restaurant and bar, but to provide both keep-fit classes for pensioners and children's holiday activities at less than cost.

Buses may be run at a loss as a policy aimed at reducing congestion.

The aim is to make services available to the residents more efficiently or more cheaply than would be possible for a private enterprise. These activities are overseen by a council committee.

Activity 2 [20 minutes]

Find out what services your local authority provides and what its departments are.

You can get this information from:

- the telephone directory;
- local news sheets published by your local authority;
- committee and council reports in public libraries.

Since 1980 the government has increased the number of local government activities that have to be put out to *competitive tender*. In order to ensure efficiency and value for money, local authority departments have to compete for work with private firms. For example, the Direct Labour Organisation maintains houses and roads and collects refuse – services that have to be competitive.

Finally in this section we look at the public services.

1.3   Public services

About seven per cent of the labour force are employed in public administration in the civil service and local government. They work in ministries and departments. Their mission is to carry out policies (for example to provide National Vocational Qualifications (NVQs) in all industries) and to administer operations. Much of the work is done by agencies, for example the Passport Agency. These agencies were established to try to bring the benefits of private-sector business efficiency to the public services. The establishment of the agencies has caused great changes in the structure of the public services since 1980.

Communication in public administration

It could be said that public administration is entirely concerned with communication. Administrators have to research, consult, inform and persuade.

Activity 3   [15 minutes]

The Department of Transport has been trying to get people to cycle rather than use their cars. List three interested parties they might consult and/or inform.

Much of the work of the public sector is done through quangos and publicly financed organisations, which play an important role in the country

2   QUANGOS

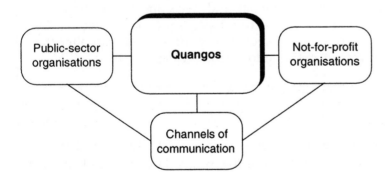

There are between 1,300 and 5,500 bodies that carry out some function on behalf of the government. The lower figure includes just the government recognised quasi-autonomous non-government organisations (QUANGOs); the higher figure includes all the National Health, opted-out schools, agencies and other bodies funded by the government.

All quangos have powers delegated to them by a Minister, who appoints the members of the Board and provides for finance. Some quangos are self financing from fees and licences; others get their income from the government.

Many quangos are not strictly business organisations, but their activities have an important impact on business.

EXAMPLES: OFT AND ACAS

The Office of Fair Trading monitors restrictions on trade and makes recommendations to the Minister on proposed mergers.

ACAS (the Advisory, Conciliation and Arbitration Service) tries to resolve disputes between employers and workers.

The wider definition of quangos includes National Health Hospital Trusts and those agencies that have taken over functions formerly performed by government departments such as the Passport Office. To some extent these are trading bodies.

For discussion

How many public-sector activities could be provided by the private sector, given that the government and local authorities can provide subsidies and supervise the firms? How might the cultural attitudes and beliefs of the organisations differ if they were privatised?

Think about the situation:

(a)   *locally;*
(b)   *nationally.*

EXAMPLES: COLLEGES AND UNIVERSITIES

Local colleges have been privatised and have become corporations that appoint their Boards of Governors. The government decided the representation on their boards. Colleges are financed and supervised by the Higher and Further Education Funding Councils. They have a dual structure. The commercial and administrative structure has had to change since local authority funding and administration ended. The academic structure continues to operate through the Academic Board and Course Committees, which oversee educational matters.

Universities also have a dual structure. Their organisation can be affected by the Higher Education Funding Council and decisions of the Research Councils, which also provide funds. Unsatisfactory departments can be closed. Changes in priorities and forecasts of staffing needs can alter the structure of a University, as can the endowment of Chairs.

Activity 4
[1 hour]

This activity requires you to do some research, which will take most of the hour allocated. This could be done as a group exercise, with individuals each looking at a different aspect.

Look at your own college or university and examine the different structures:

(a) Academic Board, Boards of Studies, Course Committees;

(b) Faculties, departments, sections;

(c) Administrative and support departments.

What are the lines of responsibility between these and to the Board of Governors and the Principal or Vice-chancellor?

We now look at not-for-profit organisations.

3   NOT-FOR-PROFIT ORGANISATIONS

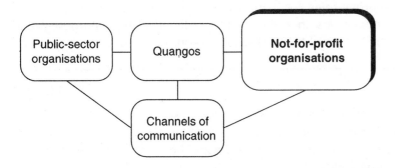

The term 'not-for-profit' includes charities, clubs and voluntary organisations. It covers political parties, religious groups, the pub darts team, and also many professional bodies, such as the Chartered Institute of Marketing and the Institute of Export (many of which are educational charities and companies limited by guarantee).

Registered charities and other bodies may have trading organisations. For example, Oxfam and Save the Children Fund have shops. Some are very large international bodies with complex structures similar to those of multinational companies. Some are small and local with a simple structure of a committee and members. Some exist for a limited period to conduct a specific campaign, such as a road protest, and may have an informal structure.

The common feature of all these bodies is that their primary purpose is not to make a profit in the business sense. The aim of the National Trust, Britain's biggest charity, is to acquire and maintain properties for the nation. Once a charity or voluntary organisation becomes more than local, it needs a structure that reflects its members' geographical span. For example, the British Red Cross is part of the international organisation and has a structure of regions, branches, centres and groups to carry on its activities from the national down to the local level.

For discussion

The purpose of a public enterprise such as the Post Office, the police and other public services and administrative departments, the NHS, the Law Society and the local bowls club will attract people who relate to it. They will subscribe to a common culture or set of attitudes, beliefs and behaviour.

Taking these bodies as examples, discuss how their different missions and cultures affect the behaviour of each of them. Why would what is right for one not suit another?

Other structures exist according to the objectives and activities of the organisation. Like business organisations, they are subject to pressures and changes that affect their structure. Some organisations have flexibility built in so that they can adapt to the changing interests of their members.

> **EXAMPLE: THE CAMPING AND CARAVANNING CLUB**
>
> The Camping and Caravanning Club has regions and district associations open to all members. It also has special interest sections and groups (for example, boating), which may be regionally organised or national. Given sufficient interest it is easy to form a new section.

All these bodies have to communicate with: their members, those they wish to attract as supporters, field workers, people they help and official bodies. The Charities Commission has to approve rules, local authorities approve flag days, and foreign governments permit operations in their countries. Even a single-purpose local organisation, such as the Friends of the Hospice, has a complex communications web.

Activity 5   [30 minutes]

You can do this as an individual exercise or, better, as a group one.

Make a list of your local not-for-profit organisations. Your list should include: a charity, a sports club, another club, a national voluntary organisation with a local branch and another not-for-profit organisation (such as a religious group).

For each organisation, give at least three specific examples of how it communicates with its members. (Don't forget to include the less obvious examples of communication, such as the local charity shop.) You may be able to list many examples for some organisations.

Get the information you need from the local paper, which lists what is on and sometimes reports on meetings, from the public library, which often has diaries of events, and by looking around and asking friends.

Next we will look at why all organisations need to communicate and the channels open to them.

4   CHANNELS OF COMMUNICATION

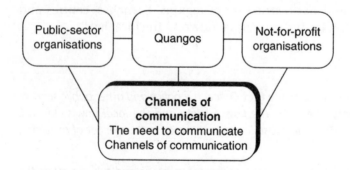

We start by looking at the reasons for communicating.

4.1   The need to communicate

People in all types of organisations, both profit making and not-for-profit, need to communicate to:

(a) inform (e.g. staff of policies);

(b) explain (e.g. changes in procedures);

(c) report (e.g. monthly results);

(d) persuade (e.g. staff to work overtime);

(e) describe (e.g. research);

(f) motivate (e.g. a team);

(g) instruct (e.g. setting out procedures);

(h) confirm (e.g. receipt of an instruction).

Activity 6   [10 minutes]

Give one example of each of the above reasons for communicating that has affected you recently.

As we have seen, organisations also have to communicate with their external environment. This involves using internal communications to interpret and act on information coming in and to send out the desired message. Information has to be gathered and used to deal with all sorts of external people and bodies, including the following activities:

(a) marketing:

(b) ordering supplies;

(c) influencing government policies;

(d) providing statutory and regulatory information.

Without speedy and accurate communication, people in an organisation may not be able to do their jobs well. The organisation may fail to carry out its aims and policies. It may not even be able to communicate its policies to its members and others and so fail to operate effectively and gain support and interest from outside.

In the next and final section, we look briefly at channels of communication, a topic that is examined in detail in Chapter 9.

4.2   Channels of communication

Formal channels

Formal communication networks follow the normal channels of authority. There is a downward flow of instructions and information through the levels of the organisation. Upward flows confirm receipt of communications and send information. Communication also travels between people at the same level.

The structure of the organisation affects the structure of the formal channels: if there are few levels and many people with the same authority there will be a lot of communication *across a level*; conversely, if there are many layers of authority there will be many *vertical* communications.

EXAMPLES: LATERAL AND VERTICAL COMMUNICATION

A partnership may demand a lot of lateral communication, as all members are equal.

Army regiments, the police and companies with many layers of authority will need many vertical communications.

Informal channels

Communication also takes place outside the official channels, through *informal* networks. Informal networks can be used effectively by managers to pass on news and listen to staff opinions and grumbles.

An informal network that moves at random between all levels, uninitiated and uncontrolled by management, is called a 'grapevine'. The grapevine passes on gossip and rumour. Workers and managers can use the grapevine to manipulate information and attitudes. Although the grapevine can cause damage, its effects can be minimised by managers giving out accurate information in good time.

Chapter roundup

- Public-sector organisations are central- and local-government public enterprises and public services.

- A large part of the work of the public sector is done through quangos, agencies and regulated enterprises.

- Not-for-profit organisations include societies, clubs, charities and voluntary bodies.

- Not-for-profit organisations often have complex structures because of the division between their administration, trading activities and members' organisation.

- Communication is external and internal to the organisation; it must pass through the necessary channels for the organisation to function effectively.

- Communication may be through formal channels, the authority structure of the organisation, or informal channels, including the grapevine.

Quick Quiz

1 What is a public corporation?

2 What is a quango?

3 Why have agencies been established to take over work previously done by government departments?

4 What is the difference between a public service and a public enterprise?

5 Give two examples of not-for-profit organisations.

6 What are formal channels of communication?

7 What is the grapevine?

Answers to Quick Quiz

1 A public corporation is established by Act of Parliament to run a government owned business.

2 A quasi autonomous non government organisation that operates a service or agency on behalf of the government but with freedom from government control.

3 To get the benefits of private business enterprise and efficiency.

4 A public enterprise is established to operate a business and could aim to make a profit; a public service provides a service to the public without any commercial aims.

5 You might have said charities, clubs and voluntary bodies or named actual organisations such as Help the Aged, the local athletics club and the Scouts.

6 Formal channels of communication follow the authority structure of the organisation.

7 The grapevine is informal; communication is often started by someone wishing to spread misinformation.

Answers to Activities

1 Your list might include, for example, the local hospital (enterprise), the parks department of the council (service), Department for Education (service), Royal Mail (enterprise). You may have found many other examples.

2 A typical structure for a County Council is as follows: a finance and general purposes committee takes a general oversight and deals in particular with the budget, borrowing and personnel. Other committees oversee specific departments,

including planning, education, social services, fire and transportation. There are also Housing and works (or technical services) to deal with maintenance and refuse collection in District Authorities. The treasurer's and personnel departments support the other departments.

3 Some of the bodies likely to be consulted would be local authorities (which are responsible for roads), the Department of the Environment (with its interest in pollution), the Countryside Commission and the Council for the Preservation of Rural England (which are likely to be interested in an increase in recreational cycling) and cycling pressure groups such as Sustrans.

4 You will probably have found structures similar to the following: course committees report to boards of studies, which report to the Academic Board, which reports to the Governors or Senate. Sections are responsible to departments, which are responsible to faculties both directly in the administrative structure of section leaders, department heads and deans of faculties and, for academic matters, to the committee structure. Ultimately they are responsible to the Principal or Vice-chancellor and the Governors or Senate. Administrative departments are responsible to the chief executive, who may be the principal, and to faculties and departments if they provide services specifically to them.

5 A club could communicate through a notice board, a report of activities in the local paper and a newsletter. A charity could use the same methods, assuming it has local branches. It could also send out mail shots soliciting funds and hold flag days. Large national organisations may use TV – either by means of adverts or by having representatives on programmes. Local radio can also be used.

6 You might have communicated to:

(a) inform a lecturer that you would be absent;

(b) explain why your assignment is late;

(c) report that you have returned the family car safely;

(d) persuade your friend to go out;

(e) describe the film you saw;

(f) motivate your project group;

(g) instruct your friend on how to do the project;

(h) confirm that you will attend an interview.

Assignment 2   [2 hours]

This can be done as an individual exercise, or as a group exercise with each member looking at a different type of organisation. It can be applied to business, public and not-for-profit organisations.

1 Take an organisation that you know, establish its ownership and find out its mission or objectives.

2 Having found out what the organisation was established to do, find out how it does it. What is the authority structure in the organisation and how is it organised – by region, product or function? Look at its sources of finance and explain how they relate to the ownership and activities. Briefly say how you think that the objectives, ownership, activities and finance shape the structure.

3 Present your findings in the form of a short report.

Chapter 3

ORGANISATION STRUCTURES

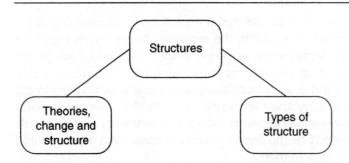

Introduction

Today you want to drive to college. You know that you can call at a BP petrol station and fill the tank, pay with your Visa credit card and go on your way along the district council's well surfaced road. If you break down, you can call out the very, very nice man from the AA.

Each of the organisations involved with your drive has *objectives*. The objectives of the organisation and what it does determine the type of structure that it has. An efficient structure for a government department would be ineffective for an advertising agency. Changes in technology, such as the development of personal computers since 1984, can radically change both organisations' ways of working and their structures.

Your objectives

After completing this chapter you should be able:

(a) to identify and describe different organisational structures;

(b) to classify organisations according to various criteria of structure;

(c) to outline how changing theories of management have led to different structures;

(d) to appreciate the effects of changes in technology and working practices on the structure of organisations.

First we look at the influences that shape organisations.

1   STRUCTURES

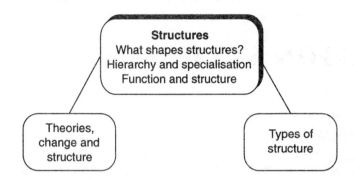

Suppose that none of the organisations involved with your journey to college outlined in the *Introduction* had a formal structure. What would happen? For a start, you could not take it for granted that you could buy petrol at a petrol station. Without having people to take the decisions to drill for oil, extract it, refine it and ship the petrol to the pumps, there is no guarantee that it would all happen. There has to be an organisational structure to carry out all the functions involved in meeting the mission of the petrol company.

Research into organisations, and theories of how organisations function, have influenced structural design. Three main factors have led to changes in management practice and new thinking about how to structure organisations:

(a) dissatisfaction with the working of traditional structures;

(b) social and economic change;

(c) technological advances.

1.1   What shapes structure?

Every organisation is established for a purpose. This is often expressed in its mission statement, which sets out its overall aim. The mission statement is supported by a set of goals or objectives, stating how the mission is to be achieved. The effective organisation will structure itself to carry out its mission.

Definition

Mission statement: a statement that sets out an organisation's purpose in society in general terms describing what it exists to achieve.

Other factors also influence structure. In total, the structure of a business organisation is determined by:

(a) its mission;

(b) what it does;

(c) its size;

(d) where it operates;

(e) who it deals with;

(f) its culture;

(g) technology;

(h) the complexity of its operations;

(i) its history and future expectations.

For example, a hairdresser who provides haircuts to men and women within a two mile radius is clearly going to have a very different structure to a company providing air travel globally to a global market.

The public and not-for-profit sectors

Organisations in the public and not-for-profit sectors also have structures determined by the factors listed above. The public services and local government have some additional factors that influence them:

(a) the extent and type of duties and obligations imposed by Parliament, which they must perform;

(b) the changing expectations of society;

(c) changes in government policies and priorities.

Because they are closely associated with government and depend on it for funding, quangos, much of the voluntary sector, many arts and environmental bodies and local clubs and societies that use the facilities of the local authority are all affected by these factors.

For discussion

In Chapter 2 you looked at your college or university's structure of faculties and departments. Which of the factors listed above have been important in shaping its structure? How do you think that they compare with those that are important for:

(a) a news agent and sub-post office;
(b) the Royal Air Force?

Next we look at the way in which organisations develop hierarchies of authority and specialisation.

1.2   Hierarchy and specialisation

An organisation is a collection of groups joined in a common mission. Each group has its own specific objectives and functions. A group is unlikely to operate successfully without a leader who can take responsibility for seeing that the group performs its tasks. Current changes in management practice are leading to collective responsibility for work being given to groups themselves; however, there must still be an individual who interacts with other groups and with managers of wider groupings.

Many decisions need to be made within an organisation, and someone must have the authority to make them at each of different levels within it. This authority should be given to people who have the appropriate knowledge and experience. Along with the authority goes responsibility, and the need to ensure that the decisions are carried out.

Organisations develop layers of authority to ensure that correct decisions are made and implemented. This results in the *organisation pyramid* as shown in Figure 3.1. The more important a decision is to an organisation, the fewer are the people entrusted with the authority to make it.

Figure 3.1 The organisation pyramid

As organisations grow specialist individuals or groups appear. These have to be co-ordinated, so further layers of management are required. Each department develops its own pyramid of authority. There can be specialism within a department, requiring more co-ordination. Thus increasing specialisation often leads to more layers of management.

EXAMPLE: BUILDING SOCIETIES

When building societies took deposits and lent as mortgages they required only a few specialist departments: deposits, lending, administration and legal. When they started to offer cheques, make personal loans and offer many types of savings, they had to develop many more specialist departments.

Activity 1   **[20 minutes]**

Think about your local department store (or visit it if you do not know it well).

1   List the departments on the sales floors.

2   Also list the support departments such as accounts.

3   Now suggest what advantages there are in having this degree of specialisation.

The structure of an organisation depends on how its specialist functions are organised.

1.3   Function and structure

The structure of an organisation arises from the need to delegate authority and responsibility and ensure co-ordination between the specialist functions.

There are three relationships between people in organisations:

(a) line;

(b) staff;

(c) function.

The line relationship

The line relationship is a direct one from the top management level to the lowest.

31

For example, there is a direct line of authority in the manufacturing function in a factory as shown in Figure 3.2.

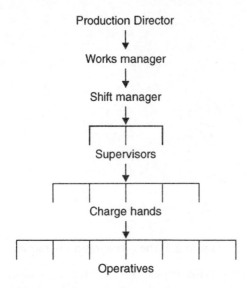

Figure 3.2 Production line management

The same could apply in a charity, as shown in Figure 3.3. This kind of line of authority applies to business organisations and also those in the public sector.

Figure 3.3 Line of authority in a charity

The staff relationship

The staff relationship refers to the work of support staff and departments. For example, production is supported by purchasing, stores and personnel. Thus production can concentrate on the manufacturing process and the organisation gets the benefit of greater expertise and efficiency through functional specialisation. Staff departments have the right to advise other departments but have no direct say.

The function relationship

The next volume in this series, *Planning and Decision Making*, describes business functions.

Chapter 3: Organisation structures

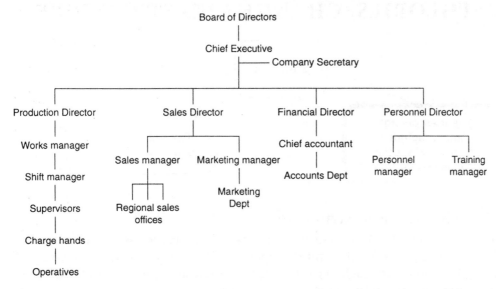

Figure 3.4 Line and staff structure

Functional authority gives one department the right to specify what goes on in other departments. For example, the personnel department lays down standard procedures for recruitment to which all departments must adhere.

EXAMPLE: FUNCTIONAL AUTHORITY

Banks have compliance officers who ensure that confidentiality is maintained between different areas.

Firms and local authorities may have equal opportunities officers.

Government departments may have security personnel.

All these functions report directly to top management.

Activity 2   [10 minutes]

Describe the departments and structure of each of the following:

(a) your college;

(b) your faculty;

(c) the BTEC section.

Next we look at how theories of organisations and technical change have influenced the structures of organisations.

2   THEORIES, CHANGE AND STRUCTURE

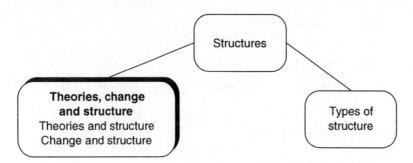

2.1   Theories and structure

Henri Fayol (1841–1925), an industrialist, is generally regarded as the first to analyse management activity. He thought that there should be only one line of command, with only one boss for each person to answer to. He also believed that division of labour and specialisation would lead to increased output. He recommended the hierarchical principle of management with clear levels of authority.

Max Weber (1864–1920), by contrast, an academic sociologist, analysed authority structures in organisations. He divided them into:

(a) those where power rests in a charismatic leader, such as the founder of a firm; such structures are inherently unstable as the founder's demise leads to conflict;

(b) traditional organisations where decisions are made according to precedent, and authority is decided by custom and status, often the case in family firms;

(c) the rational-legal organisation with a bureaucratic structure. A bureaucracy is *rational* because it is designed to achieve certain well-defined goals; it is *legal* because authority is exercised through a system of rules and procedures.

Bureaucracies

Definition

Bureaucracy: a form of organisation where tasks and duties are allocated to clearly defined positions in a hierarchy of authority which operates on the basis of rules and regulations to secure uniformity of action.

A major feature of bureaucracy is that it is impersonal: working for the organisation is paramount. Posts are filled on merit based on qualifications.

Today 'bureaucracy' is used almost as a term of abuse to be levelled at hide bound, rigid, unthinking organisations and their managements. Weber saw it as the most technically efficient form of organisation, capable of:

(a) surviving long after its founders are dead, and

(b) operating efficiently, because personal preferences or out-dated procedures do not divert it from using the best methods to reach its goals.

The bureaucratic structure is a series of steps in which each office's authority embraces all the steps below it. Managerial authority goes with the job, not with the individual who happens to hold it at any one time. Orders are obeyed because the rules say that the office holder can give these commands. This hierarchy is staffed by specialists.

As large-scale business organisations developed they adopted structures designed for efficiency and growth.

2.2 Change and structure

As technology developed and large-scale organisations appeared in business, the principles of specialisation and a rule-based system were widely adopted.

EXAMPLE: THE FIRST RAILWAYS

One hundred and fifty years ago railways were the *only* large-scale industrial organisation. They had to invent a management system almost from scratch, and turned to the only available models – the army and the church, both large bureaucracies. The railways operated single tracks, with trains going in opposite directions on the same line. Strict rules had to be laid down to ensure that trains ran to time and safely. A hierarchy of authority created powers and responsibilities to see that the rules were obeyed.

Activity 3 [5 minutes]

Match the most likely type of authority structure – charismatic, traditional, or bureaucratic – to each of the following organisations.

(a) Alanbrooke's Hospital;

(b) New Wave Advertising Ltd;

(c) C H Westlake & Son (Est. 1924).

The division of labour

In 1776 Adam Smith, a major economic theorist, described the advantages of the division of labour. He looked at the process of pin making: dividing the process into the smallest possible tasks, with specialist workers for each, enabled the workforce to increase the output of pins 250 fold.

The development of this principle reached its peak in 1908 when Henry Ford (1863–1947) used the moving assembly line to bring work to operatives who each performed one tiny, specific task in building a car. The car industry later developed the management structure essential for running a large, multi-product firm efficiently, and which enabled it to grow. Alfred Sloan (1875–1966), the head of General Motors, divided production and sales among single-model car assembly divisions and centralised all the staff functions. Head office could control the production divisions by monitoring their output and financial results. The standard pyramidal organisation allowed for growth by simply employing more workers at the base and adding management layers above them. As firms grew in size and production and administrative work was divided into smaller and smaller tasks, so the number of managers increased. More layers of management meant that senior managers became remote from their customers and markets.

Structures based on the technology of production

Joan Woodward (1916–1971), a professor who surveyed manufacturing organisations in South East Essex, found striking differences in the number of levels of management and in the number of workers supervised. She found that the objectives of a firm – what it wants to make for its chosen markets – determine its technology of production. This leads to differences in organisation structure. She identified three types of structure, ranging from the least to the most complex:

(a) production of units and small batches to customers' requirements – goods are made after the customer has ordered them and it is almost impossible to predict work loads;

(b) large-batch and mass production on assembly lines – every so often, a large quantity of an item is made, in advance of use and is stored; there is continual target setting as there are constant adjustments to variations in manufacturing capacity;

(c) process production, as in the oil and gas industries – production is continuous and never-ceasing and uncertainties in production are reduced as the equipment can be set for the desired level of output.

These descriptions can also apply to service industries and public services. For example, unit and small- batch production in advertising or a medical clinic, large-batch cheque processing in banks, and process or flow in an agency providing social security payments.

Unit production has a short hierarchy, with top managers close to production and workers taking a lot of the responsibility for output. Mass production has short lines of command within a complex hierarchy of specialist departments. Process production takes place in a continuous flow through the plant and is predictable; it has a tall hierarchy with long lines of command and a high proportion of non-production staff.

The post-entrepreneurial organisation

Global competition and the need for quick and flexible response to a rapidly changing market have concentrated attention on how the modern corporation can recover the flair and enterprise that make firms into innovative market leaders. Rosabeth Moss Kanter (born 1943), an American professor, has worked as a consultant in many organisations. She proposes that the corporation of the 1990s should be 'post-entrepreneurial', with fewer management levels and able to anticipate change and seize opportunities. Flatter structures make co-operation across divisions and departments easier. The keys are employee empowerment and strategic alliances with suppliers and customers and in joint ventures. The organisation becomes a small head office managing a network of other enterprises.

Definitions

Empowerment – employees are all given the right to take decisions relevant to their sphere of work which would previously have been taken by supervisors; teams are often empowered.

Strategic alliance – an arrangement with another organisation to co-operate in some way (for example, in jointly developing a new product).

Other modern thinkers, like Henry Mintzberg, as we shall see later, also see the form of organisations changing as they are forced to adapt to new technology, more competition and better information technology.

For discussion

Business organisations are keen to develop entrepreneurship – the willingness to innovate and take risks – among their managers. They see this quality as the essential element in being competitive and successful in the global market. The effect on the structures of organisations is to make their hierarchies flatter and to create more autonomous units. However, many organisations prefer to remain as bureaucracies, seeing certainty and control as important. They remain structured as hierarchies with clear lines of authority and control.

Consider three organisations you know: a large business, a public service and a voluntary organisation. Discuss how each might find it advantageous or disadvantageous to adopt bureaucracy or entrepreneurship.

Different organisation structures have emerged as managements try to improve co-ordination and control. Next we describe the main ways to classify structures.

3 TYPES OF STRUCTURE

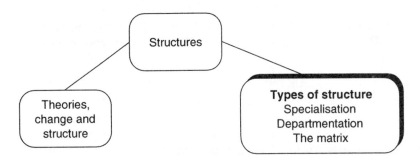

First we look at organisations with a structure based on specialisation by function.

3.1 Specialisation

Specialisation by function leads to line and staff management, as introduced in Section 2. The direct relationship between levels is based on the scalar chain, which shows the extent of authority running downwards and accountability flowing upwards (see Figure 3.4). Remember that each staff department has its own line management.

Activity 4   **[10 minutes]**

There is often friction between line and staff departments. List three possible sources of conflict between them.

Small organisations do not have all the staff functions shown in Figure 3.4. They buy in specialist services as they are required. As we shall see, modern management thinking is that firms should concentrate on their core businesses and hive off functions such as catering and cleaning to specialists. This leaves senior management free from these time absorbing but non-profit making functions.

All kinds of organisations have line and staff structures. Figure 3.5 shows such a structure for a typical charity.

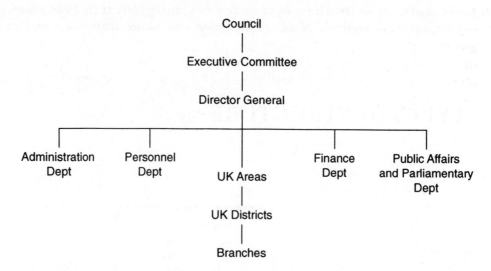

Note: This organisation is also typical for voluntary organisations

Figure 3.5 A line and staff organisation for a charity

Departments can be organised in different ways and this is the next type of structure.

3.2 Departmentation

As organisations grow they are split into divisions and sub-divisions. A division can include many departments. Often it carries out all the line and staff functions except for the strategic direction and control exercised by headquarters.

The method of departmentation depends on the nature of the organisation and its work, and could be as follows.

(a) Functional, where work is divided into specialist areas by primary function such as production, finance and marketing, each of which is sub-divided into specialist departments. This is line and staff organisation.

(b) Product, where the organisation is divided by product or service. Each division has its own line and staff structure, as shown in Figure 3.6.

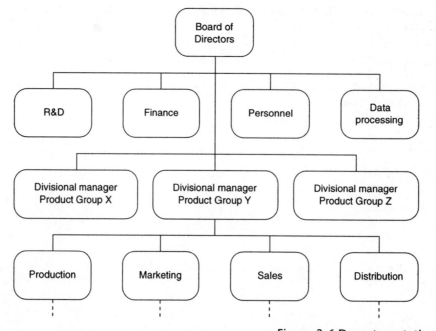

Figure 3.6 Departmentation by product

(c) Territorial departmentation is often used by multinational companies, which retain the major staff functions at headquarters and divide their operations geographically. If they are large enough, each regional subsidiary could have its own board of directors supervising a full range of line and staff functions. More often the territorial division will market all the company's products. This is shown in Figure 3.7.

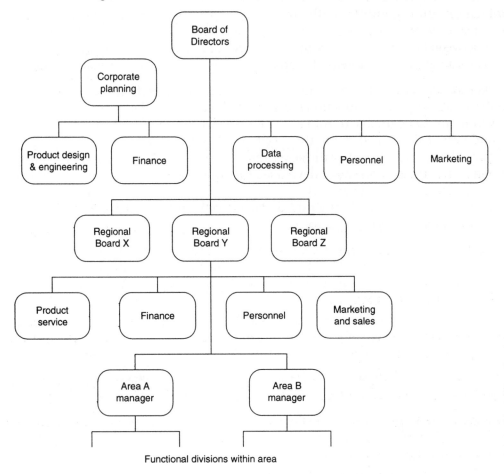

Figure 3.7 Departmentation by territory

Multinationals can also divide up their activities by product, with each product division taking responsibility for world wide production and sales, often with a territorial structure that has, in turn, a functional structure.

International charities tend to have territorial structures. For example, the Save the Children Fund has divisions for the UK, Africa, Asia and the Americas and Pacific.

Activity 5   [10 minutes]

What type of departmentation has:

(a) central government?

(b) independent television?

(c) your college?

For discussion

As you can see from these examples, an organisation can use different methods of departmentation at different levels. Why is this so? What advantages are there for a multinational firm in having a territorial structure with regional divisions each structured into product divisions that are organised into functional departments?

39

Next we examine the matrix organisation – an attempt to overcome the problems of departmentation.

3.3 The matrix structure

Despite its advantages, specialisation by department leads to problems of co-ordination and control. With increasing specialisation no-one may take responsibility, or have authority, over *all* aspects of a project. There is a traditional split between line and staff departments. Large complex developments may require the co-ordination of hundreds of production units and suppliers.

Lockheed, the American aircraft manufacturer first developed the matrix structure in the 1950s. Its previous functional organisation caused its major customer, the US government, to be unable to find a single manager to deal with problems. Project co-ordinators developed from the need to co-ordinate all the line managers involved in a project to satisfy the government's demand for a project management system. Later the co-ordinators developed functional authority and responsibility for project budgets, design and scheduling. Functional department heads remained responsible for the work of their departments; programme co-ordinators became responsible for all aspects of a project.

With this structure, an employee could expect to receive orders from both the co-ordinator and the department head. This dual command was a significant change from the principle of the single boss. An example of a matrix structure is shown in Figure 3.8.

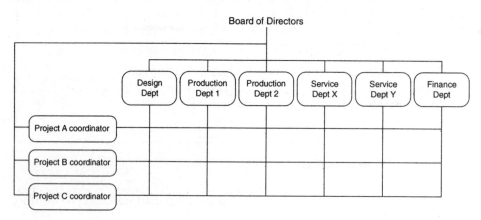

Figure 3.8 A matrix structure

Matrix organisations are primarily found in industries that handle large complex projects, such as the aerospace industry and the construction industry, and in advertising agencies (where a brand manager co-ordinates work across all the specialist functions such as copywriting, design, media buying and research).

It is also possible to have a matrix based on products, as shown in Figure 3.9. This structure is used in companies where strong brands are important.

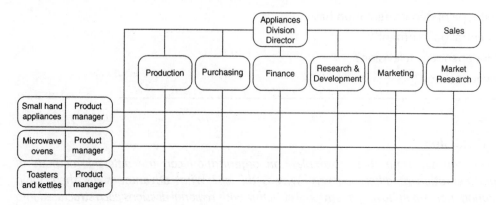

Figure 3.9 A product based matrix

Activity 6   [15 minutes]

Could the management of your course be described as part of a matrix organisation?
Draw an organisation chart for courses in your department of the college.

Chapter roundup

- The structure of an organisation is determined by influences such as its mission, operations, culture, technology and external factors like changes in government policy.

- Organisations develop the typical pyramid structure because of the need to establish lines of authority and responsibility.

- The typical relationships between people in an organisation are line, staff and function.

- As organisations grow and develop specialist departments they tend to establish a line and staff structure.

- Classical management thinking developed the principles of a hierarchy of authority and bureaucracy with its clearly defined tasks and rules and authority based on the post held, not the person.

- The length of the scalar chain of authority depends on the type of production – unit, mass or process.

- Organisation structures can be classified into the following categories:

  (a) specialisation – the typical line and staff organisation;

  (b) departmentation – functional, product or territorial;

  (c) matrix – authority is shared between the project manager and the line managers in departments.

Quick Quiz

1 Give two influences which may shape a public service's organisation structure but which may not apply to a business.

2 Why do organisations develop layers of authority?

3 What does a line relationship show?

4 Give three examples of staff departments.

5 What was Fayol's principle of command in organisations?

6 What three types of authority structure did Weber identify?

7 Why did Weber think that bureaucracy is the most efficient form of organisation?

8 What are the differences between the hierarchies of firms engaged in unit, mass and process production?

9 Why does Rosabeth Moss Kanter think that firms should have shorter hierarchies?

10 What does a scalar chain show?

11 Draw an outline organisation chart to show a line and staff organisation structure.

12 What are the three types of departmentation?

13 What are the responsibilities of project managers and department heads in a matrix structure?

14 Who is an employee's boss in a matrix structure?

Answers to Quick Quiz

1   Public services' structures may be influenced by the duties and obligations imposed by Parliament. These may change because of changes in government policy, for example reducing defence spending, and because of society's expectations, for example care for the elderly.

2   To ensure that correct decisions are made and implemented at appropriate levels of authority and responsibility.

3   It shows the direct line of authority from top management to the lowest level in the organisation.

4   You might have listed: purchasing, stores, accounts, transport, marketing, sales, personnel, training and research.

5   A single line of command with each worker having only one boss.

6   Charismatic, traditional and rational-legal.

7   Because posts are filled on merit, not personality, it is impersonal. Working for the organisation is paramount, and it uses the best methods to reach its goals uninfluenced by personal preferences or outdated procedures.

8   Unit production has a short hierarchy, with the lowest level having a lot of responsibility. Mass production has short lines of command within a complex hierarchy of specialist departments. Process production has a tall hierarchy with long lines of command.

9   Flatter structures make co-operation easier across the divisions and departments of the firm.

10 It shows the levels of authority and responsibility in a hierarchy.

11 See Figure 3.4.

12 Functional, product and territorial.

13 Project managers are responsible for all aspects of the project, including the schedule and the budget; department managers are responsible for their departments, as line managers.

14 Both the project co-ordinator and the department head. Some matrix organisations combine territorial and functional organisation.

Answers to Activities

1   You will probably have found sales-floor departments such as: ladies' outer wear, gents' outfitting, sports goods, children's clothes, stationery, ladies' shoes, linens, furniture and carpets. Service departments might include: accounts, credit, personnel, transport and warehousing and marketing. The advantages of such specialisation are greater expertise and efficiency.

2   Your answers should be as follows: (a) line and staff; (b) line and staff if there are support units such as administration and audio-visual, or line if not; (c) line.

3   Your answers should be: (a) bureaucratic; (b) charismatic; (c) traditional.

4   You might have listed: the split of authority that could cause line managers to resent staff 'interference'; line managers regarding staff as inferior; and conflict over resources.

5   The correct answers are: (a) functional; (b) territorial; (c) product.

6   You are correct if you said that your course could be described as part of a matrix organisation. See Figure 3.10 for an example organisation chart.

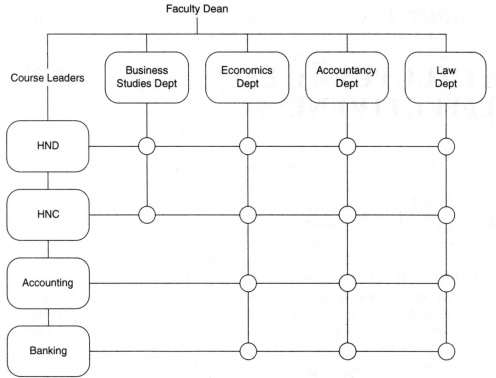

Figure 3.10 A faculty course matrix

Assignment 3 [2 hours]

Take an organisation that you know, or on which you can get the basic information required.

1 Draw an organisation chart for the organisation.

2 Explain the structure shown in the chart with reference to:

   (a) the organisation's mission;

   (b) its products;

   (c) its markets;

   (d) its method of production;

   (e) any particular external influence.

Write up your findings in the form of a list of bullet points for a presentation to be made to new recruits to the organisation.

Chapter 4

STRUCTURAL EFFICIENCY AND EFFECTIVENESS

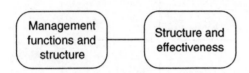

Introduction

All organisations have to reach a minimum level of efficiency to survive: business organisations have to be efficient to survive competition; public services are subject to audits and inspections; voluntary bodies have to account for their use of funds.

Most organisations have targets which they try to meet and improve on, and they have to develop a structure that is effective in delivering their objectives efficiently.

The structure that is right for one organisation may be disastrous for another. Views of what makes for an effective structure change with technological developments and changes in the external environment of organisations.

Your objectives

After completing this chapter you should be able to:

(a) recognise factors affecting the efficiency and effectiveness of organisational structures;

(b) appreciate the link between organisational structure and effectiveness in meeting organisational objectives;

(c) understand the need for different structures.

First we look at the functions of management and how they relate to the structure of organisations.

1 MANAGEMENT FUNCTIONS AND STRUCTURE

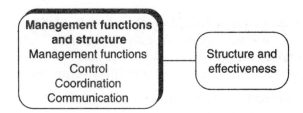

1.1 Management functions

The functions of management are:

(a) *to plan* – which includes selecting objectives and strategies;

(b) *to organise* – which includes structuring tasks and groups and motivating people to work well;

(c) *to control* – which includes directing subordinates to carry out tasks, and measuring and correcting their performance;

(e) *to co-ordinate* the activities of individuals and groups;

(f) *to communicate* objectives, plans, instructions and results and receive information.

When an organisation has decided its objectives and selected its strategies for achieving them, it requires an effective structure to implement plans and programmes. An effective structure is one that provides for the control, co-ordination and communication necessary to implement the plans and achieve the objectives.

Activity 1 [15 minutes]

You are responsible for the presentation next month of a seminar group report on the packaging industry. Briefly describe how you might apply each of these management functions.

Effective control is vital for an organisation to function efficiently, but securing control determines structures.

1.2 Control

The sole trader has little problem in controlling their business. Decision making, planning, monitoring and reporting may all be done by the same person. Most control relationships are direct and involve few staff.

Partnerships and small private companies have few problems, as they have few layers of authority. The same applies to any other organisation with a long series of steps in the scalar chain.

Span of control

How many subordinates can a manager control effectively? How many people can a manager direct, monitor and co-ordinate? This is the problem of deciding the span of control.

Definition

Span of control: the number of subordinates working to a superior. For example, if there are five workers reporting to a manager, the span of control is five.

The principle of span of control applies equally to a chargehand with a team of assembly workers, to a Local Authority Director supervising managers (for example, of planning, building inspection, technical services, works depot and surveying) and to a chief executive with half a dozen managing directors of subsidiary companies.

Management writers, especially Lyndall Urwick in his 1952 *Principles of Management*, argue that the span of control should be restricted to the number of subordinates that can be supervised effectively. The recommended span is between three and six. The arguments for a narrow span of control are that this gives:

(a) tight control and close supervision from the top of the organisation down;

(b) reduced delegation;

(c) better communication;

(d) better co-ordination.

Wide spans of control can be as many as forty. The arguments in favour are:

(a) greater decision making authority for subordinates;

(b) better motivation and greater job satisfaction;

(c) lower supervision cost.

Against these must be set some loss of control.

In practice the span of control depends on a number of factors, including:

(a) the complexity of the work of a unit and how exposed it is to change – greater complexity and rapid change call for a narrow span to ensure group effort in problem solving;

(b) how hazardous the work is – the greater the danger, the narrower the span;

(c) how good the organisation's managers are at delegating and at controlling and managing demands on their time;

(d) the extent to which staff functions can provide specialist support functions to line management;

(e) the knowledge and experience of subordinate staff and the amount of supervision they require;

(f) the consequences of mistakes by subordinates – how costly they are;

(g) whether the group is together or dispersed in different locations;

(h) the technology involved, as demonstrated by Joan Woodward;

(i) the quality of the communications network in all directions;

(j) whether the organisation's directors believe that there should be a tall or flat management structure.

There is no correct size for the span of control. What is right depends on the nature of the individual organisation. Current thinking is in favour of flat structures with few levels in the hierarchy, but some organisations require a tall structure.

Activity 2 [40 minutes]

Select an organisation you know or which you can ask someone about and find out the span of control of the management, both generally and in a specific function such as production, accounting or marketing.

With reference to the factors which determine the span of control listed above, try to give a value to each on a scale of one (unimportant) to five (very important). For example, complexity of processes = 4, ability to delegate = 2.

As organisations grow, the difficulties of co-ordinating activities between people, groups and divisions become greater and structures can become ineffective.

1.3 Co-ordination

As an organisation grows, both the number of departments and the sub-divisions within them become larger. The more complex structure makes it difficult to co-ordinate all the activities. Specialisation makes understanding more difficult between different functions and it is more difficult to share information. The nature of the organisation also changes and it is likely to become more bureaucratic. Eventually it ceases to be effective.

A simplified accounting function organisation chart is shown in Figure 4.1. Compare this with a small firm having just one Chief Accountant and a sales ledger and a bought ledger clerk. This could be multiplied many times across the different departments and divisions of a typical multinational organisation.

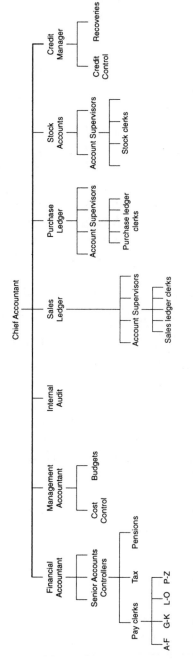

Figure 4.1 An accounting function organisation chart

Numbers of relationships

The greater the number of people or groups in an organisation, the greater the potential number of relationships between them. Graicunas' formula showed how the number of relationships increases in a geometric progression in proportion to the number of members. The formula is

$$N = \left(\frac{2^n}{2} + n - 1 \right)$$

N is the total number of relationships and n is the number of subordinates. Where $n = 1$, $N = 1$ but when n only equals 7, $N = 490$. In other words, with a manager and six subordinates the possible number of relationships among them all is 490.

Activity 3 [10 minutes]

Suppose there are ten members of your seminar group and you all have to co-operate in completing an exercise for which you each have found out some information and statistics. If you cannot all meet up in one place, how many potential relationships could there be between you to collect the results?

You might find it interesting to consider how many relationships there are in the typical matrix structure of the college department we looked at in the last chapter.

Layers of management

Do not confuse co-ordination with control in terms of layers of management. With a narrow span of control, it is quite possible for one director to control thousands of personnel. For example, if each level controls five subordinates the result is an organisation pyramid like this:

1	Chairperson
5	Vice-chairpersons
25	Managing Directors
125	Directors on boards
625	Area managers
3,125	Works managers
15,625	Department managers
78,125	Team leaders
390,625	Team members

If each team leader controlled 20 team members there would be 1,562,500 team members.

A small span of control and a tall hierarchy make it possible to have very large organisations. However, the problems of co-ordinating all the diverse parts are so great, especially when there are many different businesses, that some have taken the extreme step of breaking up the organisation to restore effectiveness. The split of ICI and Zeneca is a recent example.

The problems of control and co-ordination are made worse by the difficulties of communicating in large organisations.

1.4 Communication

Today's organisations require close co-operation, so communication is vitally important. Recent developments, such as electronic messages and computer networks, make communicating easier, faster and more accurate. However, they also lead to communication overload. The communication net becomes just as complicated as the web of relationships outlined above.

The need to control, co-ordinate and collect, store and transmit information leads to bureaucracy. The organisation's technology for communicating and monitoring can easily add rigidity to rules so that the organisation becomes inflexible and unable to cope with change.

When communications flow up and down a simple line organisation they are efficient. Once specialisation increases and many staff functions appear, the need to inform and consult means that communication becomes slow and irrelevant to many members of the organisation. The fact that more parts of the organisation communicate with outside groups, such as suppliers and shareholders, adds to the problem.

For discussion

Large organisations suffer inefficiencies that do not affect small organisations. These difficulties arise from the increasing complexity of control, co-ordination and communication. Discuss how these problems affect some large organisations you know and what the symptoms are. What have been your experiences of communicating with, and of co-ordination and communication in, a large organisation?

Next we look at the structure of an organisation in relation to its effectiveness. First with reference to its response to its environment.

2   STRUCTURE AND EFFECTIVENESS

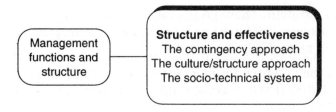

2.1   The contingency approach

The contingency approach to organisation analysis says that there is an ideal structure which can optimise the efficiency of the organisation. The ideal structure depends on the nature, objectives and circumstances of each organisation.

Differentiation

Paul Lawrence and Jay Lorsch laid the foundations for the contingency theory with their studies of organisations published in Organisation and Environment (1967), followed by other analyses with a number of other contributors. Their major finding was that, in order to cope effectively with their external environments, organisations have to develop differentiated units. Each unit has the task of dealing with an aspect of conditions outside the firm. For example, Production deals with the sources of resources – equipment, materials and labour, Design deals with market demand, technological change and government regulations and Sales deals with competition, customers and markets.

The differences between the units' functions and tasks are accompanied by differentiation between the perceptions of their managers and differences in their structures. The Design department is likely to have a long time horizon and an informal structure. Production operates on a very short timescale in a rigidly formal system. Sales looks to the medium term as dictated by competitors' actions in the market and operates a moderately formal structure.

This differentiation is essential for the organisation to operate successfully. But it is a system that must be integrated. It must be co-ordinated to secure collaboration. Thus the organisation requires both appropriate differentiation and adequate integration.

Stable/simple and dynamic/complex environments

The most appropriate structure for an organisation is also influenced by whether its environment is stable and simple or dynamic and complex. This will be discussed in Chapter 11.

Activity 4 [15 minutes]

State whether the following organisations operate in a stable or dynamic environment and give one reason for your choice in each case:

(a) a fund holding General Practice;

(b) Virgin Atlantic Airways;

(c) Microsoft Computer Software Corporation;

(d) Capital Gold Radio;

(e) Liverpool Corporation.

In stable environments there is strong pressure for uniform structures. Top management can deal effectively with comparatively rare unforeseen events. The highest performing firms in different industries have been found to have structures in which senior management have a high degree of, and middle managers have a low degree of, influence and authority.

In dynamic environments successful firms have greater diversity among their units and a structure where senior management have rather less influence and authority and middle management rather more.

Greater differentiation brings the potential for more inter-departmental conflict. Specialists develop fundamentally different ways of thinking and behaving. Their cultures are different. Their goals diverge.

For example, Sales managers are concerned with bringing a new product to market, in a given timescale, for a cost, and selling it at a competitive price. Research managers are concerned with making a new product safe, well designed and the best in its field. Production wants simplicity of machining, regular and continuous supply and stable, predictable demand. The successful firm must therefore develop machinery for conflict resolution and integration if it is to function effectively.

Such machinery includes the traditional methods of a formal managerial hierarchy, reporting and information systems and regular contact between members of different departments. Successful firms with a high degree of differentiation add such devices as:

(a) assigning the role of liaison officer to one manager in a staff department;

(b) setting up temporary teams of specialists to deal with urgent issues;

(c) establishing formal integrating teams from the various functional units to resolve conflicts.

Successful firms have an organisation structure that reduces uncertainty. They pay great attention to integration. In particular they have an appropriate organisation structure which enables people to perform their tasks well.

Next we look at the relationship between culture and structure.

2.2 The culture/structure approach

The culture/structure approach says that the ideal structure for an organisation in any situation depends on its existing culture. The culture of organisations is discussed in detail in Chapters 14 and 15 (see especially 15.2.1), but the main features are as follows.

(a) The degree of formality in management as shown by:

    (i)   the way decisions are made, by individuals or with consultation;

    (ii)   the amount of delegation and freedom of action given to subordinates;

    (iii)   the amount, freedom and type of communication between senior managers and junior employees.

(b) The degree of formality in the structure as shown by ranks and authority levels.

(c) The degree of formality in office layout, dress, modes of address and personal relationships.

Four types of corporate culture

Charles Handy (born 1932) worked for Shell before becoming a consultant and professor at the London Business School. He writes on corporate culture and organisations. Handy describes four types of corporate culture. The firm may have only one of these or a mixture in different parts of the organisation.

(a) The *power culture*, where influence and authority stem from a single source. This culture is typical of the sole proprietor or charismatic founder. It is best suited to small organisations where personal contact is possible, and is capable of flexible and swift response to change. It suffers from the defect that decisions are taken by one or a few individuals and other employees work by precedent.

(b) The *role culture* is bureaucracy. It operates through rules and precedents; status determines authority. Formal job descriptions determine the roles of post holders so that efficiency depends on the structure and not on personalities. Bureaucracy is effective in stable environments, but does not cope well with change.

(c) The *task culture* is concerned with the job. There is more concern with expertise than with an authority structure. Typically the task force or project team is flexible and constantly changing to meet new challenges. It is also found in matrix organisations.

(d) The *existential culture* is a person culture which exists to serve the interests of the individuals in the organisation. It exists in some partnerships, for example an architectural practice, and in design studios. It is also a feature of the informal organisation of many bodies. Individuals see the organisation as existing to serve their personal goals. The arts and the media are examples.

Activity 5 [15 minutes]

Identify the most likely type of culture for each of the following:

(a) your college;

(b) the Home Office;

(c) Manchester United Football Club PLC;

(d) the BBC news teams;

(e) the Michelin starred restaurant Le Manoir des Quat' Saisons;

(f) Disney Corporation.

The relationship of structure to culture

The relationship of the organisation structure to its culture depends on:

(a) its age, stage of growth and size, all of which affect how it moves from a power culture based on the founder through added management and departments to a bureaucracy;

(b) its objectives, which vary from the personal expression of an independent television producer in a task culture to a local authority department operating as a role culture;

(c) the nature of the work and the technology that it uses determine the structure, as we have seen from the work of Joan Woodward and Lawrence and Lorsch;

(d) whether the environment is stable or dynamic – the former is more likely to lead to bureaucracy, the latter to a task culture and a matrix organisation.

The organisation will adapt to growth and change in one of three ways:

(a) by reinforcement of the formal structure with committees and project teams – this may succeed, but is likely to blur authority and delay action;

(b) by decentralising and delegating authority to subordinate organisations that duplicate the original on a smaller scale, thus recreating the bureaucracy – this is only likely to be successful in a stable environment;

(c) by setting up different structures with different cultures in different parts of the organisation.

The organisation that is likely to be successful has a central decision-making body of key individuals. It sets up a power culture to deal with sudden crises, a bureaucracy where there is stability and the work is routine, a matrix or task forces where there is dynamic change in the market and there is a constant need for new developments, and an existential culture where individual flair is important, for example in research or design.

The effective organisation will differentiate to gain the strengths of the different cultures and integrate to achieve the common goal: successfully resolving conflict.

Activity 6   [5 minutes]

What are the two common features of the contingency approach and the cultures structures approach?

Finally we look briefly at the socio/technical concept which says that structure depends on technology.

2.3   The socio-technical system

Joan Woodward showed how the technology of an organisation determined its structure. The work of the Tavistock Institute in London by Trist, Emery, Rice and others focused on the work group. Their examination of the effects of technological change led them to the concept of the organisation as a socio-technical system.

This analysis rests on the concept of the *'primary work group'*. This is the smallest unit within the organisation. It is important because:

(a) it is the immediate social environment of the individual worker;

(b) the methods and team spirit in primary groups determine the working relationships and efficiency of the whole organisation.

The optimum primary group is small because the intimate personal relationships on which it depends cannot be formed among more than a dozen people.

The technology limits the type of work organisation that is possible, but the work organisation has social and psychological properties of its own that are independent of the technology.

Social and technological requirements are mutually interdependent and they must have an economic validity. Achieving the optimum for any one of these is not enough; they must be optimised as a whole. The work organisation must attempt to balance:

(a) economic advantages;

(b) technological advantages;

(c) social and psychological advantages.

Changes in technology or the organisation have to take account of all of these.

Most organisations do not provide for these groups, as the formal management hierarchy ends above their level. The result is that unofficial informal groups appear, with their own leaders and aims. They tend to be self-protective. The goals of the group may not be the same as the objectives of the organisation.

With the same technological and economic constraints, the organisation can operate different systems of work organisation with different social and psychological effects. The successful organisation will attempt to select the one that best meets the needs of the work group. The importance of this concept in organisational design is discussed in the next chapter.

Chapter roundup

In this chapter you have seen that:

- To be effective an organisation's structure should make it possible for management to control, co-ordinate and communicate in order to reach its objectives efficiently.

- A manager's span of control is the number of subordinates that he or she can direct.

- A narrow span of control not exceeding six subordinates is generally supposed to be efficient. A wide span improves motivation among the subordinates.

- The optimum span of control depends on the nature of the organisation.

- Effective co-ordination is essential in large organisations. This is made difficult by the fact that the number of relationships increases geometrically as group size increases or more departments are created. Communication becomes more difficult and more of the information becomes irrelevant to the recipient.

- The contingency approach says that the most effective structure for an organisation is determined by its external environment. More dynamic environments mean greater diversity of structure among the differentiated units that the organisation has to create. Successful organisations provide for integration of these diverse functions.

- The culture/structure approach says that the effective structure for an organisation depends on its culture – power, role, task or existential. A successful organisation will adopt the structure for each unit that best suits its culture. It will also provide for co-ordination.

- The socio-technical system examines the primary working group in terms of economic advantage, technological advantage and socio/psychological advantage. Unofficial groups will be formed if the organisation does not ensure that the social and psychological needs of the group are met. The successful organisation selects the structure that best meets the needs of the group.

Quick Quiz

1 What are the functions of management?

2 What is the span of control?

3 Why is a narrow span of control favoured?

4 Why does co-ordination become more difficult as the organisation grows?

5 Which organisation structure has the simplest communications?

6 What does the contingency approach say that organisations must do to cope effectively with their environments?

7 What sorts of structures are required in stable and in dynamic environments?

8 Complete the following sentence: 'Successful firms with a high degree of differentiation pay great attention to...'

9 What are Handy's four types of corporate culture?

10 According to the culture/structure approach, how does the successful organisation adapt to change and growth? What makes for a successful organisation?

11 What is the primary working group and why is it important?

12 According to the socio-technical approach, which three factors must be considered in deciding on an organisation structure?

13 If an organisation does not provide for the primary work group, what tends to happen?

14 What is the structure adopted by the successful organisation according to the socio/technical approach?

Answers to Quick Quiz

1 Plan, organise, control, co-ordinate and communicate.

2 It is the number of subordinates reporting to a manager.

3 A narrow span gives tight control and supervision with better communication and co-ordination.

4 Because the number of relationships increases geometrically as the group size or the number of departments increases.

5 Any line organisation, especially the sole trader with no employees!

6 They must develop differentiated units each suited to the part of the external environment it deals with.

7 Stable environments mean simple, uniform structures. Dynamic environments require highly differentiated units.

8 Integration.

9 Power, role, task and existential.

10 It sets up different structures according to the appropriate culture in each unit. Success comes from a combination of diversity and integration to achieve the common goal.

11 It is the smallest unit within the organisation of not more than twelve people. It is important because it is the social environment of the individual and the working relationships in groups that determine the efficiency of the whole organisation.

12 The economic, technological and socio/psychological.

13 Unofficial, informal groups form, which may not have the same objectives as the organisation.

14 The successful organisation adopts different structures according to the social and psychological needs of the groups.

Answers to Activities

1   You might:

(a) plan for the production of the report and the conduct of the presentation;

(b) organise the programme of work;

(c) control the work of the team by monitoring progress;

(c) co-ordinate their activities, for example by getting research results passed to members doing graphs and overheads;

(d) communicate with members to give them information about others' work and find out their progress.

2   Compare your answers with the following example of a college.

The span of control is between 3 and 5. The importance of each factor is:

(a) the complexity of the work = 4

(b) hazardous nature = 1

(c) quality of management = 5

(d) specialist support by staff functions to line management = 4

(e) quality of subordinate staff = 1

(f) the consequences of mistakes = 2

(g) whether the group is together or dispersed = 1 to 5

(h) the technology involved = 1 to 5

(i) the quality of the communications network = 3

(j) whether the organisation's directors believe that there should be a tall or flat management structure = 4.

3   Your answers should be as follows:

$$N = \left(\frac{2^n}{2} + n - 1 \right)$$

$N = 10(2^{10}/2 + 10 - 1)$

$N = 10(1024/2 + 9)$

$N = 10(512 + 9)$

$N = 10(521)$

$\quad = 5,210.$

4   (a)   A fund holding General Practice operates in a generally stable environment, but this will become dynamic if a future Labour government alters its financial basis.

(b)   Virgin Atlantic Airways operates in a dynamic environment, as a result of competition, airline mergers and changes in government policy in the USA and EC.

(c)   Microsoft Computer Software Corporation operates in a dynamic environment, because of the pace of change in the industry.

(d)   Capital Gold Radio operates in a fairly stable environment (until the next round of licensing) as competition is known and fixed.

(e)   Liverpool Corporation operates in a stable environment, as its finances and policies are set. This environment will become more dynamic if there is a Labour government with new policies.

5   The most likely cultures for each organisation are as follows:

Your college – power/existential.

The Home Office – role.

Manchester United Football Club Plc – power/task.

BBC news teams – task.

Le Manoir des Quat' Saisons – power/existential.

Disney Corporation – role for administration, task for production.

6 Both the contingency approach and the cultures/structures approach favour diversity and integration.

Assignment 4   [2.5 hours]

This can done as an individual or as a group exercise.

Analyse an organisation that you know and write a short report setting out:

(a) its objectives;

(b) its structure;

(c) its culture (or cultures);

(d) how the structure relates to the culture and technology;

(e) the span of control and how it relates to culture and technology;

(f) whether the structure makes for good co-ordination and communication;

(g) whether the organisation reacts well with its environment.

Conclude by analysing whether or not the organisation achieves its objectives and the role of the structure in this. (If you cannot get information on criteria such as market share, judge the organisation on a published measure such as profit or waiting lists).

Chapter 5

ORGANISATIONAL DESIGN AND CHANGE

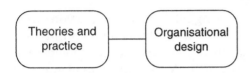

Introduction

Organisations grow and, as they do so, develop new objectives and functions. External forces can also cause change. Organisations may be prompted to redesign themselves by, for example, the restructuring of local government, the challenge of new competitors, or the promise of new technology.

The impetus for change may come from a dramatic outside intervention, such as the local government reorganisation that has created more unitary authorities and split up the Scottish regions. Alternatively, it may be an internal response to the problems of differentiation and greater bureaucracy. Redesign is also often forced on companies by their shareholders, who seek better returns. A current factor leading to change is that modern management thinking has moved away from concepts that emphasised authority and control from the top. Today's efficient organisation involves *all* its members in its success.

Organisation development is the process of bringing about the changes in attitudes, structure and operations that are necessary for success and, even, survival. Designing the organisation for success is a vital part of the process.

Your objectives

After completing this chapter you should:

(a) appreciate the context of modern business;

(b) understand the relevance of modern management theory to the modern context of business;

(c) be able to identify the aims when designing organisations in the context of modern business.

We start by discussing the modern context of business.

NOTES

1 THEORIES AND PRACTICE

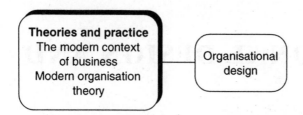

1.1 The modern context of business

Until comparatively recently 'Production was King'. Business organisations were designed to produce as much as possible. Production was broken down into ever smaller tasks which could be automated. Administration followed the same path of dividing tasks and duplicating procedures. The attitude of management was still linked to Henry Ford's famous statement: 'The customer can have any colour he wants so long as it is black.' (Black paint was the only colour to dry fast enough to keep up with output.)

Management thinking and attitudes have been transformed in many, though not all, firms in the past twenty years. Firms have become customer oriented. Quality is seen as vital. Work organisation recognises the importance of job satisfaction and job enrichment. Competition has become global. The production function itself has changed. Firms often no longer make things, but source parts and sub-assemblies from wherever they are cheapest and assemble them into final products. The personal computer on every desk has transformed administration.

Major features of modern business

The major features of modern business are as follows:

(a) *Customer orientation*. There is no longer a mass market. Each customer is unique and expects products tailored to their wants and supplied in convenient ways. Japanese firms provide quality products at competitive prices with high levels of service. Deregulation has brought competition and choice to one-time monopolies such as telecommunications. The balance of negotiating power has shifted from manufacturers to the large-scale retailers. Similarly, the banks have lost customers to deregulated building societies that offer better rates and service.

Activity 1 [20 minutes]

(i) Take a look at a motoring magazine and see how many variants there are of a popular model of a car. Why is this so?

(ii) Go into a local bank or building society and pick up a leaflet giving details of their deposit accounts. How many variants are there? Why is this so?

(b) *Competition*. Trade barriers have disappeared and local firms face competition from around the globe. Products are targeted at niche markets. New firms can easily enter many markets. A higher level of service can give a company an advantage. Information technology plays an important part – for example, IT can personalise service through access to customer databases, link the administrative processes of customers and suppliers and make possible such new approaches as customer call centres for telesales linked to TV programmes.

(c) *Change*. Change is now a constant feature. New technology and work methods have shortened the product life cycle. Competition changes the market. Former rivals seek co-operation because the cost of developing new products is too great for one to bear alone.

Activity 2 [10 minutes]

List three reasons why a supermarket would benefit from using IT to identify its customers.

Diseconomies of scale

The traditional organisation has grown on the basis of sub-dividing tasks. Each increase in the number of line workers results in a larger number of people in staff functions. There are forty steps in making a pair of shoes and at least as many spread over sales, stores, transport, finance and credit in getting them to the shop. The advantages of reducing complex processes into simple, small tasks are overwhelmed by the costs of the diseconomies of large scale. These include the cost of co-ordination, poor communications and loss of entrepreneurship.

Firms typically try to improve their performance by doing things better. They improve procedures, apply more technology, preach the virtues of customer service and promote quality circles. Working on the existing system can have only limited results. Better management can only work within the structure as given.

Success in the modern business context requires a new approach to the design of organisations.

For discussion

Take a number of firms which you know and discuss their performance in terms of customer satisfaction. Many organisations publish customer charters and similar statements. How does their actual performance compare with their stated intentions? Why is performance good or bad?

For example, you might compare a railway company with McDonald's.

Management thinkers have responded to the changed context of business by proposing new work organisation.

1.2 Modern organisation theory

As we have seen, the traditional organisation is hierarchical, with many differentiated units departmentalised by product, region or function. It spends much effort on co-ordination and integration.

Urwick's eight principles for effective organisations

Lyndall Urwick formulated eight principles, in 1952, which he felt would lead to the design of effective organisations.

(a) The principle of the *objective* – the organisation and its parts should exist to carry out a purpose.

(b) The principle of *correspondence* – formal authority and responsibility must run together and be equal at each level.

(c) The principle of *responsibility* – a superior has absolute responsibility for the acts of a subordinate.

(d) The *scalar* principle – there must be a clear line of authority running from top to bottom.

(e) The principle of the *span of control* – a superior cannot supervise the work of more than six subordinates.

(f) The principle of *specialisation* – as far as possible the work of every person should be limited to one function.

(g) The principle of *definition* – every position should be clearly described in writing.

(h) The principle of *co-ordination* – the final object of all organisation is smooth and effective co-ordination.

All but the last of these is about control.

This is the design for a typical bureaucracy. You will find it in banks, the Civil Service, supermarket companies and the army. For certain types of organisation it is effective. As we have seen, the structure of an organisation is determined by its objectives, nature, technology, culture and environment. Where there are routine tasks with a high cost of errors a bureaucracy is efficient and effective.

The post-entrepreneurial organisation

There are other types of organisation in which some sacrifice of control can make them more successful. Modern management theory has developed new ways of organising work and designing organisations.

We have seen that Rosabeth Moss Kanter proposes the post-entrepreneurial corporation with:

(a) a flatter hierarchy;

(b) decentralised authority;

(c) autonomous work groups.

Her experience of many large American corporations led to her belief that the traditional bureaucracy could not respond quickly and flexibly enough for success in the global market place. The key change is employee empowerment.

Mintzberg's five types of organisation

Like other theorists, Kanter was influenced by Henry Mintzberg (born 1939) who divided organisations into five types.

(a) The *simple structure*, with centralised control by a small hierarchy, is typical of the entrepreneur-founded company that attracts strong loyalty because of its sense of mission and its simplicity, flexibility and informality.

(b) The *machine bureaucracy* has many layers of management. Its 'technostructure' of line and staff experts is a great strength that manages mass production well, but is slow to react to change and poor at motivating employees.

(c) The *professional bureaucracy* is founded on shared expertise rather than a hierarchy. With its standards set by external professional bodies it tends to be more democratic and more highly motivated among the professionals than a machine bureaucracy.

(d) The *divisionalised form* is where a small central core controls key elements, like investment, for a number of otherwise autonomous units. It is several machine bureaucracies operating under a central staff. It is typical of multinational companies which set up geographical divisions.

(e) The *adhocracy* is characterised by flexible cross-discipline teams collaborating on specific projects. It is found most frequently in new technology industries which need to innovate constantly and respond swiftly to market changes. Mintzberg divides it into the *operating adhocracy*, which is a creative unit working in a competitive market, and the *administrative adhocracy*, which may be research based.

Activity 3   [15 minutes]

Write down three industries where an adhocracy could be expected to flourish. How do they differ from an industry where you would find a divisionalised structure?

Mintzberg divides each of these organisations into five elements:

(a) the strategic apex of top executives;

(b) the technostructure of key personnel in production, planning, finance and human relations;

(c) the operating core of staff who interface with customers and suppliers;

(d) the middle line of managers who link the strategic apex and the operating core;

(e) the support staff who work in areas such as research, public relations and salary administration.

The adhocracy is seen by some as the organisation for the future: all structures should ultimately develop this in order to cope with the external pressures of competition and change and to develop the potential of their people. However, Mintzberg recognises that adhocracy is suitable only for certain types of business activities, particularly for some newer industries. Bureaucracies are still ideal for certain types of task.

Mintzberg also considers a further type of structure, the *missionary structure*, which has a strong ideological basis. His prototype for this is the shared ideals and single status found in an Israeli kibbutz. In business it applies to innovative, research-based start-up firms, for example those linked to universities. It is common among single-issue voluntary organisations. They are likely to remain small as their success depends on personal contact.

Peters' and Waterman's analysis

Tom Peters (born 1942) and Robert Waterman (born 1936) wrote the world's best selling business book *In Search of Excellence* in 1982, and have since separately written several books on managing change, including one by Waterman which develops the concept of adhocracy as a way of structuring work to meet the need for constant change.

Peters and Waterman analysed the factors that made 43 companies the most successful of the top 500 in the US. They identified such features as: treating people as a source of value, and combining autonomy at the shop floor with a central core of values subscribed to by all. The firms had a simple structure with some of the best having a minimum of headquarters staff. They fostered innovation.

Five years later only fourteen of these firms could still be classed as excellent. The conclusion was that nothing stays constant long enough in the present business environment to enable a firm to build excellence sustained on its past and current activities.

Peters and Waterman said that an excellent company should be redefined as one that believes in constant improvement and meeting the demands of constant change. The successful firm must move from a hierarchical management pyramid to a horizontal, fast adapting, cross functional one based on co-operation across the organisation.

The core message from all these thinkers is that the successful modern organisation must be structured to encourage flexible responses to change and for innovation. The key to this is empowering its people.

Activity 4 [25 minutes]

(i) Write down three factors that you consider would show that an organisation is 'excellent'.

(ii) Choose an organisation and ask five people who use it how they rate it on each of your factors. Which is most important to them?

Next we look at how organisations can be designed to meet the context of modern business.

2 ORGANISATIONAL DESIGN

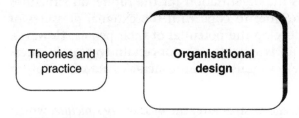

Good intentions and brilliant proposals will be dead-ended, delayed, sabotaged, massaged to death, or revised beyond recognition or usefulness by the overlayered structures at most large and all too many small firms.

Tom Peters *Thriving on Chaos*, 1987

This condemnation of the classical bureaucracy does not mean that every organisation should abandon it. For many organisations it remains the most effective structure. The armed forces, police, civil service, large manufacturing firms making mature products and some voluntary organisations seeking to co-ordinate the efforts of many branches all benefit from bureaucracy. However, they can still benefit from adapting their structures to take advantage of new approaches to organising work. Those facing competition and change must redesign their organisations if they are to succeed.

Organisations can rarely be designed from scratch. They have to be *re*designed. The process of change is called *organisation development* (OD). This is discussed in Chapter 12. It is an organisation-wide process concerned with changing people's behaviour, organisation structures and decision processes through the intervention of a 'change agent' brought in for the specific job. The aim is to enhance organisational effectiveness.

Redesign of an organisation has to take account of:

(a) increasing turbulence in the dynamic environment;

(b) greater competition and the need for constant improvement and innovation;

(c) the impact of information technology;

(d) new systems of values in society and the workplace;

(e) increasing complexity of processes that are inter-dependent and that require co-operation.

The result is that the organisation of work and the structure of organisations must change:

(a) the work unit changes from the functional department to the cross-division team;

(b) employees are empowered – authority and responsibility are shifted from the hierarchy to the team which organises its own work;

(c) jobs and skills change from simple, sub-divided tasks to multi-skilled work where the individual is involved in a whole process, not just a specific part of it.

For discussion

What are the implications for managers of these changes in work organisation?

The culture of the organisation must change to make this redesign work:

(a) the priority is to serve the 'customer' – who may be an internal part of the organisation or someone in the outside market;

(b) management's role is to facilitate the work of teams, not to direct and control;

(c) people are rewarded on the bases of results and ability, not on measures of activity.

The implications for organisation design are that structures change from tall hierarchies to flatter ones with fewer layers of management. Mintzberg's middle line of managers is not so essential when teams resolve problems and take decisions for themselves. The size of the strategic headquarters is small. Companies such as BP and Shell have pushed HQ functions out to divisions and down to operating levels.

Firms concentrate on their core activities. They constantly ask the question: what business are we in? Many of the peripheral functions that used to take up much management time are hived off to specialist organisations. For example, facilities management companies take over the work of buildings maintenance, managing the computer network and running the staff restaurants. Hospitals contract out cleaning, laundry and catering. The Olympic Games, Wimbledon and other major events are largely run by facilities management firms.

The ultimate case is the *'virtual organisation'*, where a strategic and administrative headquarters contracts out all the operations to sub-contractors and facilities managers.

Companies seek flexibility. Using specialist contractors means that staff levels can be expanded and contracted to suit seasonal variations in workload. Part-time working has increased as firms seek to tailor staffing to customer demand. BHS, the clothing and furnishings store group, introduced flexible working so that its permanent, full-time staff were available at the times of greatest customer demand.

Shareholders seek value from their investment. The investing institutions are under pressure to get the best return on their funds. Large groups are forced to examine their structures to secure efficiency and value for money. The result can be a demerger, such as the splitting of ICI into ICI and Zeneca to form separate chemicals and pharmaceutical companies each concentrating on one core business area.

Activity 5　　　　　　　　　　　　　　　　　　　　　　　[20 minutes]

Think about an organisation that you know and list those activities that you would expect it to sub-contract. Then check which of them are actually contracted out.

Chapter roundup

- The modern context of business is one of customer orientation, competition and constant change.
- The traditional organisation grew by sub-division. The modern organisation can only succeed if its structure allows it to flourish in the modern context.
- Urwick's eight principles were concerned with control and the workings of bureaucracy. They are appropriate for organisations in stable environments carrying out routine tasks.
- Modern thinking designs organisations around Mintzberg's concept of the adhocracy. Multi-discipline teams cut across functional boundaries to manage their work.
- The adhocracy approach creates the flexibility and innovation that are lacking in traditional hierarchical organisations.
- Redesigning organisations for creativity and flexibility means team working, employee empowerment and fewer layers of management.
- Firms concentrate on their core business and contract out peripheral activities. They change work patterns to gain flexibility.

Quick Quiz

1. What are the three elements in the modern context of business?
2. Of Urwick's eight principles for the design of effective organisations, how many were concerned with control?
3. What are the principal features of the post-entrepreneurial corporation?
4. List Mintzberg's categories of organisation.
5. Which of these is most likely to apply to a multinational company?
6. For a new industry such as software development which structure is most likely to create an effective organisation and what are its features?
7. After analysing the reasons for firms losing their positions as being among the most successful, what did Peters and Waterman conclude about what makes an excellent firm?
8. When an organisation is redesigned for success in modern business what cultural aspects are vital?
9. Give two examples of the work of facilities management companies.
10. What sort of hierarchy is recommended for a modern company?

Answers to Quick Quiz

1. Customer orientation, competition and change.
2. Seven.
3. Autonomous work teams in a flatter hierarchy. Authority is decentralised due to employee empowerment.
4. Simple structure, machine bureaucracy, professional bureaucracy, divisionalised structure, adhocracy, missionary.
5. The divisionalised structure.
6. Adhocracy. Flexible cross-discipline teams collaborate on specific projects.
7. They concluded that excellence depends on the quest for constant improvement and the ability to meet the demands of constant change.

8 Every unit of the organisation's priority is to serve the customer; management becomes a facilitator and rewards are based on ability and results.

9 Building maintenance, cleaning, catering, computer system management, laundry.

10 Flat.

Answers to Activities

1 (i) You could easily have found twenty variants of a popular model of a car. Taking all the possible combinations of engine, body type, trim and paint finish into account, BMW reckon they produce *thousands* of variants, and Ford can supply over two thousand varieties of Escort. The reason is to give the consumer as much choice as possible and to meet the demand for individuality.

(ii) Banks offer many deposit and savings accounts to suit the demands of customers for combinations of return and liquidity (the speed of turning assets into cash). Some people want quick access to their funds, others can wait for a year for a better rate of interest. If they did not offer this range of choice, banks would lose customers to other savings outlets.

2 A supermarket could use IT for a loyalty card scheme, such as that run by Tesco, which encourages customers to shop at the store as much as possible. IT could be used to record customers' typical individual shopping habits, so that they can be informed about special offers or new products and developments that are likely to interest them. The more information a supermarket has about its customers, the easier it is for them to adjust the stock to meet the likely pattern of demand; it is also easier to establish what new products are likely to be suitable for individual stores.

3 You might have listed computer software, television production, film making, advertising, bio-technology and fashion. These may be international organisations, but they differ from the divisionalised structure typical of the multinational firm, organised along product or geographical lines, which is involved in mass production.

4 You might have said, for example: customer service, profitability, market share, innovation, return on capital and growth. Most people are most concerned with customer service.

5 You might have chosen your own college. In this example, you might expect to find cleaning, catering, building maintenance, grounds maintenance, inter-site transport, payroll administration and security contracted out. The *most* likely to be contracted out are cleaning, security, grounds maintenance and catering.

Assignment 5 [1.5 hours]

Take the organisation which you reported on for the Assignment 4. Add a short report on whether or not it uses cross-discipline teams. You could concentrate on just one part of the overall organisation. Evaluate whether or not the organisation's performance would be improved by adopting the principle of adhocracy with employee empowerment and delayering of management. If this approach is considered unsuitable, try to explain why.

Chapter 6

THE PROCESS OF EFFECTIVE COMMUNICATION

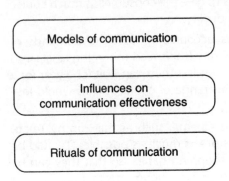

Introduction

Chapters 1–5 have described organisations, their structures and their need to communicate. In this chapter we focus on the actual process of communication, which may seem relatively simple at first glance. However, if we try to identify its component parts, in order to create a model of it, we find that there are *many* processes involved. We need to explore the individual parts of the communication process, and how they relate to one another.

The effectiveness and efficiency of communication are influenced by both internal and external elements, and we shall consider all of these. We shall then go on to examine the short cuts used in communications, the rituals associated with communications and their value to communication within organisations.

Your objectives

After completing this chapter you should be able to:

(a) describe the process of communication;

(b) identify factors that degrade and interfere with effective communication;

(c) understand the conditions required for effective communication to take place.

Before we can build a model we need to consider what happens when we communicate.

1 MODELS OF COMMUNICATION

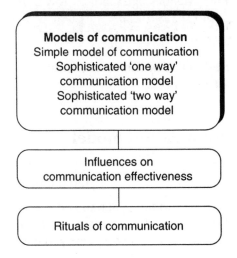

Models of communication
Simple model of communication
Sophisticated 'one way'
communication model
Sophisticated 'two way'
communication model

Influences on
communication effectiveness

Rituals of communication

Activity 1 [15 minutes]

Think of a simple sentence containing information that might need to be passed on to another person. For example; 'The meeting is at ten o'clock'.

Think about the process whereby the message is transformed from an idea in your mind to knowledge in the mind of another: write down a list of the things that happen, in the order that they occur. Concentrate on the *process*, do not consider the *media* of communications, for example, written, oral etc.

We start by looking at a simple model of communication.

1.1. Simple model of communication

The most simplistic of the communication models includes three components:

(a) the speaker;

(b) the speech;

(c) the audience.

A more complete model will include some sort of response or acknowledgement, designed to let the speaker know that the message has been received and understood. This feedback is an essential part of communications and creates the circular flow shown in Figure 6.1.

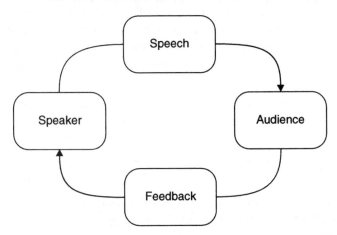

Figure 6.1 Simple model of communication

Definition

Feedback: a response to communication which lets the message sender know that the message has been received and understood (or not, as the case may be).

We will now start to build a more sophisticated model of communication. We will start by looking at a one-way communication process.

1.2 Sophisticated 'one-way' communication model

Activity 2 [20 minutes]

You wish to send the same message as in Activity 1, but this time your audience does not speak the same language as you do. How will this increase the processes required? Using your list from Activity 1, draw a diagram to include any further process you have identified.

Information in our brain is no more than a concept; it must be transferred into a tangible form before we can share it. The tangible form of communication may be speech, language, illustrations etc. – all these can be considered as codes.

More sophisticated models of communications take account of the coding process and the de-coding that is required before an audience can understand the information. Figure 6.2 shows a more sophisticated model of the path that information follows as it is transmitted from one point to another.

Figure 6.2 A sophisticated communication model (one way)

The component parts of this model are as follows.

(a) *Source* The source is the origination point of the communication. The information that the source intends to transmit may be original, or it may be the result of previous communication.

(b) *Encoder* A source becomes an encoder when it converts the information into a transmittable form.

(c) *Message* The content of the message can be anything, but, if it is to represent the concept or information originated at the source, it must be structured carefully.

(d) *Receiver* This is the point at which the message is picked up. The receiver can be, for example, the person being spoken to, or a facsimile machine. It is not necessary for the receiver to be able to decode or understand the message; the ears and eyes of humans have to pass the message on to the brain for decoding.

(e) *Decoder* This is the point where the coded message is transformed into a form that is understandable.

(f) *Meaning* The decoded message may need to be considered in the light of other knowledge to put it into perspective and allow real understanding of its implications.

Activity 3 [30 minutes]

The sophisticated one-way model can clearly be demonstrated by using it to examine the transfer of information in war time between secret agents and their masters.

Assume that the source of information is an agent in the field, and the end point (where meaning is understood) is the Chief of Staff.

Write down who would be involved and what happens at each stage in the model described above. Your answer should ensure that only the Chief of Staff fully understands the message.

We are now ready to consider a sophisticated two-way model of communication.

1.3 Sophisticated 'two way' communication model

Carrying on the example in the last activity, assume that the Chief of Staff requires clarification. A message, in the form of a question, must be transmitted in the opposite direction to that of the original communication. The original source thus receives *feedback*. For example, 'I did not understand. Please answer the following question so that I may understand better.' Feedback is the response to communication. A more complete 'two-way' model of the process would include this, as shown in Figure 6.3.

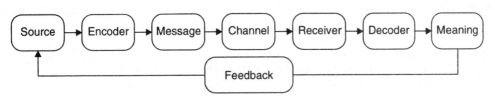

Figure 6.3 Sophisticated model of communication (two way)

If communications only involved those parts included in our models so far, then we could assume that all communication is successful. We are well aware that this is not the case, and so we must consider those factors that affect the effectiveness of communication.

2 INFLUENCES ON COMMUNICATION EFFECTIVENESS

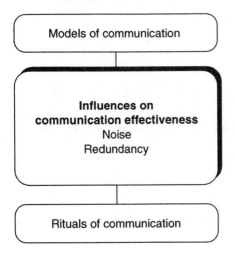

2.1 Noise

Definition

> *Noise:* a term used to describe any external influence that interferes or degrades effective communication (including, but not restricted to, audible sound).

Activity 4 [10 minutes]

You wish to pass on some information to a business contact. You arrange to meet in a pub. When you arrive you realise that there is live music playing.

Are these circumstances conducive to effective communication? At what stage in the communication process could the circumstances interfere? Draw a diagram to illustrate your answer.

If we look at each element in the communications model in turn, we can see that: the *source* can create noise if there is difficulty in describing the information to be transmitted; the *channel* may be a source of noise if it is inappropriate; the *receiver* may not be 'tuned in' to receive the message correctly; the *decoding* process maybe inefficient and the wrong *meaning* may be attached to the message. This last possibility is most common where jargon or specialist language is used.

Activity 5 [30 minutes]

Consider the following mini case study.

Nurse Brown spent two years training to nurse patients with bone problems. Many of the patients she cared for had suffered a slipped disc, technically known as prolapsed intervertebral disc (PID). These patients are treated in the first instance by complete bed rest, to encourage the disc to return to its normal position in the spine.

Nurse Brown went on to train in a general hospital. One day, Nurse Brown was asked to look after a woman with PID. For several hours Nurse Brown insisted that the patient remain flat in bed until, wanting to use the toilet, the patient asked the Ward Sister why she must have a bedpan. Realising what had happened, the Ward Sister then explained to Nurse Brown that PID also stood for Pelvic Inflammatory Disease, a medical condition requiring antibiotic therapy, not bed rest.

Write down how effective the communications were in the mini case. State why any communication was ineffective and identify the stages of the communication process at which problems occurred. Give some thought also to the method of communication and its suitability. (We shall be covering this in more depth in Chapter 7.)

Figure 6.4 shows how noise can interfere with communications at any stage.

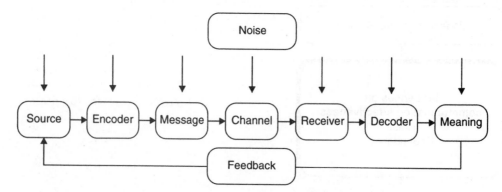

Figure 6.4. Sophisticated 'two-way' communication model showing where noise can influence effectiveness

Noise is one factor that can degrade the effectiveness of communications. We now consider another: redundancy.

2.2 Redundancy

Definition

Redundancy: the term used to describe superfluous or irrelevant information contained within a message.

Activity 6   [30 minutes]

Read the following instructions through once. Then, without looking back at them, write down as much as you can remember.

You are a sales representative for a large company. You receive the following fax detailing the calls you must make on a given day.

1st call: Mr Greening, purchasing manager
        NMP Plc
        Unit 21a Broad Field Industrial Estate
        Oxford

Your appointment is for 9.30 am. From our office you need to take the main road to Oxford, through Tiddington and on towards the M40. You will cross the M40 and then feed onto the A40 into Oxford. (Past the lay-by where you met John Sanderson.) When you reach the traffic lights where the park and ride is, go straight on. The park and ride is very useful if you have to go into the city centre because the parking is appalling. The next thing you come to is a roundabout. Turn right. You can use both nearside lanes, but watch the drivers on the inside as they have a tendency to go straight on, cutting the outer lane up in the process. Carry on, on this road, until you come to the roundabout where Cowley works used to be. I think there are two roundabouts and two sets of traffic lights. Turn right. Turn left at the second from last junction, opposite Texas or Tesco. There are some pedestrian controlled traffic lights just before or after this turn. Broadfields is down this road and unit 21a is the 3rd from the end on the left.

2nd call: Fred at Auto trade, Burford High Street

Take the A40 towards the Cotswolds; when you get to Burford roundabout, turn right. Fred's is on the right halfway down the hill. If you do this call first you turn left off the roundabout at Oxford; the A40 goes both ways. Not the last exit, the second to last. The last exit goes up to the crematorium! However it may be a good idea to come back this way if the traffic on the A40 is bad.

When you have checked the accuracy of your recollections, time how long it takes you to translate the instructions into a form that you could safely refer to whilst driving.

So far we have considered the factual elements that affect all communications. We must now consider the impact of sociological factors. These are the factors that can differ from individual to individual and organisation to organisation.

3   RITUALS OF COMMUNICATION

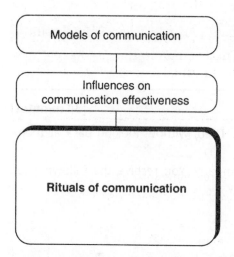

Models of communication

Influences on
communication effectiveness

Rituals of communication

Definition

Rituals: repeated patterns of behaviour that have a symbolic meaning. In life we consider religious and historical ceremonies to be rituals. Within organisations, rituals can be the office Christmas party, or the way information is passed on to various individuals within the organisation.

As in many other areas of our lives, we create patterns and rituals of communication which enable us to have a standard of behaviour to deal with specific situations. Such rituals may vary according to the social setting.

Activity 7   **[20 minutes]**

You are a student living away from home. You have the chance to spend a week shadowing a senior manager in the car industry. The manager is based at the main Volkswagen factory in Germany. You need to notify your parents and your college in order to explain your absence.

Write two short notes: one to your parents and one to your college.

Now compare the two notes and list all the differences in how you have communicated the necessary information.

Communication within organisations follows many of the social codes used in everyday life, but it also follows rituals specific to the workplace. Both the type and structure of the organisation have an influence on the nature of these rituals.

Definition

Culture: the shared values and beliefs of the members of an organisation. It encompasses codes of behaviour, levels of personal interaction and binds the members together to form a cohesive group.

There is debate over the effect of culture on an organisation's communication rituals: do the rituals help to create the culture, or does the culture create the rituals? One thing is not in doubt: there *are* communication rituals, and these can promote or inhibit effective communication, depending on their nature and how they match the other forms of communication being used.

While some rituals are common to many organisational environments, others are peculiar to particular organisational types. Rituals can be made up of the way information is passed in terms of the language (code) used and/or the media used.

Rituals do not have to be overtly based upon communication to be an effective communication aid. For example, rituals such as regular meetings between management and unions can communicate to the workforce that it is being informed and its views are being heard. Similarly, the ritual of yearly incremental pay increases communicates that management reward loyalty to the organisation: the longer you stay, the more you are paid. (This communication can be rendered ineffective if management retain this payment ritual but alter the basis for employment towards short-term contracts.)

Chapter roundup

- Communication is a complex series of interrelated processes.
- The effectiveness of communications can be affected at any stage.
- Feedback is vital to ensure understanding.
- Noise can interfere with the communication process.
- Redundancy will degrade communication effectiveness.
- Socialisation impacts on how we communicate.
- Rituals can promote effective communications by acting as a type of short hand.
- Rituals can render communications ineffectual if they are inappropriate.
- Culture and rituals are inextricably linked, one supports the other.

Quick Quiz

1 Draw a diagram to show how the process of communication can be considered circular.
2 Label the diagram with the stages that information goes through in order to be passed from origination to destination.
3 Where in this process can communication be rendered ineffective?
4 Define the term 'noise' as it applies to the communication process.
5 Define the term 'redundancy' as it applies to the communication process.
6 What are rituals?
7 Are rituals always an effective form of communication?

Answers to Quick Quiz

1 Your diagram should be similar to that shown in Figure 6.1.
2 Your diagram should be similar to that shown in Figure 6.2.
3 The communication can be rendered ineffective at any point.
4 Noise is anything that interferes with communication in a negative way.
5 Redundancy is extra information that is not specifically needed at the point when the communication is taking place.
6 Rituals are symbolic ways of behaving. They are accepted as the way things are done.
7 No, rituals are not always an effective form of communication if they are not 'in tune' with the other rituals or accepted norms within the organisation.

Answers to activities

1   You may have only identified three components in the communication process: the speaker, the speech, and the audience. You may also have considered some sort of response or acknowledgement designed to let the speaker know that the message has been received and understood. This is *feedback*.

2   Before you can pass your message you will need to find a language or method of communication that both you and the recipient of the message understand, or you will require an interpreter. The need to find a common language does not only occur when we communicate with nationalities other than our own – it happens in all communication.

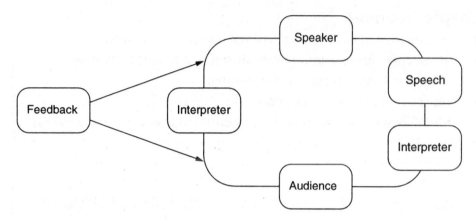

Figure 6.5 A diagram of the communication process when the audience speaks a different language from that of the speaker.

3   Your answer should be similar to the following:

Source: We can think of this as the agent preparing to pass on newly acquired military secrets.

Encoder: The secret agent will encode his/her information in such a way as to be readable only by his/her masters.

Message: In this case military secrets.

Receiver: This may be a junior member of the forces working in the radio room.

Decoder: In war time there would be specific staff to do just this job; however, they would not necessarily be able to understand the implications of a message even after decoding it.

Meaning: Think of this as the Chief of Staff in our example. Only he knows all the information that has been gathered and can therefore understand the overall picture.

4   You probably concluded that the circumstances are not conducive to effective communication (particularly if either you or your business contact has any hearing impairment). Your diagram should illustrate that noise can interfere at any stage in the communication process as shown in Figure 6.4.

5   You should have seen that there was clearly a breakdown in communications in this case. You could have identified the following causes: the use of abbreviations, the method of communication (verbal), assumptions about prior knowledge. The parts of the process where breakdown occurred differed according to the different causes, the important point being that differing causes will result in the breakdown of communication at differing points in the process. No part of the process is immune.

6   You will have found that it takes *at least* 10 minutes to translate the text into a list that is easy to refer to. The complexity of this message makes it inappropriate for the use to which it is to be put, namely, as directions to use whilst driving. You will also have found that not all the information is accurate enough to give good directions to someone who does not know the area.

Much of the information in the original version is unnecessary. Redundancy can cause a message to become distorted or make it difficult to decode and understand. Whilst the content of information required in a message can be said to be subjective, information such as the advice about the park and ride is clearly not relevant to this communication. Some information that may seem superfluous, such as the reference to a previous meeting, may be useful to fix the location in the sales person's mind; however, it makes quick referral to the document difficult.

7   Your answers to this activity may well be near the extremes of familiarity and formality. This will depend on the relationships you have with your parents and your tutor.

Your list may have included the following differences.

They way you address people:	Sir/Mum and Dad
The tone of the language you use :	familiar/formal
The format of the note:	typed letter/hand-written card
The content of the note:	'educational visit'/'trip to Germany'

Assignment 6   [1.5 hours]

For this assignment you will need to draw on past experience. Use your knowledge of a working environment, if you have experienced one, or your school, if you have not.

Write an essay of not more than 1000 words to illustrate the rituals that existed in your chosen environment and comment on the way in which these rituals enhanced or inhibited effective communications.

75

Chapter 7

THE MEDIA OF EFFECTIVE COMMUNICATIONS

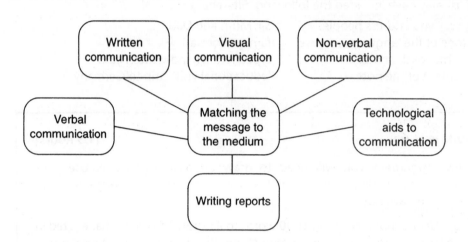

Introduction

In Chapter 6 we discussed the process by which information is communicated; we now consider one aspect of this process: *channels of communication*. The channel, or medium, of communication is the route through which the encoded message is passed to the receiver.

There are generally accepted to be four main media of communications:

(a) oral/verbal;

(b) written;

(c) visual;

(d) non verbal.

We shall consider each of these in turn, highlighting the advantages, disadvantages, skills required and any environmental factors which may have an impact on their effectiveness.

Your objectives

After completing this chapter you should be able to:

(a) identify the various communication media;

(b) select appropriate media according to the purpose of communication;

(c) produce an example of effective written communication;

(d) appreciate the impact of technology on communication, both generally and within organisations

 The first of our communication media is verbal, speaking to one another.

1   VERBAL COMMUNICATION

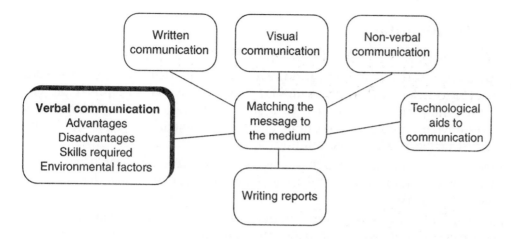

Verbal communication can be face-to-face or long-distance. Long-distance communication through such technological media as the telephone is considered in Section 5. In this section we shall consider only face-to- face verbal communication.

We start by looking at the advantages of verbal communication.

1.1   Advantages

Verbal communication has the following advantages.

(a) *Speed* Verbal communication can be the fastest way to impart information.

(b) *Clarity* Verbally it is a simple task to ask for clarification, to ensure under-standing of the message being transmitted. Even if clarification is not asked for, the communicator can receive almost instantaneous feedback.

(c) *Flexibility* New information can be quickly assimilated and used as part of the communication. For example, what began as an enquiry regarding lateness may become a reprimand when a manager hears the response to their enquiry.

(d) *Sensitivity* Delicate or personal matters can be dealt with more empathy and responsiveness verbally than with any other communication media.

(e) *Interactivity* When carried out face-to-face, verbal communication can be supple-mented by non-verbal cues. The reinforcement or denigration of the verbal message by these cues enables the sensitivity, flexibility and clarity of the communication to be heightened.

Figure 7.1 shows how body posture can act as a verbal cue.

Figure 7.1 Verbal clues from body posture

Now we consider the disadvantages of verbal communication.

1.2 Disadvantages

Verbal communication has the following disadvantages.

(a) *Articulation* Verbal communication requires both participants to be articulate. They also need to share the same language or have an interpreter present. Whilst the problems associated with sharing the same language may be the most obvious, problems of pronunciation, dialect and use of jargon can be just as destructive to effective communications.

(b) *Speed* We have already stated that speed is an advantage, however, it can also be a distinct disadvantage. Little time is available for planning the form the message will take.

(c) *Reliability* Although in law verbal contracts may be valid, the maxim that 'verbal contracts are not worth the paper they are written on' carries some merit. Certain circumstances dictate that verbal communication is not the most effective medium.

(d) *Logistics* It would be difficult, if not impossible, for all the fans at a premier league football match to hold a conversation. Similarly, if information is to be passed by word of mouth through a large number of people the message tends to get changed (as anyone who has played Chinese whispers will know). The following example, allegedly from the first World War, illustrates this point.

EXAMPLE: DISADVANTAGES OF VERBAL COMMUNICATION

The soldiers at the front line needed to get a message to their company commander; the only means available was word of mouth. The message was passed from man to man in the trenches across a long distance. It finally reached the company commander, who was baffled by the request: 'Send three and fourpence, we're going to a dance.' So bemused was he, that he mounted his horse and set off to find the source of the message. On arriving at the front line, he was greeted by the sergeant with, 'Are you the only one Sir?' 'Only one of what?' he replied. The sergeant shook his head in disbelief, 'We asked for reinforcements, we're going to advance.'

Activity 1 [30 minutes]

You are negotiating with a supplier to overcome quality problems you have had with a product. Taking into consideration the advantages and disadvantages of verbal communication, and the elements that make up the process of communication, write a short scenario to show how the proceedings may evolve.

Now identify the one component (which has not yet been mentioned) that is likely to increase the chances of your negotiations reaching a successful outcome.

(Tip: think through the scenario, focusing on what each person does at each stage.)

We have looked at the potential advantages and disadvantages of verbal communication. Now we consider the skills required to maximise its success.

1.3 Skills required

Listening

The key skill required for verbal communication is that of listening. It is commonly believed that listening is an innate skill; however, the importance it holds for effective verbal communication means that its development merits special attention. Effective listening helps to avoid many of the disadvantages of verbal communication.

(a) Concentrating on listening focuses the attention and reduces the effect of noise.

(b) Effective listening facilitates clarity of understanding.

(c) Effective listening encourages feedback.

Articulation

As we have already stated, verbal communication requires both participants to be articulate and to share the same language or have an interpreter present.

We next consider the environmental factors that can affect verbal communication.

1.4 Environmental factors

Culture

In the modern business world, language and culture are important factors. Language can be aided by the use of interpreters, but culture must be understood if effective communications are to take place.

EXAMPLE: VERBAL COMMUNICATION AND CULTURE

The Japanese have strict cultural and social rules regarding the nature of verbal exchanges. Failure to adhere to these may prevent the knowledge being imparted from being considered seriously, in the light of what may be seen by the Japanese as ineptitude at social skills.

The behaviour of women in business is of particular relevance in Japan, as their social standing is not considered to be equal to that of men. Aggressive negotiating will therefore not be taken seriously if it comes from a woman.

Activity 2 [15 minutes]

You wish to pass on some highly sensitive information to your Managing Director. His secretary gives you five alternative times when you might catch him. Rate these possible meetings in order of preference, using your knowledge of the communication process and the advantages and disadvantages of verbal communications as the basis for your choice. Give reasons for each of your ratings.

Option	Meeting	Rating	Reasons
1	5 pm Friday – en route to his car		
2	11 am Saturday – on the golf course		
3	3.30 pm Thursday – in his office (10 minute appointment)		
4	10 am Monday – at the office meeting		
5	8 pm Friday at the company Christmas dinner		

Verbal communications are used both formally and informally in organisations (See Chapter 10). They take the form of meetings, briefings and the 'grapevine'.

If we wish to refer back to what we have said, we must create some record of it. The written word is the most common medium for doing this.

2   WRITTEN COMMUNICATION

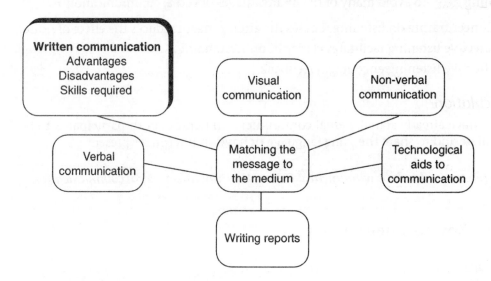

Within organisations great emphasis is placed upon written communications. This medium is used for recording information for future use, eliciting information from others, enabling more than one person to do a job by having 'silent communications' and 'talking' to others, on paper (letters and memos).

Let's look at the advantages of this medium.

2.1   Advantages

Written communication has the following advantages:

(a) *It is a lasting record of the communication* The permanence of the information given in written for allows it to be referred to at a later date.

(b) *Clarity* There is a general belief that written information prevents ambiguity.

Next we consider the disadvantages.

2.2   Disadvantages

(a) *Loss or damage* Documents can go astray or be mislaid; documents produced on a computer must be 'backed-up' to prevent loss if the system fails.

(b) *Ambiguity* The written word, if not produced with care, can still be ambiguous. For important documents, such as reports or contracts, specific training should be undertaken to improve skills.

(c) *Time* Documents take time to prepare and pass on to the intended recipient. This problem is being addressed in some measure by new technology, which we shall consider later.

Finally we look at the skills required for effective written communication.

2.3   Skills required

Writing

This may seem an obvious requirement for written communications, but it would be wrong to assume that if an individual can write, they can communicate effectively in writing. Different written skills are required for differing types of communications.

Activity 3   [45 minutes]

Prepare a short piece of written work (no more than 200 words) for an employment agency, using the title 'My ideal job'.

Now re-write the piece as if you were telling a friend about the type of job you would like.

Now list the differences between these two pieces of work, highlighting differing language, phraseology and content.

Activity 4   [15 minutes]

List at least five forms of written communications used by organisations.

We use our eyes to read the written word, but there are other ways of communicating through visual aids.

3   VISUAL COMMUNICATION

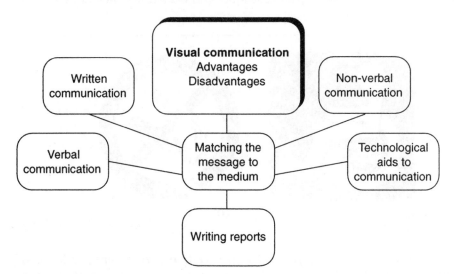

This relates to charts, graphs and tabulated data, and also to colour, design and symbols.

First we consider the advantages of visual communication.

3.1 Advantages

Visual communication has the following two main advantages.

(a) *Quantity of information* Appropriately used, a well designed graph can impart more information, with greater clarity, than several pages of text or several minutes of verbal description.

(b) *Impact* The use of symbols can act as a short cut to understanding. When driving it would be impossible to assimilate all the information given if it were all in the form of words. A symbol, once learned, will trigger understanding within the human brain.

Now let's look at the disadvantages.

3.2 Disadvantages

Visual communication has the following disadvantage.

Ambiguity Symbols and the use of colours must be learned before they can be understood. Children are not born knowing that a red light signifies stop or that a green light signifies go; they must learn these meanings. Different cultures use different symbols; for example, a symbol used to warn workers in a food factory of the dangers of dust build up would have very little meaning to a new employee or visitor. Thus symbols and colour coding must be used with care.

Activity 5 [30 minutes]

Figure 7.2 (a) and (b) show two examples of symbols. What does each one communicate to you? Write down the meaning of each.

Draw or find pictures of five other symbols in common usage (use no more than two road signs). Write down their meanings.

Now show these symbols to five of your colleagues and write down their understanding of the meanings.

(a)   (b)

Figure 7.2 Visual symbols

Communication is not always just what we write or say. There are levels of communication that hover below the conscious level, not entirely sub-conscious, but almost.

4 NON-VERBAL COMMUNICATION

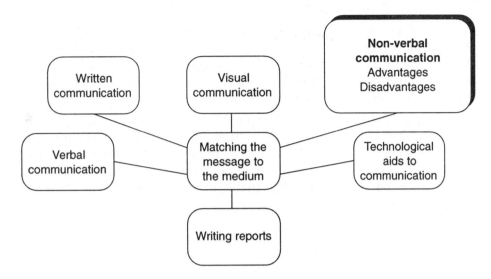

Non-verbal communication relates to the non-verbal aspect of personal interactions. It can be divided into four areas:

(a) physical appearance;

(b) paralinguistic (tone and speed of voice);

(c) kinetic (movements, gestures, facial expression and eye contact);

(d) proxemic (body proximity, orientation and posture).

Each of these areas can reinforce the message being passed, so long as they are appropriate to the verbal communication. If they are inappropriate, the message may be confused or ambiguous. Non-verbal communication is considered to be the aspect of communication over which an individual has least control; however, it is possible to become aware of the meaning of certain gestures etc. By doing so, verbal communications skills can be reinforced and understanding can be enhanced.

Non-verbal communication has a strong cultural aspect to it. Certain bodily movements in particular are unacceptable in various parts of the world. For example, it is considered a gross insult to give the thumbs up sign in South America, and in Arab countries it is unacceptable to point the soles of your feet in another person's direction. What we consider usual may not be acceptable elsewhere; many a business has run into difficulties as a result of lack of preparation before venturing abroad.

We will now look at the specific advantages of using non-verbal communication.

4.1 Advantages

Being aware of non-verbal communication brings the following advantage.

Competitive advantage Understanding and being aware of the non-verbal signals being communicated from another person can help you to ask the right questions or give the correct responses. The use of your own body language can reinforce the message you want to convey, and this can be supported by adopting a 'listening' pose. All good salespeople know that customers buy from individuals they like or identify with; this fact can be used to advantage by those in control of their own body language.

We now look at the disadvantages associated with non-verbal communication.

4.2 Disadvantages

There are two main disadvantages associated with non-verbal communication.

(a) *Concentration* Just as control of one's own body language, and an understanding of the body language of others, can be an advantage, it requires a high degree of concentration and training. A lapse in concentration during an important meeting could be unfortunate, if one is using controlled body language to reinforce a point that is not genuine.

(b) *Ambiguity* You will have seen photographs of celebrities, where the caption has been added by the publication editor. Usually designed to be amusing, these captions fit words to the body posture of the celebrity. No-one expects the caption to reflect exactly what was said, but the results are often believable. This illustrates the possible ambiguity that can be attributed to non-verbal communication.

For discussion

In seminar groups discuss the following statement:

'Non-verbal communication exists only in the minds of those who believe it to be true.'

Remember that all great actors not only say their lines convincingly, but alter their body movements, postures and facial expressions to create the illusion of another person.

We no longer rely on smoke signals to communicate over geographic distance. Now, more than ever, we are part of the technological communications revolution. Just how valuable is it?

5 TECHNOLOGICAL AIDS TO COMMUNICATIONS

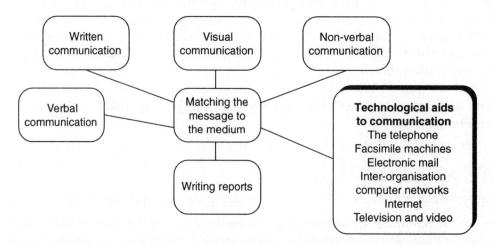

5.1 The telephone

The telephone is probably the oldest commonly used technology. We are so used to it that we consider a telephone conversation virtually as good as a conversation face-to-face.

Advantages

The telephone has three main advantages.

(a) *Speed* Communicating verbally with someone who is at a geographic distance can be time consuming in terms of travel. The telephone has made long-distance communication possible.

(b) *Convenience* Most people, and certainly all organisations, in the industrialised world are able to be contacted by telephone. The advent of the mobile phone has made it even easier to contact people, but its contribution to effective communications is debatable.

(c) *Participation* Conference calls are now a reality, and therefore calls are no longer restricted to two participants only.

Disadvantages

The telephone has the following disadvantages.

(a) *Association* The benefits that come from associating verbal and non-verbal communication are not available; although if video phones become more widespread this may change.

(b) *Distraction* There are potential problems of distraction for the participants in a telephone conversation.

Facsimile machines also make use of the telephone network. They enable any sort of visual material to be exchanged.

5.2 Facsimile machines

The facsimile machine (fax) has made it possible to send hard copies (that is, on paper) through telephone communications. In this way documents such as contracts can be passed on for perusal faster than through the post or even by courier.

Now we a look at a technology that has only recently begun to be commonplace within businesses, schools and colleges.

5.3 Electronic mail

The use of electronic mail is beginning to have an effect on cutting down the time lapse inevitable with written communications. All participants in the communication must have access to a computer and be able to link their computer into whatever network is to be used.

Email can be both formal and informal. Letters and other documents can be posted in the recipient's 'mailbox', to be read at their leisure, or conversations in written form can be conducted in real time.

Voice mail is an extension of electronic mail, it enables recorded messages to be left to be picked up at a later time.

Electronic mail involves the sending of computerised messages. Computers themselves can be linked closely using computer networks.

5.4 Inter-organisation computer networks

Computer networks within organisations have been possible, although expensive, for some years now, but the most recent development has been the ability of related companies to link up part of their computer systems with each other. This has particular implications for strategic alliances and partnership arrangements. Without this kind of system the co-operation of so many countries in the Airbus project, for example, would have been very much more complicated and difficult to achieve.

Another form of computer-based communication involves the Internet.

5.5 Internet

The Internet is the most recent addition to the technological communications tool kit. This medium can be used in two ways: firstly as an interactive communications channel and secondly as a form of notice board where information can be displayed. It is fast becoming a world wide form of communications, although the problems of differing language and culture still exist.

There is one final type of technological communication that we have not yet considered: that of television and video.

5.6 Television and video

Whilst these are not commonly seen as communication media used by organisations, they are playing an increasingly important part in the marketing function. The music business is the best example. Once songs were sold purely as sheet music, to be played by those who had mastered an instrument. Then came the various recording devices, allowing music to be enjoyed by even those with no musical ability. Now, for a song to become popular enough to be worth money, a video is needed as part of the promotion.

Similarly, television has become probably the most important advertising medium, having access as it does to millions of people at once. Its outward appearance is of a medium that fits with our 'one way' communication model. However, one could regard the purchase of advertised products as a form of feedback. The message has got across and has been understood: 'Buy BPP's other HND books , they're great!'. Whether the consumer believes the message or not is irrelevant, they bought the product. Thus television and video can be considered to be true two-way communications (and are likely to become even more interactive in the future).

Within organisations the use of videos for training (either produced 'in house' or bought in) and facilities for video conferencing are becoming more common.

Activity 6   [15 minutes]

List all the methods you can think of for finding out the day's news – local, national and international. Identify each medium and show which methods facilitate feedback.

With such a vast array of different media to chose from, how do we know which to choose?

6 MATCHING THE MESSAGE TO THE MEDIUM

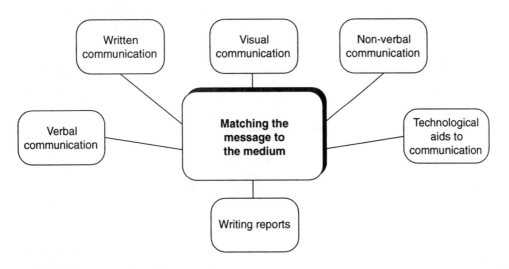

Activity 7 [10 minutes]

You are marketing manager for a major retailer; you wish to tell your customers of an amazing offer. What media could you use?

Would you use the same media if you wished to warn your customers of a wet floor in your store? Write down a list of alternatives.

The choice of medium depends upon a variety of factors including the following.

(a) *Urgency* Some media, by their nature, take longer than others. The time span available must be considered. A request for the fire brigade to attend a fire at your office would not be effective if done by letter!

(b) *Permanency* Some pieces of information are required to be repeatedly proven. Your qualification from this course might not be of much use to you if it existed only in verbal form. Other pieces of information may need to be referred to over and over again to ensure accuracy.

(c) *Complexity* Detailed information regarding last year's sales would be too complex to impart over the phone. On the other hand, you would not consider it appropriate to use an internal memo to inform your secretary that you take one sugar in your coffee.

(d) *Sensitivity* This can be in the emotional sense or in the sense of secrecy. You would not post strategic marketing plans on the Internet, for fear that your competitors would see them. Nor would a purely verbal plan be appropriate, as there are issues of complexity and permanence.

(e) *Cost* Lengthy analysis and formal report production can be an expensive business. (If similar information is to be gathered from many sources then *forms* may be an inexpensive and appropriate method.)

None of these factors can be considered in isolation. Often several factors need to be considered when deciding upon the best medium, each factor having a varying degree of importance to the specific decision.

In your career as a student and in business you will be asked to focus on one medium in particular: the written word, specifically written reports. We shall now consider how to make your reports communicate effectively.

7   WRITING REPORTS

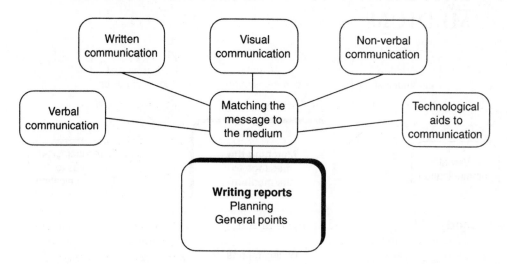

Report writing is the most intricate form of written communication and requires a high degree of skill. As a business student you will be required to produce reports in preparation for your entry into the world of organisations. This section contains guidelines to help you to ensure that your reports are effective in imparting the information you wish to impart.

We start by examining how to plan a report.

7.1   Planning

Before putting pen to paper you should consider the following.

(a) Who is the report for? (Who is the user?)

(b) What information is required?

(c) For what purpose is the information to be used?

(d) Are recommendations required?

(e) What time span and budget are available to produce the report?

A basic report format is given below.

Title page	Title/subject of the report, author, recipient and date.	The title should be descriptive of the contents, not poetic or ambiguous.
Contents page	List of contents with page and paragraph numbers.	This must be clear and concise, the aim is to enable sections to be found quickly.
Terms of reference	Purpose of the report and the scope of the investigation made.	Terms of reference will sometimes be given, but on occasion it is up to the author to define the parameters. Methodology can be included here in academic pieces of work, or can be a separate section. (It is not usual in commercial reports to detail methodology in this way.) Detailed findings may be included as an appendix.

Executive summary	Brief description of the key issues and/or recommendations.	When you write this consider the needs of a busy executive who wishes to 'skim' the main points before reading the full report.
Introduction	Background information	Only include that which is *necessary* in order to make sense of the rest of the report. Begin to 'tell a story'(though not in the poetic sense).
Main body	Concise analysis of the subject.	Key words here are *concise* and *analysis*. Do not be descriptive or include redundant information. More detail can be included in the appendices.
Conclusion	Round up of key points to this stage.	Do not introduce any *new* information. Reiterate the key points which lead on to the recommendations.
Recommendations	If this is within the terms of reference, recommend changes, improvements etc.	All recommendations must be backed up by solid reasoning and evaluated for their feasibility, suitability and acceptability.
Appendices	Detailed information gathered and analysed in the process of writing the report.	May contain financial analysis, tables and graphs. Used as supporting information should the reader wish to use them. Of paramount important when undertaking reports for academic purposes.

Now we look at some general aspects of report writing.

7.2 General points

Analysis

It is usually best to make your analysis objective. It is sometimes necessary to make subjective judgements; if so, you should make sure that you clearly indicate where this is the case. For example, you might use informal interviews to gain information; this is a valid method of data collection. However, when you come to interpret what has been said, you should indicate that your conclusions are inevitably subject to your own values and beliefs.

Writing style

Each individual has his or her own writing style. Style can include the way sentences are structured and the phraseology used. Some writing styles are more effective in reports than others. General points to remember about good report writing style include the following.

(a) Short sentences are easier to understand; they reduce the potential for ambiguity and make reading easier.

(b) It is best to avoid emotional and value judgements.

(c) You should avoid colloquialisms and abbreviated forms of language (which may seem inappropriately informal).

(d) Only use technical jargon if the report is intended for use within an organisation where this jargon is in common usage.

(e) It is usual to de-personalise language and avoid the use of 'I' or 'we'.

Layout

Reports are presented in a formal layout. Ensure that key points are highlighted by the use of emboldening, italics, type size, spacing or underlining. Sections and paragraphs should be numbered. This helps users to find specific sections and makes it easier for a group of people to discuss the contents. Sections should be clearly headed and the use of sub-section headings is recommended.

Activity 8   [30 minutes]

Read the following case study. As you read, make notes on any important information about the company (for example, size, type of organisation). Take particular note of any information regarding the communications within this organisation. Try to structure your notes into issues that arise and actions which you think should be taken. (You will need these notes later for this chapter's assignment.)

John Gibb, the owner of Gibbs Motors, a small second-hand car garage, needed to invest in more stock. John usually obtained cars from Wally's Car Auctions, a local car auctioneers, but, although John had never had any problems with the cars he bought, rumour had it that some of the cars that Wally's sold were of dubious ownership. John decided to look around for a more reputable car auctioneer.

After visiting many car auctions, John came across Quality, a car auctioneers selling second-hand cars of extremely high quality. John told the Peter Gold, the owner, that he was interested in obtaining cars and said he would phone the next day to confirm the order and specify which cars he wanted.

John spent a couple of days deciding the cars to buy. Before he could contact Quality, Peter rang to ask John whether he still wanted to place an order. John specified the models he wanted and told Peter that his price limit was a maximum of two thousand pounds for each car. There was a lot of interference on the phone lines that day, so both parties found it difficult to understand each other. John told Peter that he would fax through a confirmed order in writing. Before leaving the office that day, John left a note for his secretary to confirm the order.

Within the week five cars were delivered to John's garage. John was delighted with the quality of these cars and thought them good value for money. He advertised them in the local paper the next evening. Before the paper came out, the invoice for the cars arrived. To John's amazement the invoice was for £15,000. Thinking there must be some mistake, John rang Peter Gold and asked why the bill was for £15,000 when it should have only been for a maximum of £10,000. Peter said that once vehicles had been delivered to their new owner, whether this was a member of the public or another garage, they could not be returned and had to be paid for. John sought legal advice and found that, as he had confirmed the order in writing, Quality would either have to charge him the agreed price or accept the cars back. When John spoke to his secretary she denied all knowledge of his note and said she had not confirmed the order at all. John realised that short of being able to prove a verbal contract over the agreed price, he was stuck with five cars he could barely afford to pay for.

Chapter roundup

- Communication can be conducted through four main types of media: verbal, written, visual and non-verbal.
- Each medium has its own distinct advantages and disadvantages.
- Each medium requires different skills.
- Some media are affected by environmental factors, such as culture.
- Non-verbal communication can reinforce or confuse verbal communications.
- Technology has expanded the media available for communication, particularly the verbal and written forms.
- Reports play an important part in organisational life. If written with care they can provide easily accessible information.

Quick Quiz

1 Name the four main media of communications.
2 What is the difference between verbal and oral communications?
3 List three methods of written communication used in organisations.
4 What is the Internet?
5 Name two disadvantages of verbal communications.
6 How do we know that red means stop or danger?
7 How can written communications help more than one person to do a job?
8 What should you consider *before* writing a report?
9 In verbal communication, what can you do to facilitate feedback?

Answers to Quick Quiz

1 Verbal, non verbal, written and visual. Technology aids the use of these media.
2 None!
3 Letters, memoranda, reports, forms, leaflets, posters, payslips and many more.
4 The Internet is an international web of communication links. It can be accessed by any computer owner, through the use of telephone satellite links and a modem. It can be used for either active or passive forms of communication.
5 It cannot be relied upon for future reference and allows little time for planning one's message.
6 We know that red means stop or danger because we were taught this as a child. It is not inborn knowledge.
7 Lists of instructions can help to ensure that whoever is doing the job they will do it in the same way.
8 Check your answer against Section 7.
9 Listen.

Answers to activities

1   Your scenario should highlight the 'to and fro' nature of conversation, with one party appearing passive while the other is active and then roles reversing. You should have recognised that the passive party *must* be listening to the active party for the communication to be effective and an amicable result to be negotiated.

2   The following shows the best and worst scenarios; those in between may vary depending upon your relationship with the MD.

Option	Rating	Reasons
1		
2		
3	1	Privacy, chance of distraction low, feedback facilitated
4		
5	5	Distraction from many forms of noise, lack of privacy, feedback inhibited

3   The piece written for the employment agency will be more formal in style, the language will be more correct and the description of the job will be what you think they would like to hear. To a friend you are likely to be more honest, the phraseology will be more relaxed and the expression of ambition may be less realistic, but more enthusiastic.

4   Your list could include the following: reports, memoranda, leaflets, posters, notices, payslips, signs, letters, handbooks/manuals, mail shots, forms.

5   Figure 7.2 (a) indicates 'disabled facilities available'; Figure 7.2 (b) indicates 'no smoking'. You may have found many other symbols, some easy for everyone to understand, and others that are more obscure.

6

Medium	Feedback
Local papers	Some possible but slow
Local radio	Some possible but slow
National papers	Some possible but slow
National radio	Some possible but slow
National television	Some possible but slow
Internet	Yes
Teletext	No
Other people	Yes

(This is not a comprehensive list, there are many more)

7   You could tell people about the offer by using written media (posters, leaflets, signs), or verbal communication (radio advertising, costermongering (market traders)). You could warn about the wet floor by using written media, or by telling people verbally.

8   Your notes could include the following points.

● Gibbs Motors seems to be a small company; there is an owner and a secretary, but no-one else mentioned.

● Gibbs has used a local supplier and never had any problems.

● John Gibb listens to rumours.

● John Gibb has time to visit many auctioneers.

- John Gibb is not in a hurry for new stock.
- John Gibb placed the order when prompted.
- The deal was agreed over the phone.
- John Gibb did not confirm his own order.
- John Gibb communicated by a note to his secretary.
- The cars were of good quality.
- John Gibb is in a hurry to sell them.
- Is the secretary telling the truth?
- Gibbs Motors has a low cash flow.
- Communications – John Gibb does not seem to like written communications.

Assignment 7   [2 hours]

Using your notes from Activity 8, write a report for John identifying the communication problems within his company. Make recommendations as to how communications could be improved to prevent a similar situation in the future.

Chapter 8

COMMUNICATIONS IN ORGANISATIONS

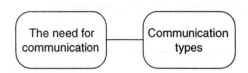

Introduction

So far we have explored how, and through which media, we communicate. For us to understand fully the benefits of effective communication, it is necessary to discover why communication is so necessary to the success of an organisation. To do this we shall first consider the need for communications at three levels:

(a) the individual level;

(b) the group level;

(c) the organisational level.

We shall also look at how you can attempt to ensure that other people communicate effectively with you, especially when using a written medium.

Your objectives

After completing this chapter, you should be able to:

(a) understand the need for, and the use of, different types of communication between individuals, groups and organisations;

(b) recognise how to facilitate effective communications in the written form;

(c) produce effective forms of communications.

Why do we need to communicate? Before we continue to examine how communication works, lets us review the need for it.

1 THE NEED FOR COMMUNICATION

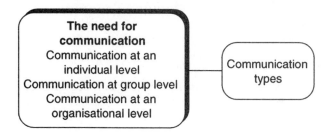

The need for communication
Communication at an individual level
Communication at group level
Communication at an organisational level

→ Communication types

We all need information, whether it is the basis for an academic piece of work, or information about when the local buses run. Without information we cannot make decisions. If we have no information we are unable to choose between the available options as we are unaware that those options exist.

Activity 1 [10 minutes]

You are going to the cinema. You are unable to discover what film is showing, by any means. When you arrive there are no posters or other advertising to give you this information. Tickets have to be purchased out of a machine. Do you:

(a) Buy a ticket and take a risk that the film is enjoyable?

(b) Wait for the film to end and ask someone who is leaving what the film is? (And hope that the next showing is of the same film.)

(c) Leave, and watch the television at home instead?

How would your decision affect the profitability of the cinema? Compile a list of possibilities for each of the decisions.

It is said that education creates choice, but, as education is the gaining of knowledge (information), then it can be said that information *equals* choice. This applies as much to organisations as it does to individuals.

> *Communication takes place at individual, group and organisational levels. We start with the individual.*

1.1 Communication at an individual level

Activity 2 [20 minutes]

It is you first day of work at a small office. You are deaf, dumb and blind. You are employed as a filing clerk. The filing cabinets are on the third floor of the building, but the offices where you must collect documents for filing are on the ground floor. Documents are filed by date, not alphabetically. Write a few paragraphs indicating how you think your first day at work will go.

Activity 3 [10 minutes]

Now consider a similar scenario to that in Activity 2. In this case you have all the physical attributes necessary for communicating, but the office manager is hostile, aggressive and intimidating.

How would you go about completing your task under these new circumstances?

Individuals need to be able to communicate in order that they may:

(a) carry out the job they are employed to do;

(b) deal with problems as they arise;

(c) prevent problems occurring;

(d) become committed to the organisation or work group.

Effective communication also gives a job meaning; it allows for personal development and helps to motivate the individual.

Next we look at communication at group level.

1.2 Communication at group level

One would be right to assume that communication within groups depends upon individuals being able to communicate. However, you should be aware by now that there is a difference between communicating and communicating *effectively*. Sometimes individuals are able to communicate effectively in some circumstances but not in others.

Activity 4 [30 minutes]

You are one of two researchers for a local radio station. You have a good relationship with your colleague, which shows in the way you are often in tune with each other's lines of thought. Your radio station is soon expected to be amalgamated with several other small stations. In future there will be ten researchers to cover the broader programme base and larger listening audience.

Write a letter to the Broadcasting Director explaining what difference this increase in numbers will have on the efficiency of the research team.

Group structure will have an impact on the efficacy of communications within the group. Formal design, in terms of leadership and individual areas of responsibility, is just as important as the personality of group members and their interpersonal relationships. Groups need effective communications within themselves for the same reasons as individuals; in addition, the more effective the communication between group members, the greater the sense of identity that the group will develop. In many organisational settings this closeness is a vital part of making the organisation work.

Activity 5 [10 minutes]

Identify five scenarios where you consider closeness of team work, brought about by good communications, is vital to the achievement of an organisation's objectives.

Groups within organisations also need to communicate with each other. The differing functions must co-ordinate their activities to achieve common objectives.

Activity 6 [20 minutes]

You are the sales director for a small firm producing a range of high quality paints. You manage to secure a large order from a national hotel chain to supply the paint for their forthcoming total refurbishment programme. This order is subsequently lost, because your company's range of colours no longer contains those required by the hotel chain.

Identify ways to avoid this kind of situation; make a list of the actions to be taken and the personnel who would need to be involved.

Finally, we look at communication at the organisation level.

1.3   Communication at an organisational level

The communication of information is a basic necessity in any organisation, as it is this which enables decisions to be made. From strategic objectives to hiring new staff, all decisions must be made with the best and most accurate information. Without this a decision may be inappropriate.

Information is also required for staff to perform to the standard required. Job descriptions, training and day-to-day instructions are all valid ways for the organisation to communicate with individuals. These methods make clear what is expected, what will be rewarded, and what will not be tolerated.

Activity 7 [25 minutes]

You run a small company manufacturing electrical plugs. List all those organisations which your company is likely to need to communicate with.

Communication between organisations is just as important as the communication that goes on inside an organisation. Inter-organisation communication can include communication between an organisation and:

(a) suppliers;

(b) customers;

(c) organisations providing support activities;

(d) legal organisations such as the Inland revenue and Customs & Excise;

(e) professional organisations and trades unions;

(f) the media;

(g) the local community.

This is not a definitive list, there are many more examples.

Activity 8 [30 minutes]

Consider the types of organisation discussed in Chapter 1. Pick three categories and find an example from your own experience of each of these types. (For example, your Students Union could be an example of a 'not-for-profit' organisation).

Write a list for each of your examples showing who the organisation needs to communicate with. Use your own judgement to place the items on the list in order of importance.

We shall now take two of the examples from the list above and examine why communication with these agents in particular is necessary.

Suppliers

The basic need for communication with suppliers comes from the necessity of procuring the correct supplies, to the required standard, at the appropriate time, in a predetermined quantity and at an acceptable cost. The closer the links with suppliers, and the better the communication links, the more likely it is that these five criteria will be fulfilled. The recent *total quality management* (TQM) approach to production places particular importance on communication with suppliers. Any organisation wishing to become TQM oriented must first address the communications problems that commonly exist with suppliers.

Professional organisations and trades unions

Throughout the 1980s there were countless examples of a lack of communication between employers and employees (as represented by trade unions and professional organisations). The resulting industrial havoc tended to be blamed solely on militant trade unions making unreasonable demands. The reality of the situation was that adversarial relationships had built up over many generations; the nature of these relationships prevented good communications (a form of noise). Thus the needs of the individual were isolated from the needs of the organisation, and management claims to require certain behaviour in order to remain competitive were disbelieved and generally mistrusted. Effective communications could have prevented some of these problems.

Legal curbs on union power have since reduced industrial relations problems. However, this was a case of treating the symptoms rather than the cause of the disease. Organisations that communicate well and consistently with their employees, whether they do so through trade unions or not, tend to have fewer industrial relations problems. This can be attributed to the partnership relationship that effective two-way communications can foster.

Activity 9 [45 minutes]

Write a short paragraph on each of the other examples (b), (c), (d), (f) and (g) of inter-organisation communication, identifying the needs for, and the effects of, effective communications.

Just as with individuals and groups, organisations communicate with each other through all the media we have considered. The greatest emphasis here is placed upon communication in the written form, for reasons of permanence and proof. We shall now consider the differing forms the written medium can take.

2 COMMUNICATION TYPES

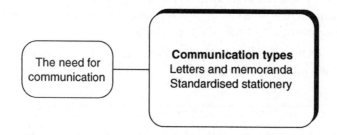

We discussed in Chapter 7 the various media of communications. Each of these media can provide several different types of communications. Written communications are the most widely accepted form, especially in legal terms, and it is these that we shall concentrate upon. Some examples of types of written communication are:

(a) letters/memoranda;

(b) reports (see Chapter 7);

(c) standardised stationary (forms).

We start with the first of these: letters and memos.

2.1 Letters and memoranda

We are not concerned here with the *format* of a letter, but with the need for it to *communicate information*, or *requests for information*, effectively. There are four good general rules to follow:

(a) plan what you intend to say based on what needs to be said;

(b) assume the reader is as busy as you are and keep the letter brief;

(c) avoid redundancy;

(d) pay attention to layout, paper type, logos and so on. Badly used, these things can act as noise and distract from the message; used correctly they can reinforce the message.

Eliciting information can be particularly complex. To gain the right information you have to ask the right questions.

Activity 10 [25 minutes]

Read the following mini case study.

A young boy arrives home in a dishevelled state. His father is in the garden and calls out to ask what is the matter. 'Dad', said the boy, 'I've had a smash on my bike.' After establishing that the boy is unhurt, father and son sit down to discuss the incident. 'What happened?', asks the father. 'Mr Jones opened his car door just as I was passing', is the reply. The father carefully explains that when riding a bicycle one has to be aware that these things can happen. Nevertheless, he is furious that his son has been put at risk in this way and decides to speak to Mr Jones as soon as he gets the opportunity. 'Make sure you only pass a parked car when there is no traffic coming the other way, so that you can go out far enough into the road to avoid being hit by a door suddenly flung open', he says. 'But Dad', said the boy, 'I was riding on the pavement'.

Re-write this scenario as told by *Mr Jones* to his wife. Highlight the differences in the two versions of events.

In any communication of information, verbal or written, be aware of two important points.

(a) You will be told what the *other person* thinks is important. This may differ from what you consider to be important.

(b) Most misunderstandings in communications occur when people make assumptions. Ask the right questions to establish the facts or gain the information that you consider is important. This is more difficult in written form, as spontaneity is lost, but there is the advantage that you do have a chance to consider what the important questions are.

A word of caution, just as listening is one of the most important skills in verbal communication, so reading and interpreting are vital skills in communicating in written form.

Reports have been dealt with in Chapter 7, so we shall now continue with standardised stationery.

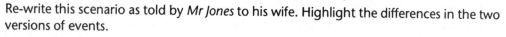

2.2 Standardised stationery

The most common type of standardised stationery is the dreaded 'form'. These can contain a variety of elements, ranging from short tick boxes to long complicated questions. Whatever their format, their purpose is the same: forms elicit information. In particular, forms can be effective ways to gain a large amount of information swiftly.

As we have seen above, to gain the correct information, we must ask the right questions in an unambiguous way. There are many texts dedicated to the subject of form design alone. Here are some basic guidelines.

(a) Before putting pen to paper, consider what information is required and for what purpose.

(b) Do not make assumptions regarding language or phraseology. For example, you may consider dinner to be an evening meal; others may consider it to be eaten around midday.

(c) Be specific.

(d) Phrase questions in such a way that a clear answer can be given.

(e) Do not ask more than one question at a time.

(f) Consider possible answers. These may lead you to further questions. (If Fred says ABC, I will have the information I need, but if he says DEF, I will need to know XYZ.)

The same guidelines can be used for eliciting information in any circumstances. One of the most common difficulties with forms is the way in which questions are asked. We each have our own outlook on life and perceive things differently; therefore we understand things differently. Even badly placed punctuation can cause difficulties.

EXAMPLE: AMBIGUOUS QUESTIONS

The following examples are from questionnaires:

Q. Where do you live?..................................... A. In a house.

Q. Do you always purchase the same car?   A. No, when I buy one I like it to be new.

Here are two examples from life:

(Overheard in a hospital ward) 'Mrs Brown, have you always had these veins?'

(Child caught in the tennis club) 'Do you belong to this tennis club?' 'No sir, I belong to my Mum and Dad.'

Activity 11   [30 minutes + research time]

Working with a partner, obtain a copy of the student loan application form. (If the student loan form is unavailable, any form containing questions will do.) Read the questions out to each other and write down answers to each.

Make a note of any questions you find hard to answer and for which you require more explanation. Try to re-write them so that they are easier to understand.

Now consider each question carefully and write down what information it is designed to elicit and the purpose to which you think this information will be put.

Chapter roundup

- Before we can use the media of communication we need to identify the purpose of the communication.
- Communication can be considered at three levels: individual, group and organisation.
- All levels need communication to gain information in order that they may make decisions.
- Communication facilitates choice.
- Communication bonds groups together.
- Communication allows productive interaction between groups and organisations.
- Effective communication can prevent problems.
- Written communication can be as ambiguous as verbal communication.
- Written communications need to be specific to be effective.
- In order to gain all the information required, the right questions must be asked.
- Forms can be used to gather a large amount of information quickly.
- Forms can gather the wrong information if not designed with care.
- Individuals differ in what they regard as important information.

Quick Quiz

1 What do we require in order to make decisions?
2 Give five reasons why communications are necessary.
3 Identify which of these reasons apply to individuals, groups and organisations, respectively.
4 How can effective communications within a group affect its performance, and why?
5 Why do organisations need to communicate effectively with their suppliers? (Give five reasons.)
6 How do the letters you may be required to write on behalf of an organisation differ from those you may write to friends and family?
7 What is the most important point to remember when eliciting information?
8 Give three guidelines you should use when designing forms to gain information.
9 What are the advantages of using forms to gain information?

Answers to Quick Quiz

1 Information
2 There are many reasons to be found throughout the chapter, here are a selection. Communications are necessary in order to: (a) perform a job; (b) become committed to the organisation; (c) build partnership relationships; (d) procure appropriate supplies; (e) know what the customer wants.
3 All the above can be relevant to the individual, groups and organisations. In particular (a) and (b) apply to individuals; (c) especially applies to groups within an organisation; (d) and (e) are strongly associated with organisations.
4 Effective communication within a group can improve the group's performance by: (a) ensuring clarity of purpose; (b) creating commitment to each other member.

5 Organisations need to communicate effectively with suppliers in order that they may: (a) get the right goods; (b) get the right quality; (c) get the right quantity; (d) at the right time; (e) at a reasonable price.

6 | **Family and friends** | **Organisation** |
|---|---|
| Informal | Formal |
| 'Chatty' with no concern about redundancy | Focused and to the point |
| Often hand written | Usually typed |

7 Ask the right questions!

8 You could chose any from Section 2.2.

9 Forms can be used to gather large amounts of information from a large number of sources in a relatively short time.

Answers to Activities

1 If you do purchase a ticket this will add to the cinema's profitability, but if you are disappointed with the film you may not return. This will cause a loss of profits in the long term.

 As you do not know what time the film starts you could have a long wait. Most people would be unlikely to be patient enough to do this and thus profits would suffer. If all customers refuse to wait, the cinema will go out of business.

2 You will probably have concluded that it is impossible for you to carry out the task. You do not know what the task is or how to go about it. Worse still, you are unable to communicate your difficulties to other people.

3 Your task is less difficult than it was in Activity 2. Your answer will largely depend on your personality. If you tend to be shy you are less likely to be able to complete the task. If you are reasonably extrovert you will probably ask someone other than the office manager for advice.

4 You should have concluded that the efficiency of the team will be reduced, in terms of output per person, in the initial period whilst new relationships are formed. Communications effectiveness may be reduced as a result of personal jealousies and insecurities acting as noise.

5 Your examples could include the following: (a) the armed services (especially in times of hostilities), (b) cave and mountain rescue teams, (c) ambulance crews, (d) fire fighters, (e) project teams (consider a team planning the design and launch of a major new product, for example Concorde). You could have identified many others. You might assess your answers by asking three questions.

 (i) What are the organisation's objectives?

 (ii) Are a variety of skills required to achieve them?

 (iii) If the team do not communicate effectively, will the objectives be met?

6 This situation may leave the individual feeling frustrated and de-motivated, but the most important impact in commercial terms is the loss of the contract. Too many episodes like this will affect profitability and turnover, with the long-term result that the organisation will be unable to sustain itself. For the individual this may mean redundancy. The following actions could be taken.

 (a) Discontinuation of colours should be discussed at Board level. As sales director, you would then have an input into this decision.

 (b) Board decisions should be communicated to whomever they affect, in this case all the sales staff in particular.

 (c) In future, proposed changes to the range should be discussed as widely as possible. Decisions need input from the accounts, purchasing, sales and marketing departments.

7 Your list could be extensive, but you should have identified the following:

 (a) suppliers who provide any parts, such as the fuses;

(b) suppliers who provide raw materials, plastic, metals and so on;

(c) suppliers of your machinery;

(d) utility suppliers (for example, electricity);

(e) customers, in this case retailers or wholesalers of your product, and/or a white goods manufacturer to whom you supply the plugs;

(f) the local council (concerning taxes, waste collection and local bylaws);

(g) trades unions or other collective methods of communicating with the workforce;

(h) industry 'watch dogs' (concerning production standards, safety standards and so on);

(i) government departments and agencies (health and safety, tax, customs and excise (VAT)).

8 Examples of the kind of organisations you could have identified are as follows.

(a) Sole trader – local fish and chip shop.

(b) Partnership – many of the trades are partnerships (builders, plumbers, electricians). You may also have identified your dentist as a partnership.

(c) Private companies – many of these are to be found in the small to medium manufacturing sector. (If you have trouble identifying one, look in your local Yellow Pages for companies with 'Ltd' after the name. Public companies are easily recognisable by Plc after the name. Many of the large retail chains are Plcs.

(d) Mutual societies – be careful if you choose a building society to establish whether or not it is still a mutual society, many have changed their status to compete in the modern commercial world. Your local co-operative society would probably be the best example.

(e) Public-sector organisations – again be careful here. Many organisations that have been public-sector organisations are no longer so in the pure sense and thus must fall into the next category. Ensure that you choose an organisation which is solely in public ownership, such as the armed forces.

(f) Mixed organisations – these are the hybrids between public-sector and private organisations. Your university or college is a good example.

(g) Not-for-profit – these range from very large international organisations to very small local clubs. You should have no difficulty in identifying one of these.

The second part of your answer should include all or most of the list preceding the activity. Your prioritisation of the list will depend upon the organisation you choose and your perception of their activities.

9 Your answers should be as follows.

(a) *Customers*: without communication with its customers a company will very quickly become out of touch with their requirements and thus lose business.

(b) *Support activities*: these are any services outside the organisation which are used by it. If an organisation has outsourced any of its secondary activities, then communication with the organisations performing them will be the only way to ensure it gets what it requires.

(c) *Legal organisations*: failure to communicate with these bodies can have dramatic results. Non payment of income tax can bring interest charges and forced liquidation. Contravention of VAT regulations can result in imprisonment for the Directors.

(d) *The media*: whilst not all organisations communicate with the media, the successful ones do use it to ensure that the activities of the organisation are commonly known about. The media may also be used for advertising in the accepted sense.

(e) *The local community*: good communication with the local community, either through the council or local organisations, can avoid difficulties over such matters as expansion.

10 Mr Jones is likely to be angry that the boy almost knocked him over/damaged his car door. He possibly considers the boy's actions to be an example of the inconsiderate attitude of youth. He would probably not believe it if he were told that the boy did not know better.

11 In a professionally designed form the likelihood of finding ambiguous questions should be negligible. However, because we all have differing perceptions and understanding, designing the perfect form is almost impossible.

Assignment 8 [2 hours]

As a line manager you have been asked to implement a new shift pattern, involving your staff working a night shift, which they have never had to do before. The details have yet to be finalised.

Design a questionnaire to gauge the feelings of the staff. You wish to use the information you gain to design a method of introduction that will cause the least disruption. You *cannot* go to senior management and say that introduction of the new system is impossible. (This is a real problem which had a satisfactory outcome.)

Chapter 9

COMMUNICATION NETWORKS

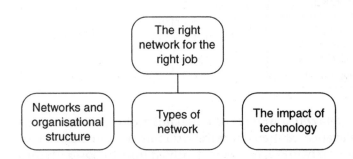

Introduction

We have looked at what happens when we communicate, and what means we use to communicate. We know that communication is important to individuals, groups and organisations and that the approach to communication varies depending upon the interaction taking place. Now we consider who, within organisations, we communicate with.

This chapter looks at the different ways in which communications evolve, and how we can use this process of evolution to establish more effective communications within an organisation. We shall concentrate on the formal communications networks, although the same principles will apply when we consider informal communication in Chapter 10.

Your objectives

By the end of this chapter you will be able to:

(a) describe the nature of communication networks;

(b) relate communication networks to organisation and group types;

(c) appreciate the impact of technology on communication networks.

To understand how communication networks function, we first need to find out how they are structured.

1   TYPES OF NETWORK

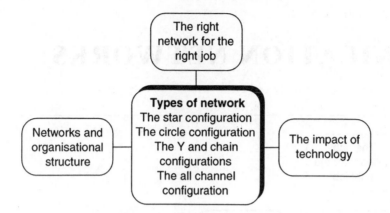

With the development of *team-centred working*, the dynamics of communications within groups become of relevance, as they affect the structure of these teams. Five main types of communication networks have been identified through research into group interactions:

(a) the star configuration;

(b) the circle configuration;

(c) the Y configuration;

(d) the chain configuration;

(e) the all channel configuration.

We will look at each of these in turn, starting with the star.

1.1   The star configuration

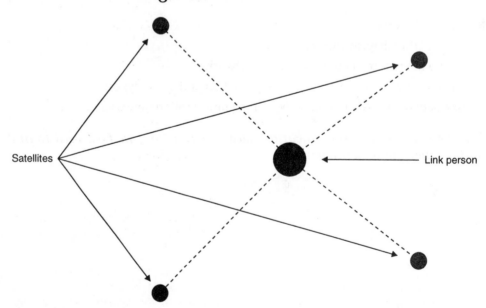

Figure 9.1 The star configuration

Definition

Star configuration: also known as the 'wheel' configuration, the star is the most centralised of the communications networks. It includes a 'link' person through whom all communications must travel. The 'satellite' individuals communicate only with the 'link' person (or department) and not with each other.

The star configuration has been found to be an efficient system for simple tasks; however, if the complexity of tasks is increased the subsequent increased pressure on the link person reduces the overall efficiency of the group.

This is a group with a clear leader. The level of satisfaction and motivation is highest for the group leader, with the other members gaining very little satisfaction. Star networks can evolve through the interrelationships within the group if there is one dominant individual. Star networks may be specifically implemented where contact between the various satellites is not desirable. (Think back to the war time scenario in Chapter 6: it is best for security if only one person knows everything that is going on.)

Activity 1   [10 minutes]

Identify and draw two examples of star networks from your own experience: one from a work or educational setting and one from your social life. Which was the easiest to identify? What do these two examples have in common?

Star networks have a strong leader. Next we consider a type of network which has no leader.

1.2   The circle configuration

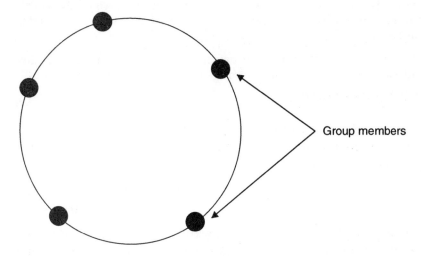

Figure 9.2 The circle configuration

Definition

Circle configuration: in this configuration the group has no defined leader. All members communicate with their immediate neighbours only.

The result of a circle configuration is an unorganised group, which tends to be slow and erratic in problem solving. However, with complex problems, this type of network does have greater efficiency than the star, with its reliance upon a single individual. Group members within a circle network gain satisfaction and motivation through perceived participation.

The next two types of network can usefully be considered together.

1.3 The Y and chain configurations

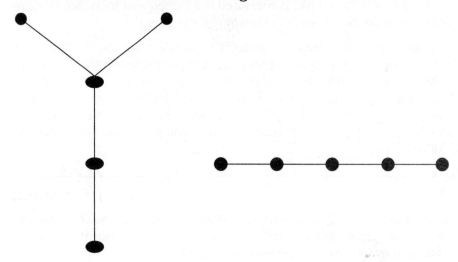

Figure 9.3 The Y and chain configurations

Both these types of communications network are commonly found in large organisations, although this does not preclude their use in organisations of all types and sizes.

Definitions

Y configuration: in this network there is a key person at the linkage of the three arms of communication, but this does not result in clear leadership of the kind found in the star configuration.

Chain configuration: with this network the situation is much the same as with the circle, with individuals only communicating with their immediate chain neighbours.

These configurations are often artificially produced. The purpose of their production is related to the structure of the organisation and the way in which the culture has been developed to achieve the corporate objectives.

Activity 2   [30 minutes]

Consider a large, multi-departmental organisation, with a centralised purchasing and supply function. All requests for inputs into the company – from raw materials to toilet paper for the lavatories – are required to go through this department. New suppliers have no access to the engineering, research and development or other departments, only to purchasing.

Write a few paragraphs on the advantages and disadvantages of this situation. Ensure that you substantiate your arguments.

The final type of network to consider is the all channel configuration.

1.4 The all channel configuration

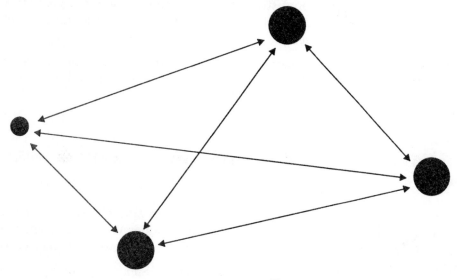

Figure 9.4 The all channel configuration

Definition

All channel configuration: all members of the group can freely communicate with other members.

This has been found to be the most effective network for complex problems. The participatory style leads to this being the chosen network for project teams in most organisations.

Having established how networks operate, we must now consider their relevance within particular organisational structures.

2 NETWORKS AND ORGANISATIONAL STRUCTURE

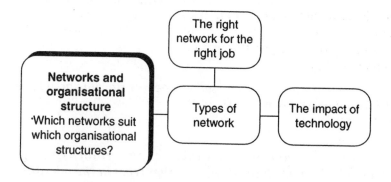

The line and staff organisation can be related to the hierarchical structure described in Chapter 3. As we have seen, the direction of communication flow can be diagonal, vertical, or horizontal. Although the networks we have seen give the illusion of being two dimensional, you should remember that they can encompass any layer of the organisational structure.

We will now look at how networks can be matched with structures.

2.1 Which networks suit which organisational structures?

All networks suit all organisational structures to a greater or lesser degree. As a heuristic, the shorter the scalar chain, the more opportunity there is for all channel communication networks to develop.

Many organisations today are changing their structures to allow for increased empowerment of employees at all levels. This has been most evident at 'shop floor' level.

Definition

Shop floor level: all those at the lower end of the scalar chain, not only those in the manufacturing industries.

In an effort to increase flexibility and the ability to react towards changing markets, structural changes are needed to speed up communications. As we have seen, the more rigid and inflexible the communications network, the slower it is to react to external change.

Nowhere has this been more evident than in the UK motor car manufacturing industry. The time taken from inception to production has been cut by half in recent years. Not only is this due to the formation of easily adaptable production techniques, it is also due to the involvement of and communication between all departments from a very early stage. For example, production of a new car model used to be driven mainly by the advancing technology of the time. How the product would be marketed was seen as a process to be considered well after the design stage, as was the sourcing of materials. Now production of a new model is very much consumer led, with marketing having input in the early stages as to the type of product that would suit the market. Similarly, sourcing of materials during the design stage highlights potential problems before manufacture is imminent.

This increase in all channel communication has been facilitated by the formation of design and project teams that cover all the aspects of the organisation that have a bearing on the product at any stage of its life cycle.

However, increasing the use of all channel communication networks is not without its problems. Interdepartmental rivalry, which may have developed over many years, is hard to break down, and the resulting attitudes and behaviour can act as noise, preventing the accurate exchange of information. The reasons for and implications of this kind of noise are complex, involving the *culture* of the organisation. This is a subject we shall return to in later chapters.

For discussion

In order to improve communications within an organisation, does the structure need to be changed first? Or should the culture be changed first?

The predisposition of certain organisational structures to certain types of communication network does not preclude the use of other types in the relevant circumstances. We must now look at the environmental and operational issues which determine the style of network used.

3 THE RIGHT NETWORK FOR THE RIGHT JOB

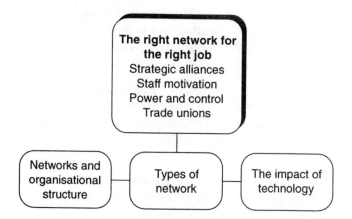

There are many environmental and operational issues that impact on the choice of network for a particular purpose. We shall consider here those which are most topical:

(a) strategic alliances;

(b) staff motivation;

(c) power and control;

(d) trade unions.

For discussion

Discuss other environmental and operational issues which impact on the choice of communication network, using real life examples where possible.

We start by looking at strategic alliances.

3.1 Strategic alliances

Strategic alliances are seen by many organisations as the route forward into the next millennium. One of the dangers of strategic alliances is that one organisation may become subjugated to the culture and character of the other. This can be avoided by the careful flow of information from one company to another. The Japanese have become past masters of this art, as was seen in the Rover/Honda alliance of the 1980s. The concept is not one of total secrecy or of trying to mislead the partner organisation, it is more a question of working on a 'need to know' basis. Providing the information that is necessary, but no more. This sort of control is difficult to achieve by conscious individual effort, thus the way in which the communication networks are structured is vital. An all channel network is predisposed to the free flow of information and would thus not be suitable.

Activity 3   [20 minutes]

Identify the most suitable network for a strategic alliance. By the use of a labelled diagram, show how this network would span the two organisations involved.

Now we consider staff motivation.

3.2   Staff motivation

The increasing trend towards fixed-term contracts and the high level of job redundancies over the past few years have led to increasing job insecurity amongst all levels of the workforce. It has been observed that this insecurity can have a de-motivating effect. One means of improving the motivation of the workforce can be by increasing their sense of *participation* in the organisation. This can take many forms and be implemented to varying degrees.

However increased participation is achieved, communication must play a central part. Communication networks where the workforce is deliberately fragmented and discouraged from free communications have the effect of isolating individuals and departments, and increasing adversarial relationships. Mistrust becomes a prominent feature and motivation is low.

Not only must communications improve in order to achieve any form of participation, improving and encouraging free communications can itself engender a feeling of participation even without any other measures being taken.

Whereas free communication can create feelings of participation, restricted communication can allow those who control the network to exercise power and control over those who are purely members of the network.

3.3   Power and control

Restricted communication is often used at the second level in an organisation to keep power and control with those who control the network. The armed forces are a good example: at unit and regimental level communication networks are designed to create closely knit teams; however, higher up the chain of command, rivalry is encouraged between regiments by limiting the contact and communication between their members. This rivalry is considered beneficial to the overall performance of the army.

This philosophy can also be found in commercial organisations which have individual branches nationwide; contact and communication are limited to the branch managers, with the rest of the workforce being isolated in order to improve competition between branches and thus the overall performance of the organisation.

Issues of power and control are also at stake when considering the communication networks that affect trade unions.

3.4   Trade unions

In the past, the activities of trade unions have been undermined by the careful use of communication networks. Some organisations have gone so far as to design production sites and shift patterns to inhibit free communications by fragmenting the workforce in a physical sense.

On the other side of the coin, collective bargaining is an example of trade unions using a specific type of communication network to ensure that they are at the hub of any negotiations.

Activity 4   **[15 minutes]**

Identify and illustrate, by means of a labelled diagram, the communication network that best fits the collective bargaining scenario.

Technological innovations have improved the contact between people, but have they improved communications? To answer this question we must look at the impact of technology on communication networks.

4 THE IMPACT OF TECHNOLOGY

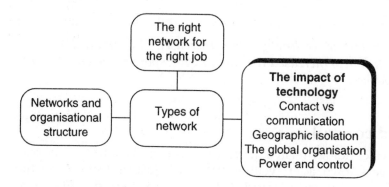

First, we should make a distinction between contact and communication.

4.1 Contact vs. communication

One might assume that, with the recent surges in information technology, the need for face-to-face communication would have been greatly reduced. This is, in fact, what has been projected to happen. Technology will allow us to work from home with minimal direct contact with our employers and with communication being conducted through computers and telephone lines. However, the undoubted growth in communication through technological means has not been as swift as anticipated.

It is certainly already true that it is very easy for contact to be made between individuals and organisations worldwide. Note the use of the word 'contact': these technological aids facilitate communication by allowing us contact with one another; they do not ensure the effectiveness of that communication. (See Chapter 7 for examples of technological aids and their associated problems.)

One sphere where technology has improved communications is in remote geographic areas.

4.2 Geographic isolation

Technology has improved, and is likely to continue to improve, opportunities for paid employment in areas of less dense population. The financial services industry has been quick to take advantage of this opportunity. Although this use of technology is mostly in evidence in the western world at present, the ability to provide communication links anywhere in the world is now a reality.

A recent concept – the global organisation – depends on technology for its existence.

4.3 The global organisation

The concept of a global organisation would not be possible without the advances that have been made in information technology. The ability to communicate regularly, and at will, with the core organisation, enables the entity to act as one, whilst allowing room for different branches to act independently, as local conditions dictate.

Activity 5 [45 minutes]

By means of labelled diagrams, show which networks would be most effective in the cases of geographic isolation and the global organisation. Below each diagram list the reasons for your choice of network.

Whilst the advancement of technology has increased the amount of free communications, it has also increased the way in which power and control can be exerted over employees.

4.4 Power and control

The best example of a technology-related increase in power and control can be seen with what used to be known as 'travelling salesmen'. Just as technology has improved the speed and distance of travel, it has enabled the individual to be contacted at almost any time. Earlier technologies, such as the telephone, enabled the individual to contact the organisation, but not visa versa. The mobile telephone has changed this. The widespread use of computers and modems now allows sales data to be downloaded to an organisation's computer from vast distances, and the facsimile machine has facilitated the transmission of documents bearing legitimate signatures. Pagers and message services mean that is possible to keep track of employees in the field with much more accuracy, appointments can be centrally booked and changes to a schedule made at short notice.

Employees working away from the office in this way now have little need to spend any time at the organisation's base. This has the effect of further isolating them from their working colleagues and so makes management control of the individual easier.

Activity 6 [20 minutes]

You are the Sales Director of a large corporation. List the technological means you could employ to keep in touch with your sales staff who are distributed nationwide.

Chapter roundup

- Networks represent the way in which communication points are connected.
- Each network type has purposes for which it is best suited; there is no one best network.
- Some types of network occur with more frequency than others in specific organisational types.
- All channel communication networks allow free communications between all and any level in an organisation.
- Faster communications lead to flexibility for the organisation.
- Networks do not necessarily follow the lines of authority.
- In many of the contemporary issues facing organisations today, the type of network employed can have an impact on the success or otherwise of the operation.
- For employees to participate in the management of the organisation, communication must play a vital part. The type of network used will either facilitate or hinder this.
- A combination of network types is often found within organisations.
- Technology has made communication easier and faster than ever before.
- Without the advances in technology that have been made over recent decades, the global organisation would be impossible to control.
- Improvements in communications technology have brought employment to areas of geographic isolation.

Quick Quiz

1. Name three types of communication network.
2. Which networks are more suited to a participatory style of management?
3. Give an example of how communication networks can be used to influence the behaviour of the workforce.
4. How many types of network can be used in one organisation?
5. Choose one network and state how its structure influences the motivation of the participants.
6. List three ways in which technology has affected the working environment.

Answers to Quick quiz

1. You could have names the star, circle, Y, chain or all channel networks.
2. All channel networks, because all members of the network have the same rights of access to all other members.
3. Networks which isolate sections of the workforce can create internal friction, which may be a good or bad thing depending on the organisational objectives. See also Section 3.3 of this chapter.
4. All of them.
5. The use of the all channel network can increase feelings of commitment in staff towards the organisation in which they work. See Section 3.2 of this chapter.
6. Technology has influenced the working environment by: (a) increasing the ability to contact people; (b) allowing outworking to take place; (c) increasing the number of global organisations.

Answers to Activities

1   In a university, for example, a star network exists between students from various colleges within the university, tutors and external examiners.

You may have found it difficult to identify a star network from your personal life, unless you have a dominant personality in your circle of friends or family. This type of network is more common in families with a strong 'figurehead' culture.

2   You could have stated the following advantages.

(a) The purchasing department has specialist expertise in negotiating with suppliers.

(b) Other departments are not disrupted by reps calling.

(c) There is less opportunity for suppliers to influence the organisation's purchasing by using incentives and inducements.

(d) All departments will receive standard supplies. Costs can be more easily controlled.

(e) Economies of scale can be achieved.

You could have stated the following disadvantages.

(a) Departmental managers have no autonomy over the supplies they require and receive.

(b) Internal paperwork will slow the supply process.

(c) High cost and low cost items will receive the same scrutiny, or more likely neither will.

(d) Specification must be detailed in order to receive suitable products.

(e) Departments will be slow to become aware of new products or technological developments.

3   If you think in terms of departments or committees communicating, it becomes easier to see that the most suitable network is one with a hub at the centre. This could be a joint management board or a project team.

Your diagram should be similar to that shown in Figure 9.5.

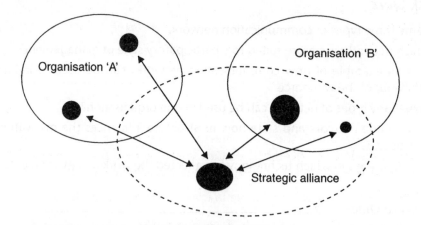

Of course, there would be many more satellites, but the important point is the central hub, filtering and censoring information.

4   This scenario is best suited to the Y configuration. Your diagram should be similar to that shown in Figure 9.6.

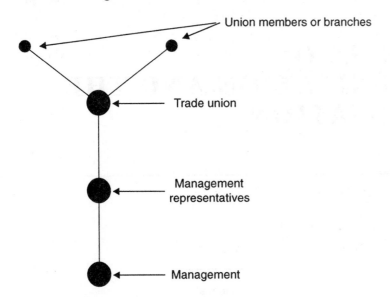

5   Geographic isolation is best suited to the Y configuration or the star. The Y configuration shows us that the point of contact with the organisation may lead on to communication with other departments or levels of management. The star illustrates nicely the isolation that the individual feels. Either would be correct if the reasons given include these factors.

    The global organisation could make use of the star or the all channel configurations. However, the point should be made that often the core organisation wants to discourage communication between satellites, except at the highest levels of management. Reasons for this are to do with power and control (divide and rule).

6   You could have suggested the following: (a) land-based telephone; (b) mobile telephone; (c) pagers; (d) conference calls; (e) video phones; (f) email (to laptop computers), (g) internet bulletin boards (again using a modem and a laptop computer).

Assignment 9   **[1.5 hours]**

As in Activity 6, you are the Sales Director of a large corporation. One of your regions has been performing below target levels for the past three months. From what you have learned in the past chapters decide on the following.

(a) What information do you require to investigate the reasons for this?

(b) Who do you need to communicate with and why?

(c) What are the most appropriate media for gaining this information? Comment on ways in which communication networks could help or hinder your investigation.

Write down your plan of campaign and give reasons for each of your decisions.

Chapter 10

CHANNELS OF COMMUNICATION AND THE ORGANISATION

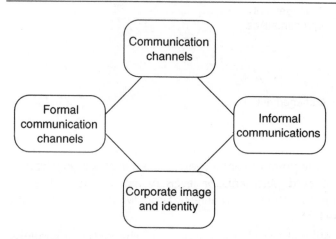

Introduction

Definition

Communication channel: a route along which communication may travel.

We are all aware of the phrase 'going through the correct channels'. This can be translated as 'following the correct route'. In this chapter we shall consider the nature of these routes, as distinct from the communication networks we identified earlier. We shall also see how the structure, culture and information needs of an organisation can affect the use of communication channels.

Your objectives

After completing this chapter, you should be able to:

(a) describe channels of communication;

(b) relate and evaluate the relationship between communication channels, the organisational structure and the needs of the organisation;

(c) discuss the importance of communication in forming corporate image and identity.

The medium of communication tells us by what method we communicate; the channel of communication indicates the direction of the communication flow.

1 COMMUNICATION CHANNELS

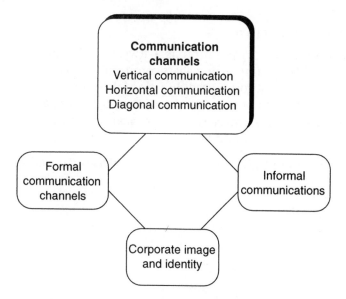

There are three potential directions for communication:

(a) vertical communication;

(b) horizontal communication;

(c) diagonal communication.

We start with vertical communication.

1.1 Vertical communication

Vertical channels of communication tend to follows chains of authority up and down the organisational structure. Remember that communication takes place in many forms: the channels of communication not only include people giving verbal instructions to each other, but may include such things as sending in time sheets and receiving data for computer input.

In most organisations (though not all) there is some sort of hierarchy. The vertical channels of communications in such organisations can be represented as shown in Figure 10.1

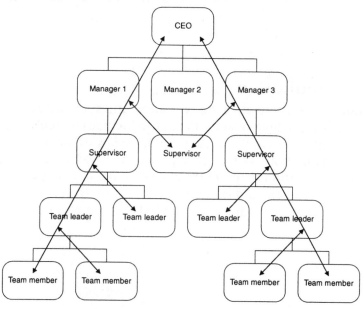

Figure 10.1 Vertical communication within a stylised hierarchical organisation

Next we look at horizontal communication.

1.2 Horizontal communication

Horizontal communication within an organisation is between individuals or groups of the same or similar rank. For example, managers communicate with other managers. This is possibly the most commonly used direction of communication within an organisation. It is needed for co-ordination of activities, but it also allows the individual to gain support from peers - more so than vertical communication does, as it is not constrained by differences in rank.

Horizontal communication is shown in Figure 10.2 for an hierarchical organisation.

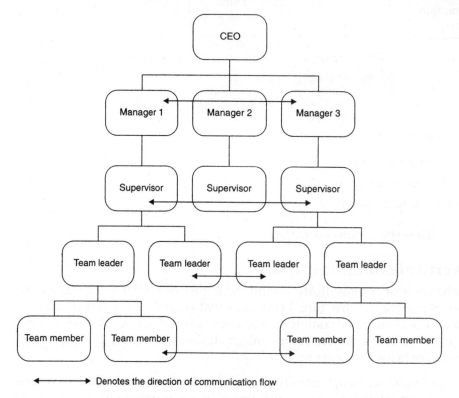

Figure 10.2 Horizontal communication within a stylised hierarchical organisation.

Finally, we consider diagonal communication.

1.3 Diagonal communication

Diagonal communication is, as its name suggests, communication across the organisation with no regard for the lines of authority. It can include any rank. This does occur in hierarchical organisations; it is usually conducted by departments or individuals who serve the organisation in a support capacity and who have no strict lines of access, either to them or from them. Examples would be: the salaries and wages part of the accounts department and the personnel function within Human Resource Management. Diagonal communication can also be shown on a diagram, as in Figure 10.3.

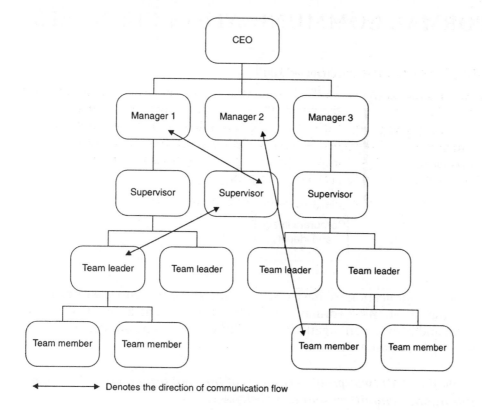

Denotes the direction of communication flow

Figure 10.3 Diagonal communication within a stylised hierarchical organisation

Activity 1   [30 minutes]

With the aid of a diagram, identify the directions of communication flow within the following organisation structure.

(a) George is the parks supervisor at the council offices.

(b) Fred and Jim are area supervisors for the towns parks, each taking responsibility for three parks.

(c) Alf, Ben, Simon, Alison, Betty and Mike each take care of one park. Each one has two part-time assistants to help with planting out, watering and weeding.

(d) Don is in charge of the council greenhouses, where plants for all the parks are grown from seed. He has three women who work full time to help him.

(e) Andy is the council grass cutter, along with Graham who is part time.

Activity 2   [15 minutes]

You are unhappy about a mark you receive for an assignment. Make a list of who you are *likely* to talk to about this (not necessarily the same as who you *should* talk to) and note what direction of communication flow is occurring in each case.

So far we have discussed communication as if it is always pre-planned and formalised. We must now go on to look at the differences between formal and informal communications, starting with the one we know most about: the formal channels.

NOTES

2 FORMAL COMMUNICATION CHANNELS

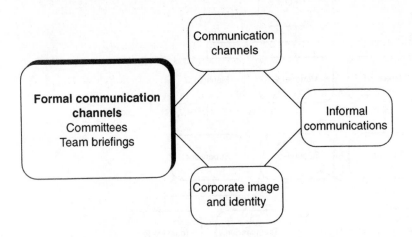

Much of the communication we have discussed already comes into the category of 'formal communications'. Formal channels of communication within an organisation and between an organisation and its environment can use any of the media described in Chapter 7.

Here we shall look at two specific examples of internal formal organisational communications: committees and team briefings.

2.1 Committees

Committees are a commonly used and useful way of communicating effectively with those who are committee members. They provide a forum for the dissemination of information and the exchange of ideas before decision making takes place. They also encourage participation in the communication process by enhancing the sense of group involvement.

Committees are a good way of combining capabilities and co-ordinating activities beyond the committee room. They can, however, be slow in decision making and can cause an organisation to be conservative in its strategic thinking as a result of the need for a consensus decision.

Activity 3   **[30 minutes 'in committee' + discussion time]**

Form groups of no more than six people. Democratically choose a committee leader to be your spokesperson once a decision has been reached. Try to have an even number of groups within the class so that your group can be paired with another.

Your paired group has £500 to spend on the following items: food for one week, three different text books to which they will all require free access (cost £20 each), road tax for six months on one car (cost £77), two items of clothing (total cost £50), a visit to the launderette (cost £10) and a college dance (cost £15 per ticket) which each member of the group wants to go to.

Reach a consensus decision within 30 minutes as to how the money is to be allocated to each of these items.

Compare your decisions between groups and discuss the difficulties you encountered in reaching them.

Now we look at the second type of formal communication: team briefings.

2.2 Team briefings

Team briefings are aimed to increase the downward flow of information from management to the workforce. They operate on a cascade principle, with more senior members of staff briefing those below them. As far as possible briefings are co-ordinated to occur at the same time, to ensure that all staff of a similar grade receive information at the same time. Briefings are held on a regular basis, usually once a month. They are not a forum for discussion or feedback, therefore the motivating benefits of such one-way communication are debatable.

For discussion

In groups, consider the benefits and disadvantages of introducing a system of team briefings into an organisation. In particular look at the improvements in communications which could be gained by:

(a) introducing team briefings as part of a package of measures;
(b) introducing team briefings as the sole attempt to improve communications.

Formal communication channels are established within an organisation in order that the flow of information can be regulated in the desired direction. Informal channels evolve to fill the gaps left by the formal communication network.

3   INFORMAL COMMUNICATIONS

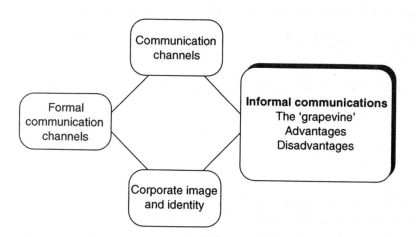

In this section we consider the grapevine of information communication that exists in all organisations, as introduced in Chapter 2. We then examine its advantages and disadvantages.

First of all, what is the grapevine?

3.1   The 'grapevine'

The grapevine is a supplementary system of communication channels and exists, without exception, in all organisations. You will be familiar with the grapevine at your own college. The grapevine tends to rely on word of mouth rather than the written medium, but can also work very successfully using computer-based communications. For example, Internet bulletin boards can now extend the grapevine to more than one geographic site, in a way that the telephone has been able to do in the past. Computer-based 'conversations' cannot be overheard, and information can be posted anonymously, or in such a way that only the participants of the grapevine know where it originates.

In order for a grapevine to function there need to be linkages between the different sections of an organisation. Some individuals move freely from one department to another (for example, the tea lady, car park or security staff) and can pick up and pass on information. Alternatively, there may be areas of the organisation where workers from all departments congregate (for example the staff canteen).

Organisational grapevines work on the 'domino principle'. You have probably seen dominoes set up in such a way that when one tumbles a chain reaction is started. If you imagine a room full of dominoes going in many directions, the removal of one or two strategically placed individual dominoes will halt the chain reaction.

Activity 4   [One day of observation; 30 minutes discussion]

This is a group activity and, as such, should be co-ordinated by your tutor.

Spend one day making a note of every piece of information you acquire through informal channels at college. It is important that you record exactly what you hear.

During your subsequent discussion period, identify how many people have the same information and find out if there are variations in it.

Try to classify the information into types, such as: general gossip, news regarding impending college activities, and requests or instructions.

From the pattern within the group attempt to identify which classification of information spreads the furthest and the fastest.

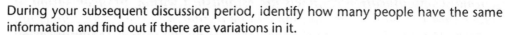

Now let's consider the potential advantages of the grapevine to an organisation.

3.2   Advantages

The grapevine can be used by the management of an organisation to supplement formal channels of communication. This is often done because of the following advantages;

(a) the grapevine is remarkably swift at transmitting information throughout an organisation;

(b) the grapevine often carries information that is not communicated through formal channels, such as internal politics;

(c) the grapevine is usually contained within the organisation;

(d) the boundaries of the grapevine go beyond shift patterns and other formal lines of demarcation.

And what about the disadvantage?

3.3   Disadvantages

The grapevine has three distinct disadvantages which prevent it from becoming the only form of communication channel within an organisation:

(a) the information carried may be inaccurate for various reasons;

(b) transmission of information is in a random fashion – not every member of an organisation may receive all the information that is being passed on;

(c) sub-grapevines can develop that are confined to a small section of the organisation; these may not have established linkages between them.

Activity 5 [30 minutes]

Draw up a list of reasons why the grapevine may carry inaccurate information. Give an example of each one.

Much of what has been discussed so far has been centred around the internal communications of an organisation. We now consider one very important aspect of organisational communication with the environment: corporate image and identity.

4 CORPORATE IMAGE AND IDENTITY

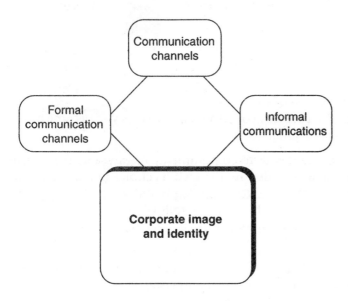

Definitions

Corporate image: the way in which an organisation is perceived by those outside it.

Corporate identity: the way in which an organisation presents itself to those outside by the use of such things as logos, livery etc.

The organisation communicates with its environment knowingly and unknowingly by the face it presents to the outside world. It is then for the environment to interpret these signals to gain an image of the organisation, what it is like and what it stands for.

The importance of a positive image to the success of the organisation cannot be over emphasised. A poor image is easy to achieve and very hard to get rid of. Ratners, the jewellers, found that once their image had been dented by their Chairman's unwise discrediting of their products, it was impossible to undo the damage. British Rail has for years had an image of expense and inefficiency which it is now extremely hard for the newly privatised companies to dispel. Many organisations have now realised that manipulating the image they project so that it is a positive one can lead to competitive advantage; conversely, ignoring their image can put them at a competitive disadvantage.

Once an organisation has decided upon the image it would like to project, it is the way in which it communicates this message that determines success or failure. As always, the content of the message is vital, but in this case the content of the message may vary depending upon the target audience. For example, a financial target audience may have different information requirements to those of the end consumer. Thus it is important to identify the information needs of the target audience before deciding on how the message will be communicated. Excess information, required by one group but not by another, may cause noise through the effects of redundancy.

Target audiences for an organisation may include the following.

(a) Customers

(b) Employees

(c) Trades unions

(d) Shareholders

(e) Distributors

(f) Suppliers

(g) Government (local and central)

(h) The media

(i) Local communities

(j) Education bodies

(k) Overseas audiences

(l) Industry commentators

This is by no means a comprehensive list; you should add to it as you become aware of other bodies who may be target audiences.

The organisation can use many methods to communicate its message. Firstly, the organisation will want to establish an identity through its choice of name and the way in which it portrays itself through advertising, logos and so on. Secondly, the image will be created by the use of such things as the following.

Press releases

A credible and cost-efficient method of gaining favourable media coverage. Final control of the message is in the hands of the media however.

Printed literature

Printed literature such as direct mail and brochures can be a good way of gaining broad coverage, with the organisation having editorial control over the layout design and content.

Videos, films and visual aids

These are being used more and more by the larger companies using schools and colleges as the forum.

Exhibitions and displays

A good way of making contact with potential buyers and suppliers.

Personal contact

Personal contact is mainly used for highly influential contacts, such as government representatives and key opinion formers within the industry.

Sponsorship

Sponsorship has become a popular way to raise public awareness of an organisation, although there is a degree of risk involved: if the event is a failure any adverse publicity could reflect on the organisation.

Corporate media advertising

This is probably the best known of all the ways in which organisations communicate with a wide audience. It is costly, however, and its results can be unpredictable.

> **EXAMPLE: BENETTON**
>
> A recent Benetton advertising campaign was thought to be in bad taste and was not shown in many areas. However, the resulting media coverage raised the name of the company in the public's awareness.

Corporate image can also be affected by the way in which an organisation deals with the circumstances in which it finds itself. Companies are often presented with a double-edged sword.

> **EXAMPLE: MCDONALDS**
>
> When faced with the BSE scare McDonalds had the option to continue to use British beef, and risk seeing their sales go down as a result of customer fears about the chances of contracting the disease. Alternatively, they could stop using British beef but perhaps still see sales go down in the short term as a protest by the British public against McDonalds' lack of support of a British product. In the event their decision was to stop using British beef and this turned out to be best for them from a financial point of view.

Activity 6 [45 minutes]

Read the following case study a write a short discussion (no more than 500 words) on the way in which this organisation has communicated with its external environment. Draw conclusions from your discussion concerning how effective you think the approach taken would be for use in another organisation of your choice.

The Body Shop

Anita Roddick set out to create the 'most honest cosmetic company around'. When the opening of her first shop was imminent, she encountered difficulties with the business located next door. As a funeral directors they objected to her choice of company name. Anita dealt with this (according to corporate legend) by contacting the local press anonymously to tell them that a mafia of local funeral directors were engaged in a vendetta against a woman who wanted to open a herbal cosmetic shop. The resulting publicity ensured a full house on the day of the shop opening.

As the company has grown, regular contact has been kept with members of the beauty press by holding regular lunches and providing samples of new products to all who requested them. Information literature is also sent to individuals in the industry.

The Body Shop has not entered the arena of expensive 'faces' to advertise their products; in fact next to nothing has been spent on advertising at all. No television campaigns, no glossy magazine adverts, just constant contact with the opinion formers within the industry. One wonders how it is that we have all heard of the Body Shop.

Chapter roundup

- Communication within organisations can flow horizontally, vertically or diagonally.
- Each direction of flow serves a purpose and has its own advantages and disadvantages.
- Formal communication channels exist in all types of organisation.
- Formal and informal communication channels coexist in the same organisation.
- Formal communication channels can use any medium.
- Informal communication channels are usually verbal.
- Informal communication channels are not always accurate.
- Informal communication channels can be used by management to supplement the formal ones.
- Organisations need to use communication to establish their identity and project a predetermined image.
- The image of an organisation can be manipulated by the management, but not with absolute certainty.

Quick Quiz

1 Complete the sentence: communication can be either formal or ... .
2 Give three directions of communication flow.
3 Give a non-verbal example of vertical communication within an organisation.
4 Which direction of information flow allows peer group support to develop?
5 Give three advantages of committees as a means of formal communications.
6 What is the main disadvantage of team briefings?
7 What is the grapevine?
8 Give two advantages of the grapevine over formal communication channels.
9 What is the difference between corporate image and corporate identity?
10 List five individuals, groups or organisations which may be target audiences for a company wishing to project a message regarding their corporate image.

Answers to Quick Quiz

1 Informal.
2 (a) Horizontal, (b) vertical, and (c) diagonal.
3 Time sheets, forms and sales data.
4 Horizontal.
5 (a) They provide a forum for discussion. (b) They engender feelings of participation. (c) They combine individual capabilities
6 There is no chance for feedback.
7 The grapevine is an informal channel of communication which complements the formal channels within an organisation.
8 (a) Speed, (b) information not carried by the formal channels is communicated.
9 Image is how the organisation is perceived by others; identity is the sum of the ways in which an organisation identifies itself, for example, a company logo.
10 See Section 4 of this chapter.

Answers to Activities

1   Check your answer against the following notes. George should be at the top of the heap. Andy, Don, Jim and Fred are each below and responsible to Graham. Horizontal communication at this level will be limited by the geographic separation of each one. Andy will communicate with Jim and Fred regarding the cutting of the grass in the parks they are responsible for. There may be some horizontal communication between Don, Fred and Jim over plants for the parks. Horizontal communication between the individual park supervisors will also be limited by geographic location, but there may be horizontal communication with Graham, and diagonal communication with Andy. Vertical communication will take place between George and all members of the team.

2   You are most likely to talk to your colleagues: this is a horizontal channel. You may then talk to your tutor: this would be a vertical channel. You are less likely to talk to the catering manager in his official capacity! If you did, this would be a diagonal communication channel.

3   You will have come to a variety of decisions, the difficulties you may have faced in reaching those decisions could include the following.

  (a) You may have taken so long to decide over some items that others had to be agreed upon without discussion. In a real committee time limits may be longer, but they often exist.

  (b) Certain members of your group may have played very little part in the discussions, either because of apathy or as a result of the stronger personality of another group member(s).

  (c) Your group is likely to have had little conscience over the decisions it made as it was not going to apply to the members of the group, but to the paired group.

4   You are likely to find that it is the gossip which spreads furthest and fastest. With college activities, especially those of a social nature, coming second. Instructions and requests are likely to come last. Why do you think this is?

5   The grapevine may carry inaccurate information as a result of the following.

  (a) Noise in any form may interfere with the accurate transmission of information. Remember 'Send three and fourpence, we're going to a dance.'

  (b) Linkages in the grapevine may filter the information, being selective about what is passed on. In doing so the accuracy or emphasis may be changed.

  (c) Linkages in the grapevine may add their own interpretation of the information, which again changes the accuracy or emphasis.

  (d) There may be malicious intent on the part of a staff member who could knowingly pass on untrue information.

  (e) Fear of something happening, passed on to a colleague, can be changed into a certainty that the event will actually happen.

6   Your discussion should include the following points.

  (a) The Body Shop has chosen a particular target audience.

  (b) The message has been tailored to that audience.

  (c) The simplicity of the media used reflects the image the Body Shop wishes to present - the simplicity of their product.

    The suitability of using similar tactics with another organisation will depend on the organisation you choose; the important point is that communication with the environment should be in keeping with the image the organisation wishes to present.

Assignment 10   [2 hours]

Read the following case study and make notes on the way in which you think the situation should be handled. You will need to make a list of individuals groups and organisations with whom you will have to communicate, both internally and externally. In your notes, identify which channels should be used (formal or informal) and which media you consider to be the most appropriate. You should make your decisions based on a long-term view of how your business will be affected, with particular reference to the impact on your corporate image.

Product failure

You are a UK-based pharmaceutical manufacturer. You have been producing and marketing a new drug for the past two years in the UK, and the same drug is produced under licence in the US.

A personal friend who lives in the US telephones you to talk about a series of disturbing newspaper articles which have appeared in his local newspaper over the previous week. A journalist is claiming that two deaths in a small mid-American town have been associated with the use of your drug, and investigations by the drug licensing authorities are imminent.

You are well aware that it is a matter of days at most before this story is published coast to coast and also in the UK. The drug in question is only available on prescription, and those patients taking it would require alternative drug therapy to control what could be a life threatening condition if they were to stop taking your medication.

Your company has also just had a new drug licensed which is being heralded as something of a miracle cure and is due to be launched in two weeks.

As an organisation, what do you do?

Chapter 11

ENVIRONMENT AND THE ORGANISATION

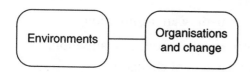

Introduction

Every organisation exists within its environment and has to adapt to change within that environment. An organisation that ignores such change is likely to become ineffective. Its structures will become irrelevant to the changed circumstances in which it must operate. An unresponsive organisation is likely to wither away. Alternatively, it may be taken over by a predator who can see the underlying value waiting to be released by selling parts of the business and restructuring the rest.

Change in the environment may arise from political, economic, social or technical sources. Do you expect to retire with a pension? Start saving now as politicians of all shades realise that government finances cannot provide the level of welfare required to meet population changes and people's aspirations. Do you expect that, as an employee, you will be able to sneak off to Wimbledon after meeting a client? The new generation of mobile phones will be able to pin point your location to within thirty feet. The only certainty is change.

Your objectives

After completing this chapter you should:

(a) be able to describe different environments within which the organisation operates;

(b) appreciate the importance of environmental change;

(c) understand how environmental change affects the organisation;

(d) be able to relate the design of organisations to their environments.

First we look at the types of environment in which the organisation may operate.

1 ENVIRONMENTS

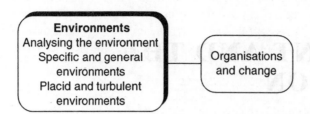

1.1 Analysing the environment

There two main ways of looking at the environment of an organisation:

(a) it can be analysed in terms of its immediate relevance to the organisation;

(b) it can be analysed in terms of the speed and extent of change.

It is important to understand the effects of change in the environment. All organisations exist in an environment. They interact with their environments in many ways. Unless they do so effectively, they disappear.

The organisation is an 'open system': it consists of people and resources in a structure that reacts with the environment by taking in inputs, processing them and providing outputs to the environment. For example, a business has inputs and outputs of goods and services, as shown in Figure 11.1.

Figure 11.1 Business processes

Charities and voluntary bodies have a similar relationship with the environment, as shown in Figure 11.2.

Figure 11.2 The charity relationship

Activity 1 [10 minutes]

Using Figures 11.1 and 11.2 as examples, draw a similar diagram for a college.

Inputs and outputs both influence the organisation. As you saw in Chapter 4, the contingency approach to the organisation states that the need to interface with the external environment determines the appropriate structure for an organisation.

The organisation can be regarded as operating in both a specific and a general environment.

1.2   Specific and general environments

The *specific environment* of an organisation is its immediate circle of contacts. This includes suppliers, customers, services, trade unions and the official bodies which it deals with. The simpler the operations of the organisation, the less complex will be its network of contacts. However, the scope for complexity is still extensive for even the smallest enterprise.

EXAMPLE: A SPECIFIC ENVIRONMENT

For a sole proprietor plumber the specific environment includes the following.

Suppliers: heating boiler manufacturers, bath and sink suppliers, builders' merchants.

Services: garage, accountant, local newspaper, phone messaging company.

Customers: householders, businesses, builders.

Others: water, gas and electricity companies, competing plumbers, Institute of Plumbing, building inspectors.

Activity 2   [15 minutes]

List, under suitable headings, the members of the specific environment of your local department store.

The organisation's specific environment is surrounded by the *general environment*. This includes the *political*, *economic*, *social* and *technological* elements which make up the environment. *PEST analysis* studies their impact on the organisation.

The relationship between the organisation and its specific and general environments is shown in Figure 11.3.

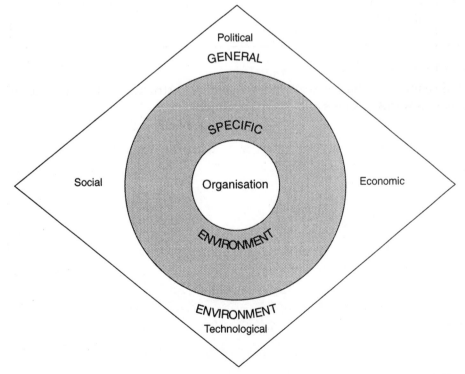

Figure 11.3 The organisation in its environments

Political change

Political change may bring more or less regulation. Legislation may change requirements for products.

EXAMPLES: REGULATION BY LEGISLATION

The decision of the European Court of Justice that the maximum working week of 48 hours applies in the UK brought a sudden change to UK employment regulations.

The UK government decision to limit the expansion of out of town shopping will change town centres and may lead to take-overs as chains try to fill gaps in their locations.

EU rules on computer products and electrical interference are causing a change in the requirements for these products.

Economic change

Economic change may result from government policy or may come from market or international changes.

EXAMPLES: EFFECTS OF ECONOMIC CHANGES

Interest rates may rise to control inflation, making borrowing more expensive, cutting investment, reducing demand for products and, by strengthening the pound, reducing exports.

If the economy slips into recession, employment and demand will be reduced.

A fall in the sterling exchange rate makes UK assets appear relatively cheap and attracts foreign investment in UK businesses.

Tough trading conditions in foreign countries may bring more imports to compete with UK firms.

Social change

Social change includes change in attitudes to work, the structure of the population and attitudes towards business and the environment.

EXAMPLES: SOCIAL CHANGES

Since 1983 more women have entered the labour force, more men have taken on what were previously regarded as women's jobs and, partly as a result of economic factors, part-time work has become sought after by large numbers of men and women.

People are now more interested in environmental matters, and this affects business by generating changes in the demand for products and altering the social expectations of how firms should behave.

Population changes can happen quickly. Many people have already left Hong Kong. Fijian Indians have left Fiji in large numbers since the 1987 coup gave more power to the 51% of the population who are indigenous Fijians.

Gradual change, as in the UK with an ageing population, can change markets and the structure of the labour force.

An increase in the numbers of graduates from higher education leads employees to have higher expectations of their jobs.

Technological change

Technological change affects organisations in many ways – from changing products and the organisation of work to creating links between companies.

EXAMPLES: TECHNOLOGICAL CHANGES

Bio-technology has created many new products in medicine and improvements to plants to make them disease resistant and to increase yields.

Computer advances have transformed the way we work and communicate. Processes can be automated and information can be stored and accessed in ways that are impossible without IT. A network can link everyone in an organisation and give them access to data. Firms link their networks so that suppliers are constantly updated about their customers' needs. Electronic data interchange (EDI) is used to track exports across the world.

For discussion

Below are four specific examples of PEST changes that could have big effects on organisations. Explain how they might affect the following.

(a)   A DIY chain
(b)   A borough council
(c)   A building society
(d)   A hospital trust

Political: *the government changes and the UK adopts the social chapter of the Maastricht Treaty.*
Economic: *interest rates double.*
Social: *the trend to single-person households reverses and family size increases.*
Technological: *everyone is issued with a 'smart card' which carries personal details including driving licence, health and fingerprint as well as a photograph.*

The relationship between the general and the specific environments

Changes in the general environment have an impact on the specific environment. For example:

135

(a) customers' tastes, disposable income and spending patterns;

(b) suppliers' products, sources and links;

(c) service operations such as automatic repair scheduling, availability and range of work that can be sourced externally;

(d) competitors' products, prices and promotions;

(e) unions' power, co-operativeness and members;

(f) regulatory bodies' scope, powers and attitudes.

The specific environment feeds back information and pressures to the general environment. Social changes affect the pattern of demand, along with economic influences such as changes in interest rates. The organisation's recruitment and investment intentions feed back into the general economic environment as part of the emerging trends; for example, increased demand for part-time workers has social repercussions.

Activity 3 [15 minutes]

Name the PEST factors that would be relevant to the following.

(a) Consumers' disposable income

(b) Supplier links

(c) Service outsourcing

(d) Competitors' prices

(e) Union power

(f) The scope of regulatory bodies

The nature of its environment significantly affects the organisation and how it should be structured.

1.3   Placid and turbulent environments

In general organisations have very little, if any, control over their specific or general environments. An organisation can ensure that it responds to changes in a way that minimises their bad effects, and it can try to use change for its benefit. Large organisations, or small ones acting together in a trade association, may be able to influence political factors. They are unlikely to be able to affect other elements of PEST.

The effect of the environment on an organisation's structure and operations depends on the level of uncertainty in its environment. Uncertainty may exist because the environment is:

(a) dynamic because it is subject to rapid and random changes;

(b) complex with many and varied factors acting strongly in it.

An organisation may exist in a static and simple environment, or it could face a dynamic and complex one that is subject to frequent technological change, strong competition and market swings.

FE Emery and Eric Trist of the Tavistock Institute identified four kinds of environments of increasing complexity.

(a) *Placid, randomised* with low uncertainty, little change over a long time and randomly distributed demands. This corresponds to the economic model of perfect competition, where no member can influence the market and the impact of external changes is to move the system to a new equilibrium. It also applies to traditional areas and organisations in religious and government areas. There is little threat to the organisation.

(b) *Placid, clustered* with little change over time but with threats and rewards that appear in clusters. This happens, for example, when a few companies effectively control the market (oligopoly) and a sudden take over or strategic alliance upsets the balance of power. It could also apply to a monopoly that loses its legal protection, as happened to British Telecom when telecommunications were opened up to competition.

(c) *Disturbed, reactive* is a more complex situation when the environment is dominated by one or a few large organisations which can control it. Microsoft, in the computer software industry, is an example: other companies have to watch what Microsoft is doing and react to it. Competition is a feature of this type of environment.

(d) *Turbulent field* is a dynamic and rapidly changing environment, with a resulting high level of uncertainty. Fashion, software, IT, foreign exchange and commodities dealing and advertising are all examples. Organisations must continually change to survive.

Activity 4 [10 minutes]

Which kind of environment are the following organisations operating in?

(a) British Gas

(b) Compaq Computers

(c) The Church of England

(d) Virgin Airways

Change is constant. An organisation can adopt strategies for coping with change and it can design its structure to suit its environment.

2 ORGANISATIONS AND CHANGE

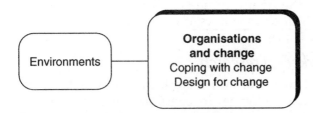

Organisations are facing increasingly complex and dynamic environments. Technology develops faster – the remotest rural village in a developing country is now exposed to global social change through its satellite TV set. More information is readily available, tempting people to try new ideas and products. Competition is global.

The organisation can react to its environment and try to cope with it, or it can redesign itself.

2.1 Coping with change

Organisations can adopt a number of strategies to try to anticipate and exploit change or limit its effects. How effective these can be depends on the complexity and dynamism of the environment, the power of the organisation to influence its specific environment and the PEST factors and the quality of its planning.

Scenario building

Forecasting trends is a vital activity. Scenario building can be used to predict the future environment. Analysis of trends can be used to prepare different scenarios of the future, assuming no change or all change in the environment. These are then refined from the general PEST-based scenarios into focused scenarios relevant to the organisation and action scenarios on which to base strategy.

Contingency planning

Contingency planning can be used to prepare for change. Some changes can be anticipated and plans put in place. For example, transport strikes can be planned for in detail and instructions issued to all staff. Some changes are random. An emergency such as the collapse of a dam and flooding of a factory could be dealt with by having procedures for senior staff to take control and act as required. Manufacturers usually try to ensure that they have alternative sources of supplies in case a supplier suffers a fire or a strike.

Hedging risks

Exporters can guard against a change in the exchange rate by entering into a forward exchange contract with a bank. This contract guarantees that the company can buy the foreign currency at a fixed price on a date in the future. Hedging also applies in financial markets. A company treasurer can buy 'futures contracts' on the London International Financial Futures Exchange (LIFFE) to protect against interest rate changes. 'Forward contracts' can be used in the commodities market. These methods limit short-term risk (generally of up to a year).

Activity 5 [15 minutes]

Take a look at the *Financial Times* or the business pages of a quality newspaper. Look at the foreign exchange report showing spot and forward rates and see how they compare. (Spot rates are for settlement at today's price.) You will also find information on the financial and commodities futures. If your library has *Economic Trends* or *The Monthly Digest of Statistics* you will find tables showing fluctuations in exchange and interest rates over a long period.

Competitor analysis and marketing research

Competitor analysis can be used to try to anticipate tactical moves by rivals. Marketing research is used to analyse changes in consumer tastes and market trends. Non-business organisations can use the same techniques to find out what is happening in their specific environments as part of a scenario planning exercise.

EXAMPLE: MARKETING RESEARCH

A professional body commissioned a survey of its members to find out what they wanted, why people left and what might attract non-members to join. This was combined with forecasts about developments in industry recruitment, education trends, likely initiatives by a potential competitor institution and demographic trends in the membership. The result was an enhanced package of services and benefits, changes in qualifications and a drive to recruit younger members who would change the age profile.

Mergers and joint ventures

A merger or joint venture can improve the competitive position.

EXAMPLE: BRITISH AIRWAYS AND AMERICAN AIRLINES

British Airways' link with American Airlines in 1996 and its joint ventures with others around the world were intended to reduce uncertainty. A passenger can now book a through ticket from Australia to the UK to any of the destinations in the US served by American Airlines. Without the link of the booking systems, a passenger was likely to switch between airlines for each leg of the journey and not choose one of the partners.

Moving to a different environment

An organisation can move to a more favourable environment.

EXAMPLE: CHLORIDE PLC

Chloride at one time made dry batteries. This industry became subject to intense competition from low-cost East European and Far East competitors. Developments in battery technology to meet the demands of the photographic, audio and computer industries required high investment in R&D. Chloride moved into electronics and, by 1996, into profit after selling off all but its Egyptian battery making operations.

Mergers, take overs and diversification can be used to move into less turbulent and complex environments. A firm can enter new markets where there is more certainty. It can spread its risk by diversifying into new products and markets.

EXAMPLES: AMSTRAD AND UTILITY MERGERS

Alan Sugar of Amstrad started in car aerials, moved to audio equipment, added word processors, computers, satellite TV receivers and mobile phones. Amstrad moved out of supplying high street retailers to direct selling of its office products and took over Viglen, the direct sales computer manufacturer.

The privatised utility companies have merged to form water and power firms and have sought overseas ventures to escape the restrictions of their regulators. Their mergers give *synergy* through reductions in the costs of meter reading, billing and administration.

Definition

Synergy: the phenomenon by which the combination of two units produces more than the separate parts added together. Synergy can arise from a merger when the new firm can shed costs and increase profits by cutting out duplication of activities, for example one of the sales forces.

For discussion

What could the following organisations do to cope with change in their environments?

(a)   P&O Channel Ferries
(b)   Madame Tussaud's
(c)   The County Council Education Department
(d)   The Bradford and Bingley Building Society

NOTES

Those organisations that cope successfully with their environments will survive and prosper. They have a better chance of success if their structures are designed for their environments.

2.2 Design for change

We have seen how Lawrence and Lorsch proposed that firms in diverse and dynamic environments should have a high degree of differentiation to cope with the interface with their complex environment. This requires a high degree of integration to maintain the focus on the organisation's objective. Less changeable environments require less differentiation, but still need a high level of integration.

T Burns and G Stalker studied firms to see how they adapted themselves to deal with changing market and technical conditions. They proposed two distinct types of management system which mark the boundaries within which intermediate forms can exist.

(a) *Mechanistic systems* are appropriate for stable environments. Their features are:

    (i) a hierarchical structure of authority, control, responsibility and communication with centralised decision making;

    (ii) vertical rather than horizontal interaction between staff;

    (iii) specialised differentiation of tasks;

    (iv) precise definitions of tasks and roles;

    (v) working behaviour and operations are dominated by superiors who expect to be obeyed.

(b) *Organic systems* are appropriate for dynamic environments. Their features are:

    (i) a network structure of authority, control and communication, with decentralised decision making;

    (ii) lateral and horizontal communication rather than vertical;

    (iii) individual tasks are adjusted as required;

    (iv) knowledge of commercial and technical aspects of tasks may be located anywhere in the network, there is no strict demarcation;

    (v) superiors give information and advice rather than instructions and decisions.

The two systems are not mutually exclusive. Organisations exist along a spectrum between the two and they can both be present within the same organisation at the same time. Large organisations have to be differentiated and mechanistic to make their diversity manageable. Delegation, staff involvement and group working can exist in units within the overall structure. What is important is that the structure is appropriate for the conditions in the environment.

Activity 6 [15 minutes]

For organisations with (a) a mechanistic structure and (b) an organic structure, list the nature of their environments and its level of uncertainty, their degree of differentiation and integration and location of decision making.

Burns and Stalker studied the attempt to introduce electronics development work into traditional Scottish firms where their well established products were facing declining markets. There was an almost complete failure to absorb electronics research and development engineers into these firms. This led Burns to question whether a mechanistic firm can ever develop into an organic one. He attributed this to the culture that develops from individuals to a group and its sectional interests. The importance of culture is examined in Chapter 14. However, Ferranti, in Edinburgh, became a leading exponent of group working and matrix organisation and developed into a world-class electronics firm.

The lesson for the design of the modern firm is to design a structure that can cope with change. The differences are summarised in Table 11.1.

Old approach	New approach
Technological imperative	Joint optimisation *of technical and social factors*
People as extensions to machines	People as complementary to machines
Maximum task breakdown, simple narrow skills	Optimum task grouping, multiple broad skills
External controls (supervisors, specialist staffs, procedures)	Internal controls (self regulating sub-systems)
Tall organisation chart, autocratic style	Flat organisation chart, participative style
Competition, gamesmanship	Collaboration, collegiality
Organisation's purposes only	Stakeholders' and society's purposes also
Alienation	Commitment
Low risk taking	Innovation

Table 11.1 Features of old and new approaches to organisation design. (From Trist, E L 'The Socio-technical perspective' in van de Ven, A and Joyce, WF (eds) *Perspectives on Organization Design and Behaviour*, Wiley 1981.)

The advantage of the new approach is that the organisation can respond quickly and flexibly to changes in both the general and specific environments. Although many firms have adopted this philosophy of organisation design it has not been without great problems, as to do so requires the culture of the organisation to change.

Chapter roundup

- Organisations exist in a specific environment of their immediate circle of contacts.

- They are also in a general environment of political, economic, social and technological (PEST) factors.

- The general environment affects and interacts with the specific environment.

- Environments may be simple or complex, static or dynamic. They are classified from placid-randomised, through placid-clustered, disturbed-reactive, to turbulent-field.

- Organisations can cope with change by planning, hedging, moving into more placid environments and by mergers and join ventures.

- They can have a mechanistic structure characterised by a rigid hierarchy and vertical authority and communications.

- They can have an organic system characterised by networking, flexibility and lateral communication. This structure can cope better with turbulence.

- An organisation may have both types of system and be anywhere along a spectrum between them. It will succeed if its structure is appropriate to its environment.

Quick Quiz

1 What is the specific environment of an organisation?

2 What are the four elements of the organisation's general environment?

3 How do the general and specific environments relate to one another?

4 What are the characteristics of a placid, randomised environment?

5 What are the features of a turbulent field environment?

6 Which type of specific environment would you expect to be complex and dominated by a large organisation?

7 How might an organisation attempt to cope with change?

8 What are the features of a mechanistic system?

9 What are the features of an organic system?

Answers to Quick Quiz

1 Its immediate circle of contacts with suppliers, customers, services, unions and trade bodies and regulators.

2 Political, economic, social and technological.

3 The general environment influences the specific, which has a feedback effect to the general environment.

4 Low uncertainty, little change, randomly distributed demands and little threat to the organisation.

5 High uncertainty, rapid change and constant threats to the organisation.

6 Disturbed, reactive.

7 Forecasting, hedging risk, competitor analysis, mergers and joint ventures and moving to a less turbulent environment.

8 A strict hierarchy of authority and control, vertical communication and interaction, closely defined specific tasks and supervisors who give orders and instructions.

9 A network structure with diffuse authority, a distribution of tasks according to current needs, lateral and horizontal communication and superiors who inform and support.

Answers to Activities

1 Your diagram should be similar to that shown in Figure 11.4.

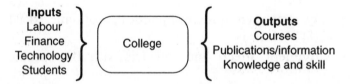

2 Your list should be similar to the following. (a) Customers. (b) Suppliers: producers, wholesalers, distributors. (c) Services: transport, maintenance, cleaning, banks, capital market. (d) Unions: USDAW. (e) Shareholders: individuals and investing institutions. (f) Competitors. (g) Inspectors: health and safety, weights and measures, food hygiene.

3 (a) Economic. (b) Economic and technological. (c) Economic and social. (d) Economic. (e) Political, economic and social. (f) Political.

4 (a) British Gas's environment is probably changing from placid clustered to turbulent field, as the gas market is opened to competition in 1996.

(b) Disturbed reactive, as Compaq is one of the 'big four' computer manufacturers and technological change, though rapid, is predictable.

(c) Placid randomised, certainly for a local church and possibly for the whole organisation. Sudden upheavals, such as the ordination of women, shift it to placid clustered.

(d) Disturbed reactive as it must watch what the big airlines, and especially British Airways, are doing. With European-wide deregulation and world-wide mergers, the environment becomes a turbulent field.

5 The sort of information which you will find shows how important it is to hedge against exchange rate changes. Especially if you sell to Turkey! Forward contracts in commodities enable companies to guard against risks such as frost affecting the coffee or orange crop.

6

	Mechanistic	Organic
Environment	Placid, simple	Turbulent, complex
Uncertainty	Low	High
Differentiation	High	Low
Integration	High	High
Decisions	Centralised	Decentralised

Assignment 11 [2 hours]

The computer industry

Assume that you are employed by a firm which is starting to manufacture computers in the UK. Write a short report on the general and specific environments of the firm. Recommend a structure for the company.

Use the following information.

The UK economy is recovering from recession and sales of computers are rising. However, competition is fierce between mail order original manufacturers, mail order resellers, high street stores and specialist computer supermarkets such as PC World.

Computer manufacture appears to be a widespread and fairly placid industry. In fact there are several potential areas of turbulence.

US manufacturers have set up plants in Europe and Asia, particularly Singapore and Malaya.

Japanese, Korean and Taiwanese firms have established subsidiaries in Asia, Europe and the USA.

The manufacture of key components is as follows.

(a) Central processing units (CPUs) – Intel in US only; others globally.

(b) Casings and power supplies – small Taiwanese companies.

(c) Motherboards – high specification Intel; others Taiwan.

(d) Memory – Korea, Japan, US, Europe. High and rising development costs mean joint ventures between even the largest firms like IBM, NEC, Toshiba, Samsung and Siemens.

(e) Disk and CD-ROM drives – rapid technological innovation has not suited Japanese companies and major firms are American, with one in the UK and a lot of factories in South East Asia, but not Taiwan. Disks and CD-ROMs are cheap to produce in China, Malaysia and Thailand.

(f) Liquid crystal diodes (LCD) – concentrated in Japan with a joint venture between IBM and Toshiba and Korea and Taiwan trying to catch up.

(g) Monitors – Japanese and Korean firms make them everywhere computers are made.

Continued ...

(h) Keyboards – most from Taiwan, but some from Intel and IBM.

The environment is largely stable, but there could be problems.

(a) The US in 1996 only just avoided a trade war with Japan and sanctions against China because of pirate manufacturers copying American products. An agreement that Japanese firms will use 20% of memory chips from overseas expired in 1996 and Japan does not want to renew it, while the US wants more access to the Japanese market. The problems are not solved, only put on hold until after the American election in November 1996. On a previous occasion American sanctions on Japan led to a cut in memory output and a sharp rise in prices. Import controls on LCDs stopped imports for US firms, but not the import of finished machines from outside Japan.

(b) Taiwan suffered a military confrontation when China objected to its first democratic elections in 1996. Chinese manoeuvres off the coast could turn into invasion if the aged Chinese leadership collapses into a military take over and the claimed sovereignty over the island is enforced. The US would intervene.

(c) South Korea is still technically (and occasionally actually) at war with North Korea forty years after the Korean War ended. The North's communist regime could attack the South as a survival measure brought on by the 1996 collapse of its economy and near famine in the country.

(d) China is waiting for Chairman Deng to die. Its special economic zones attract a lot of foreign investment and low costs have brought in Japanese, Korean and American firms. Instability is a real prospect when Deng dies and could arise from the reversion of Hong Kong in 1997 as other regions bid for the freedoms enjoyed by the ex-colony. China is criticised for its human rights record and suppression of Tibet and a new regime could turn in on itself.

(e) European Union (EU) legislation requires a local content, but this could be eroded by the World Trade Organisation agreement to liberalise trade. The US and developing countries attack EU protectionism in agriculture as well as industry and there are constant threats of trade sanctions by the US. A war between Greece and Turkey is a possibility because of disputes over Mediterranean islands and Cyprus.

(f) Eastern Europe is likely to attract more investment as several countries have highly educated technicians paid as little as a tenth of German rates. Stable nations like the Czech Republic and Poland are likely to attract firms from Germany. There could be outbreaks of fighting in some other ex-Russian countries.

Chapter 12

CHANGE AND COMMUNICATION

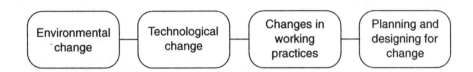

| Environmental change | Technological change | Changes in working practices | Planning and designing for change |

Introduction

Change in organisations is always the result of some external influence. Even seemingly small internal changes can be traced back to an external source. In this chapter we shall consider the environment of the organisation, specifically those influences stemming from the political, economic and social forces introduced in Chapter 11. We shall then consider the technological influences, focusing on information technology and changes in production technology. Technology has helped to cause various changes in working practices (although technology is not the only stimulus for these). We will look at the examples of down sizing, outsourcing and outworking. All these changes require certain factors to ensure success; arguably, the most important factor is effective communication.

Your objectives

After completing this chapter you should:

(a) appreciate the effects of changes in the external environment on communication within organisations;

(b) understand the impact of technological changes and changes in working practices on communications;

(c) relate changes in organisations to changes in communication systems and methods;

(d) evaluate the effectiveness of communication and recommend improvements to it;

(e) be able to describe the aims of organisational development;

(f) be able to outline a programme of organisational development;

(g) understand the methods used.

Any change that is external to the organisation is said to be a change in the organisational environment. Such external changes may or may not have an impact on the internal fabric of the organisation.

1 ENVIRONMENTAL CHANGE

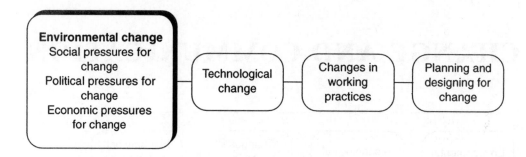

Environmental change can affect the strategy, structure or culture of an organisation. It may affect a combination of them all. Environmental changes are sometimes dramatic, such as a sudden change in public opinion, but it is more frequently the case that changes are insidious and gradual. Organisations which communicate effectively with their environment are well placed to become aware of changes as they occur. Organisations that have become insular may take longer to pick up on such changes.

You saw in Chapter 11 that the pressure for change can come from a variety of sources – political, economic, social and technological. We start by looking at the effects of social pressures.

1.1 Social pressures for change

As described in Chapter 11, there are many examples of changes brought about by social pressures for change.

EXAMPLES: CHANGE THROUGH SOCIAL PRESSURE

Green issues

Recent changes in the awareness of the public concerning the potential destruction of various parts of the flora or fauna of our planet have had an impact on many industries. In some of these both the products made and the production processes have had to be changed. For example, paper production may now be from sustainable forests, and canned tuna may be caught by methods that are dolphin friendly.

The National Health Service

The National Health Service has undergone major changes in terms of waiting times and clients' expectations of level of service. Whilst some of this change can be attributed to changes in government policy (political pressures), it is the pressure from the population that has increased the impetus for change.

Communication is important in enabling social pressure for change to grow and to have an effect. Effective communication within the organisations concerned is essential to enable these changes to occur. It is also the case that growth in world-wide communication has increased the social pressures themselves.

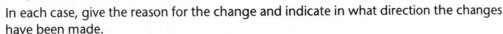

Activity 1   [20 minutes]

Make a list of four products or industries which have been forced to change in the last ten years as a result of social pressures.

In each case, give the reason for the change and indicate in what direction the changes have been made.

Social and political pressures are often interrelated. Here we focus on the effects of political pressures emanating from outside the UK.

1.2   Political pressures for change

European directives have considerable effect on the way UK organisations are run, especially as many UK companies now have links outside this country. The integration process that is occurring between EU member states in respect of working conditions within organisations is forcing many established firms to rethink their staff management policies.

Activity 2   [1 hour + research]

The European Union recently issued a directive concerning works councils. Although the UK has not become party to the Maastricht Treaty from which this directive stems, the directive will have implications for UK firms. For the purpose of this activity, assume that the directive is equally valid in the UK as in other European countries (as it is likely to be should a Labour government be returned at the next general election).

The directive instructs that all organisations over a specified size (based on number of employees) must set up works councils through which employees will be kept informed of anything affecting them (directly or indirectly) and at which employees can have their say over working conditions. The works councils will not deal with remuneration matters or other subjects covered by existing collective bargaining agreements.

Write a short essay (500-1000 words) on how you think this directive will change the emphasis of communication within UK organisations.

For organisations to be successful in introducing these changes in a beneficial way, there must be effective communication between all those involved.

> ### EXAMPLE: THE BRITISH CIVIL SERVICE
>
> One of the best examples of radical change within an organisation as a result of political pressure, in recent years, has been the transformation of the British Civil Service. This seemingly self-perpetuating bureaucratic organisation was decimated by the introduction of semi-autonomous government agencies as a result of the Ibbs report. The new structure challenged all that the old system stood for, intending instead to replace it with a flexible, less bureaucratic structure.
>
> Success has been limited by the nature of the communication networks in operation before the changes. Some would argue that, because of the culture of the organisation, the nature of these networks is unlikely to change.

We now look at economic pressures.

1.3 Economic pressures for change

External competition has always been a driving force behind changes in product design and innovation of new products. However, in the economic climate of the recent past, there has been even greater pressure on organisations to find ways to change and to adapt to fierce competition. One of the ways some organisations have achieved this is by the use of *strategic alliances*. The example of Rover and Honda was mentioned in Chapter 9. This alliance was driven by two factors.

(a) The desire by Honda to move into the European market at a time when quotas for non-EU imports were in place.

(b) The declining ability of the UK car manufacturing industry in general, and Rover in particular, to compete in the market, and the necessity of improving competitiveness in order to survive.

The alliance of these two companies allowed them both to achieve their objectives. The continued success of the Rover/Honda alliance depended upon trust built from effective communications. Once these communications broke down, the alliance was doomed to failure.

For discussion

Discuss the following statement in groups.

Increasing competitive pressure will result in greater openness in communications between rivals. The eventual outcome will be such close alliance that each sector of the market will become an effective monopoly.

In order for an organisation to have an innovative culture, the structure needs to be organic (see Chapter 11). By definition, these structures cannot exist without free and effective communications. Swift action and reaction require the fast flow of information and rapid decision making.

One of the greatest recent changes in the environment of organisations is in the area of technological advances. Technological changes have also had impacts on the strategy, structure and culture of organisations.

2 TECHNOLOGICAL CHANGE

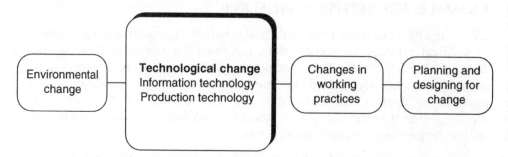

In this section we concentrate on information and production technology. This does not imply that other technological advances do not have an impact on the organisation; these are just intended as two examples of changes in technology that generate pressure on organisations to change.

2.1 Information technology

We have already considered how technological innovation in information dissemination has expanded the means to communicate; here we concentrate on how these advances have (a) pushed organisations to change, and (b) facilitated that change.

Technology has had an impact on the whole strategy of organisations. As stated in Chapter 9, the globalisation of organisations would have been impossible without present day means and methods of communications. Similarly, the concept of selling to a customer you never see would have remained a small niche market if technological innovation had not allowed television shopping. The growing interest of the UK food retailing industry in the concept of home shopping is testament to the viability of such changes.

Activity 3 [30 minutes]

How has improved communications technology facilitated the expansion of the global organisation? Make a list of the factors you consider to be important.

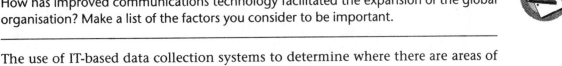

The use of IT-based data collection systems to determine where there are areas of waste has allowed organisations to realise their ambitions to cut costs. This represents a change in the values of the organisation and thus a change in its culture.

Improved communications technology has helped to improve partnership relationships with suppliers to such an extent that raw materials and components can now be delivered exactly when they are needed. This reduces the need for manufacturers to hold large stocks and thus saves money. This is one of the few areas when it is easy to quantify the benefits of highly developed and effective communications systems.

A major impact of information technology has been on working practices, which we shall consider below.

2.2 Production technology

The introduction of automated production and robotics has resulted in a reduction in the size of the shop floor workforce. From the organisation's point of view (although not the workers'), this is a benefit, where costs are cut. This reduction in the numbers of the workforce requires more and better communications between those who remain. When this type of new technology is being introduced, the process of increased communication needs to commence before its introduction. Otherwise, the transformation of the production plant is likely to be hindered by such things as trade union intervention. After the introduction of the new technology, continued communications are necessary to identify training needs and skills shortages.

Activity 4 [45 minutes]

Robert and Son is a small factory producing components for the electrical industry. Their system of production has for many years taken the form of a series of production lines, with each line producing a different sub-section of the finished component.

The development of new technology, which partly automates the production of the sub-sections, now means that it is possible to increase the production capacity. The old system required a large factory floor to house the production lines and a final assembly line where the components were put together and packaged. The new technology reduces the

---

amount of space required, so that all operations can be housed in one building. The production manager has put forward two separate layout plans for the 'new look' plant as shown in Figures 12.2 and 12.3. Figure 12.1 shows the existing layout.

Based on what you know about communications, draw up an advantages and disadvantages list for each of the three layouts. Make a final decision as to which layout to choose. Give reasons for your choice.

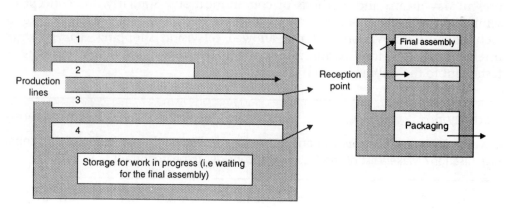

Figure 12.1 Existing layout

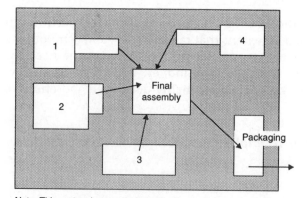

Figure 12.2 Possible new layout (a)

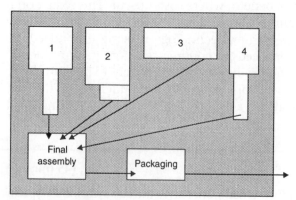

Figure 12.3 Possible new layout (b)

Whatever pressures are exerted by the external environment, the changes that occur within the organisation almost always lead, in some way, to changes in working practices. We shall consider just three of the possibilities.

3 CHANGES IN WORKING PRACTICES

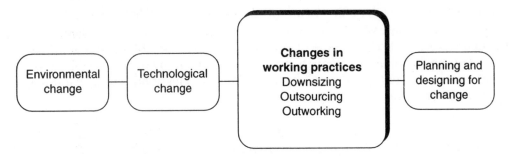

Changes in working practices can be a simple as introducing a new information collection form or as complex as transferring from a paper to computer-based system. However great or small the change, communication plays its part in its introduction and ultimate success.

Effective communication will:

(a) allay fear and suspicion about the motivation for the change;

(b) involve the workforce and gain their commitment;

(c) highlight potential problems;

(d) ensure that the change is appropriate;

(e) encourage feedback regarding unexpected side effects of the change;

(f) monitor the results of the change;

(g) facilitate the adaptation of the original plans.

We concentrate here on three contemporary and far reaching changes to working practices. The first of these is 'downsizing'.

3. 1 Downsizing

Definitions

Downsizing: the term used to describe the contraction of an organisation so that it concentrates on its core activities.

De-layering: the removal of one or more layers of middle management, accompanied by the devolving of responsibility and authority further down the organisation structure.

It is important to note the distinction between downsizing and de-layering. Although they are quite separate concepts, both can have similar effects on the motivation of the workforce, although within differing groups of workers. If communications are poor, the workforce do not understand the strategy that is being followed and the only effect they see is redundancies. This undermines their security and their commitment to the organisation, and, in turn, their performance is likely to suffer. Effective communications can reduce these effects and actively generate a stronger commitment to the change from those workers who remain after the process is complete.

Activity 5 [25 minutes]

You are the chief executive officer of a large group of companies. You have decided that, in order to consolidate your business with a view to expansion of your core activities in the future, you must sell off some of your smaller enterprises. Make a list of who you think you should communicate with in your environment to ensure that this will be a positive action for your company. Give reasons for communicating with each individual, group or organisation on your list.

We now look at the second of the three changes: 'outsourcing'.

3. 2 Outsourcing

Definition

Outsourcing: the term use to describe the process of employing outside contractors to perform tasks which, although not core activities of the organisation, were formerly performed in house. Examples can be cleaning, security, legal work and occupational health.

Outsourcing is often the result of downsizing and, as such, can encounter the same problems. Effective communication is especially important to ensure that the outsourced service is to the same standard, or better, and at lower cost than that previously provided in house. Partnership relationships are required with these service providers, and effective communications are the only way to achieve these. (There can be other influencing factors, but without effective communications they will not ensure success.) A great deal of outsourcing has been carried out in public-sector organisations, especially as a result of compulsory competitive tendering.

Definition

Compulsory competitive tendering: a process that has been forced onto public-sector organisations by central government. It entails the obligation to ask for tenders to carry out specific activities on behalf of the organisation. This process has to be repeated at regular intervals (yearly or three yearly, typically).

The nature of compulsory competitive tendering inhibits the possibility of developing partnership relationships, and thus the communication is not always as effective as it could be. These problems are just beginning to be highlighted, and may be addressed in the future.

Activity 6 [25 minutes]

In groups, consider the following.

(a) A local hospital

(b) The council for your locality

Make a list of any activities associated with the above which are outsourced.

Make a second list of activities that you think could be outsourced.

Now we look at the last of our three examples of change.

3.3 Outworking

Definition

> *Outworking*: the term used to describe a formerly office-based function being carried out primarily from the home of the job holder. This form of working has become popular in the financial services and data processing industries. The effects on the organisation are (a) to reduce overheads on expensive office accommodation and (b) to access the pool of (predominantly) female labour who have child care commitments that prevent them from taking office-based work. Outworking should not be confused with outsourcing.

The advent of the home computer and advances in telecommunications have facilitated the move towards home working. Critics of this working method claim that it will be a passing phase, as the effects of lack of communication on the worker become more evident. However, advances in all technological communication methods mean that the only area that cannot be satisfied is that of face-to-face personal interaction with others. Whilst there is debate as to the importance of interpersonal communication on the performance of the worker, it is clear that it does play a part in job satisfaction and motivation. It remains to be seen whether communications can be so carefully structured and facilitated as to remove this problem.

4 PLANNING AND DESIGNING FOR CHANGE

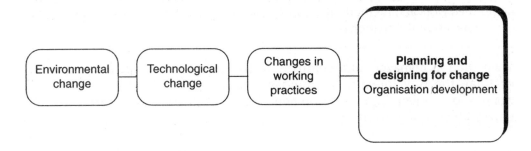

Organisations have to adapt to external and internal change. As an organisation grows its structure may not adapt to the changing demands for differentiation and integration. The environment changes but the organisation may not. It may continue with old structures and ways of working long after they have become a liability rather than an asset.

When did your own local tennis or snooker club last shake itself up and make a fresh start? Can you think of any local firms that have restructured themselves? Has their response to the economic changes of the last five years been to try to do more of the same with fewer people?

When organisations become incapable of reaching their potential, they should seek development to improve their effectiveness. This is extremely difficult to do because of the extent of the change in culture and structure that is usually necessary. Any change has to overcome the natural inertia of staff operating in a role in the existing structure. They are busy with their existing jobs. The only way to implement change is to bring in an outsider. Worthwhile change only happens if it is organisation wide.

First we look at what is involved in organisation development.

4.1   Organisation development

Organisation development has become important in the last decade. The pace of change in the environment has quickened. Privatisation, deregulation, recession and global competition have affected public- and private-sector organisations of all types. Social and political changes have been widespread. A policy such as 'Care in the Community' has affected hospitals, general practice, social services, local government, charities and voluntary bodies. The rapid development of the personal computer has transformed work. In 1980 computing power meant a multi-million pound Cray super computer operated by a separate IT department. Fifteen years later anyone can have a desk top PC with more calculating power than the Cray at a cost of around £7,000. You can get one capable of most operations for £700. Organisations have been forced to re-examine every aspect of their existence.

Activity 7   [30 minutes]

Ask some members of older generations if they can remember how clerical and accounts work were done thirty years ago. Specifically ask them about:

(a) adding up figures in accounts;

(b) how tills operated in shops;

(c) how letters and invoices were prepared.

You may have heard some of this before in the context of how the present generation cannot add up! You should also ask how many people could use a computer, or knew how it worked, in the 1960s.

Compare your findings with how jobs are done today and note how technology has transformed work and methods. It is easy to take today's technology for granted and to forget how recent the change is.

When the top managers of a company realise that it is not operating up to its potential, the way forward is a fundamental reappraisal and redesign of the organisation. Organisation development is the whole process of carrying out a strategy for adapting to change.

Definition

Organisation development is a strategy for improving organisational effectiveness by changing the beliefs, values and structure of organisations through collaboration between an external consultant and the management of the organisation.

There are three features of organisation development (OD).

(a) It is an organisation-wide process.

(b) It is concerned with more than the redesign of the structure and is essentially an education process.

(c) It relies on an external third party consultant – the change agent.

OD programmes have seven distinct stages and we look next at what they involve.

The programme

Each OD programme must be unique because each organisation is different, but they are all likely to follow much the same sequence in introducing and carrying through the required changes. Before the programme can begin, it is essential that senior management recognise the need for development and agree that it should be organisation wide.

Stage 1: preliminary planning

Senior management start by discussing the problem and choosing the change agent. There is then more detailed discussion about the aims and methods of the proposed programme with the agent. This is likely to include:

(a) the aims, methods and potential outcome of the programme;

(b) the role of the consultant and relationship with the management;

(c) the implications for the organisation.

The change agent could have different roles, according to circumstances, as:

(a) educator and facilitator of change;

(b) a catalyst for introducing new ideas and practices;

(c) an expert guiding and leading management in making changes.

Once all these are agreed, the staff of the organisation must be fully informed about the programme. So that their trust is maintained, they must be kept fully informed throughout all its stages. The consultant has to win the trust of all concerned and gain their co-operation.

Stage 2: analysis

The change agent designs a programme for obtaining information. This includes:

(a) documented information such as job descriptions, staff personnel records, budgets and control data;

(b) questionnaires dealing with all aspects;

(c) surveys;

(d) interviews of individuals and/or groups;

(e) collecting statistics;

(f) staff suggestions and proposals.

Activity 8   [45 minutes]

Assume that your course is involved in an OD exercise.

Design a short questionnaire to find out how well course members are informed about their results when they complete assignments. You should cover methods of feedback, the time scale and corrective action.

Try your questionnaire on four or five people and from the results say if it shows that there is anything unsatisfactory in the present system and make a suggestion for its improvement.

Stage 3: Diagnosis

All this information is used to build up a picture of the culture, staff attitudes and operations of the organisation. It is important that staff are involved because they must feel committed to the process. Staff participation may lead them to realise for themselves what is wrong and propose solutions.

The results are discussed with management. An agreed diagnosis of the situation is produced. It is essential that this honestly faces up to the situation. The result is reported back to top management so that the strategy for change can be agreed.

Stage 4: Aims and objectives

When the diagnosis is agreed the change agent and management agree the aims and objectives of the programme of OD. The aims might include improving profitability, increasing market share, entering new markets, changing the culture of the organisation and improving staff motivation. These are then translated into specific objectives, for example:

(a) to achieve a market share of 8% within one year;

(b) to reduce operating costs in marketing and sales by 7% in each of the next three years;

(c) to reduce manufacturing rejects by 15% in six months;

(d) to establish project teams operating in a matrix structure throughout the small appliances division within fifteen months;

(e) to put all staff through specified training programmes within the next three years.

Note that all these objectives are specific, quantifiable and have a timescale for their achievement. Progress can thus be monitored and corrective action taken if required. The outcome of the programme can be checked against the aims.

Stage 5: Action plans

The content and sequence of all the actions required to meet the objectives are set out in a master plan. This could include specific programmes for:

(a) creating an open, problem-solving environment;

(b) increasing knowledge and competence both in specific job-related areas and in general management skills;

(c) building trust and collaboration among groups;

(d) developing reward systems based on personal development as much as on achieving organisational goals;

(e) increasing employee empowerment and the degree of personal autonomy.

Stage 6: Implementation and review

All the plans are put into effect and progress is constantly monitored by the consultant and the management. Progress is reviewed and any necessary changes are made. Parts of a programme may have to be dropped because they have adverse effects. Some parts may lag behind and require more resources of management time to speed them up. Objectives and aims may have to be revised and programmes amended.

Stage 7: Completion and evaluation

As the programme is completed, the results are evaluated against the original aims. At the end of the programme the change agent leaves the organisation.

Activity 9 [10 minutes]

A new chairman of W H Smith, the news, book, record and DIY chain, announced that the culture of the firm had to change to a more commercial one. He proposed dropping many marginal product lines as part of a complete shake up of the company. Do you consider this is a good preliminary to introducing OD?

The success of any OD programme depends on the change agent; we examine this role next.

The change agent

External or internal?

An external consultant is preferred for the following reasons.

(a) A consultant will have previous experience of OD, which an internal manager is unlikely to have.

(b) An outsider is not bound by status and can operate across all levels of the hierarchy.

(c) The change agent can be expected to take a more objective view than an insider.

(d) The consultant has more time for the exercise as it is a full-time job, whereas a manager is likely to have other tasks.

(e) The change agent leaves at the end of the programme and does not have to live with the results, unlike a manager who must be wary of making trouble within the organisation.

There are also arguments against using an outsider. These include the following.

(a) An outsider lacks knowledge and understanding of the organisation.

(b) An outsider will take time taken to become familiar with the organisation.

(c) There is the possibility that a consultant will be resented as a meddler and tool of top management.

Timespan
Successful OD programmes have sometimes been spread over several years, so that the consultant could become thoroughly familiar with the organisation. The minimum time required for an effective programme is likely to be two years.

Relationships
The consultant must be capable of building an effective relationship with staff in the organisation and winning over all grades to support the project. The change agent has to build a sound relationship with the management team and establish the trust of all employees. Full information to everyone at all stages is essential.

Roles
The change agent has many roles, including the following.

(a) Expert and skilled adviser

(b) Analyst

(c) Listener

(d) Catalyst for change

(e) Counsellor

(f) Problem solver

Activity 10 [5 minutes]

Why is it that so many change agents brought in by major companies are academics, like Rosabeth Moss Kanter and Tom Peters?

Establishing the starting point
The consultant has first to establish whether the organisation is ready for OD. This means examining the organisation and asking the following questions.

(a) Are the learning goals of OD appropriate?

(b) Are the key people involved and committed?

(c) Are the culture and values of the organisation such as to make OD feasible?

(d) What are the problems?

Problems in the organisation can be analysed under the following main headings.

(a) Power and authority

(b) Differentiation and integration

(c) Co-operation and conflict

(d) Adaptation to change

(e) Culture and identity

It is not enough for the change agent to concentrate on broad questions of organisation structure and strategy, there must be a process of change at all levels down to individual processes.

Re-engineering

It is because of the potential problems of bringing in an outsider, and the need to commit members of the organisation to change, that many companies prefer the approach of '*re-engineering the company*'. This involves the same basic process as OD but is started by a leader who is a senior executive who authorises and motivates the overall effort. The process is supervised by a steering committee, composed of senior managers, which develops the overall strategy and monitors progress. Each process is led by a 'process owner' who is a manager with authority for the specific process and the re-engineering effort focused on it. The process owner is supported by a 're-engineering team', a group dedicated to diagnosis, planning the redesign and implementing the programme for that particular process. Each team includes at least one outsider who does not work in the process. There could also be outsiders who are effectively suppliers and customers of the process. Their purpose is to pose awkward questions and initiate new thinking. The objective is to find new and effective ways of doing things.

Re-engineering often starts with the appointment of a new chief executive who is effectively a change agent.

EXAMPLE: MAZDA

In 1996 Mazda, the Japanese car manufacturer, appointed Henry Wallace as its new president. Wallace was a British manager in Ford who gained experience in several countries before being appointed Executive Vice-president of Mazda in 1994. Ford and Mazda have co-operated since the 1960s and Ford took a 25% shareholding in 1979 and raised it to 33.4% in 1996. Mazda made losses in each of the three previous years and lost market share in Japan as well as seeing a drop in exports. Benefits are expected from linking Mazda's research and development with Ford's design capacity. The essential step is to re-engineer Mazda to revitalise it.

For discussion

Many organisations have undergone a transformation when they have moved from the public- to the private-sector, merged or, like building societies, changed from mutual status to Plcs.

How might OD help in these transformations?

We now consider the methods and outcomes of OD.

Methods and results

Areas of action

There are three main areas of action programmes in OD:

(a) programmes to change behaviour, including team building, improving inter-personal skills, better communication and training in coaching and counselling;

(b) programmes to improve problem solving, including training in goal setting, planning and evaluation;

(c) programmes to make structures effective, including training in systems diagnosis, role analysis and job design.

All these aspects are involved in an OD programme. There is no point in trying to fit new solutions into an inappropriate system. There may have to be radical redesign of the organisation, including delayering of management, outsourcing activities and even selling off parts of the organisation, possibly through a management buy-out.

Factors leading to success
An OD programme is likely to succeed where:

(a) top management is committed to action;

(b) there is some new element, such as a new chief executive or a merger which brings a reappraisal of internal problems;

(c) problem areas are honestly and fully analysed and diagnosed;

(d) there is collaboration between line and staff and departments in identifying problems and implementing solutions;

(e) there is a willingness to take risks;

(f) there are new solutions which produce a commitment to action;

(g) there is a reward system that rewards people for the effort of changing;

(h) positive results reinforce the acceptance of new practices.

Factors preventing success
Effective organisation development is unlikely to occur where:

(a) top management is not totally committed to improvement;

(b) there is impatience for quick results and the timescale necessary (usually at least two years) is not allowed;

(c) top management fails to secure the commitment and support of middle and lower managers;

(d) there is an attempt to fit a major change into an old structure;

(e) ends and means are confused, this includes:

  (i) assuming that training will bring about change in itself without the changes in attitudes, culture and structure that are necessary;

  (ii) assuming that simply using OD activities, such as management development programmes, constitutes a programme;

  (iii) letting consultants solve problems without management commitment to continuing the changes after the change agent leaves.

Chapter roundup
Changes affecting organisations and communications are inextricably linked for the following reasons.

- Requirements to change can be identified by communications with the organisational environment.
- The nature of the change needed requires effective communications within the organisation as well as externally.
- The way in which changes are be implemented *should* be ascertained by internal communication.
- Failure in internal communications can render changes ineffective in reaching the objective.
- Poor communications may lead to increased resistance to change.
- Organisation development is a strategy for improving organisational effectiveness by changing the beliefs, values and structure of organisations through collaboration between an external consultant and the management of the organisation.
- OD is an organisation-wide process concerned with more than the redesign of the structure.
- OD relies on an external third party consultant – the change agent.

159

- The seven stages of an OD programme are: (a) preliminary planning, (b) analysis of the organisation, (c) diagnosis of problems, (d) setting aims and objectives, (e) preparing an action plan, (f) implementing the plan and reviewing progress, (g) completion of the programme and evaluation of the results.
- The change agent leaves after the end of the programme.
- Process re-engineering is similar to OD but depends more on internal teams which look at specific processes.
- OD consists of programmes to change behaviour, improve competencies and restructure the organisation.
- Management commitment to action is essential for the success of OD.

Quick Quiz

1   What external factors can give rise to the need for change?
2   How do organisations know if change is required?
3   Define 'outworking'.
4   List the differences between outworking and outsourcing.
5   Give three reasons why communication should be considered when contemplating introducing change into an organisation.
6   Why can compulsory competitive tendering cause communications to be ineffective?
7   With ineffective communications, what is likely to be the view of the workforce when a process of downsizing is embarked upon?
8   How can effective communications overcome resistance to change?
9   Define 'organisation development'.
10 What should be the scope of an OD programme?
11 What is a change agent?
12 Why is an outsider used?
13 What is process re-engineering?
14 What is the essential precondition for the success of an OD programme?
15 Who agrees the aims and objectives of an OD programme?
16 List the main areas of OD action programmes.
17 Give three reasons why an OD programme may fail.

Answers to Quick Quiz

1   Any change in the environment of the organisation: political, social, technological or economic.
2   Organisations know if changes are required through communicating effectively with their environment.
3   Outworking is when a job is done from home rather than from an office.
4   Outworkers are (a) employed directly by the organisation, (b) may perform core activities and are usually individuals. Outsourcing is the practice of contracting out work; such work is usually peripheral or a support activity and is often contracted out to another organisation.
5   Communication should be considered when contemplating change in an organisation because:

    (a) resistance to change may be increased if communications are ineffective

(b) changes may occur only 'on paper'

(c) effective communications can evaluate the suitability of change for the circumstance.

6 Compulsory competitive tendering can result in communications being ineffective because the constant renewal of contracts inhibits the building of partnership relationships.

7 The workforce will only see the effects of downsizing in terms of redundancies, which will create feelings of job insecurity.

8 Effective communications can over come resistance to change by involving the worker in the change process and by increasing understanding between workforce and management.

9 A strategy for improving organisational effectiveness.

10 Organisation wide.

11 An external consultant brought in to manage the OD programme.

12 Because of the combination of previous experience, objectivity, ability to give the job full attention, freedom from status constraints and, because the consultant leaves at the end of the programme, lack of a personal stake in the results.

13 A strategy for improving operations by setting up process teams under a process owner to find new effective ways of doing things.

14 All levels of management must be committed to it.

15 The change agent and management.

16 (a) Changing behaviour, (b) improving problem solving, (c) restructuring.

17 You could have given any of the following. (a) Lack of management commitment. (b) Insufficient time. (c) Confusion of ends and means. (d) Trying to fit major change into an old, inappropriate structure.

Answers to Activities

1 Here are four products/industries that have been forced to change in the last ten years. You may have thought of other equally valid examples.

(a) The major players in the retail food industry have had to change the focus of their product ranges as a result of pressure from consumers to reduce prices. They have done this by introducing 'own brand' labels.

(b) Building societies have found that they cannot compete against the range of services provided by high street banks, and have thus changed from the traditional mutual society (see Chapter 1).

(c) Lucozade became less fashionable as concern regarding the sugar contents of food and drink grew. The target market of the drink changed away from the wider consumer towards the young and sporting fraternity.

(d) Fewer fur coats are now sold in the UK as a result of social pressures regarding animal cruelty.

2 Your essay should include the following points.

(a) Works councils could raise the awareness of management regarding the importance of communication with their workforce.

(b) The workforce could begin to feel that their views are important.

(c) Adversarial relationships between workers and management should begin to be broken down.

(d) Greater commitment towards the organisation may result.

(e) No change may occur in attitudes.

(f) Works councils may be 'window dressing' with no substance or commitment from management.

(g) Adversarial relationships could be created between works council and unions.

(h) Union power could be further decreased.

161

3 Technology has facilitated the expansion of the global organisation by:

(a) speeding up the communication process;

(b) increasing the ability to co-ordinate activities;

(c) facilitating data collection to raise awareness of customers' needs;

(d) allowing standardisation of response;

(e) enabling decision making to be better informed.

4 The relative merits of the two possible new layouts are as follows.

	Advantages	*Disadvantages*
Present layout (Figure 12.1)	Logical sequence to production	Cost of larger premises
	Production lines do not interfere with each other	Communication difficult between production lines
		Isolation from final assembly stops workers from feeling part of the final product
		Communication difficult along assembly lines
Layout (a) (Figure 12.2)	Savings on space	All workers will be affected by disruption to one area, even if only mentally
	Less work-in-progress	
	Central final assembly gives all workers a feeling of completing the product	
	Communication between all workers easier	
	'Shorter' and 'fatter' production lines make communication and team building easier	
Layout (b) (Figure 12.3)		Lines 3 and 4 are more isolated from final assembly
		Communication between lines 3 and 4 and final assembly more difficult

Based on these factors, your choice of layout should be layout (a) (Figure 12.2.) The reasons are that communications are easier, work-in-progress is reduced, team spirit is facilitated and there is a lower cost from the size of the facilities.

5   You could have included the following in your list.

   (a) Trade unions – Effective communications with unions can avoid misinterpretation of your actions and the militant reaction that often accompanies such misunderstandings.

   (b) Shareholders, including the money markets in general if a Plc is involved – you may need the agreement of shareholders in order to carry out your strategy. Failure to have your reasons for change understood may result in the strategy being seen as a symptom of financial difficulties. The effects of this on share prices would be detrimental to the proposed sale.

   (c) The media – much of the potential misinterpretation can be averted if regular accurate information is communicated to the media.

   Note: the activity asked for communication with your environment, so your answer should not include internal communication, such as with the workforce.

6   Your lists could have included the following:

   (a) Hospital: security, cleaning services, laundry, sterilisation of instruments, non-emergency transport, portering.

   (b) Council: gardening, refuse collection, street lighting, house and footpath maintenance, snow clearance and road gritting, library services, the running of any leisure facility.

7   You will have found that many calculations and operations were still done manually 30 years ago. The first four-function electronic calculator was produced by Sir Clive Sinclair in 1968 and cost about £70, more than a week's wages. Even bank statements were prepared by hand with cheques being posted and cleared manually. Tills printed till rolls but did not calculate change – that required mental arithmetic. The whole array of credit, cash and other plastic cards did not exist. Nor did cash machines and, if they had, the computer systems to manage the accounts did not. Telephones were land line based and the telex was the only way to send documents, with each one being typed in. Letters and documents were produced by typing pools, either from hand-written drafts or from shorthand dictation. Electric typewriters did not have spell checkers. Compare this with today's office.

8   Features you could include in a questionnaire include the following.

   (a) Methods of feedback – formal/informal, written/verbal.

   (b) Quality of feedback – marks, written report, comments on papers, verbal discussion and their extent and relevance.

   (c) Timescale – time from submission to return of assignment and to feedback.

   (d) Relevance of feedback to future work.

   You might have suggested more written comments for reference or more discussion according to your findings.

9   They new chairman's statement is not a good start as it is likely to cause staff to fear change and redundancies. Also, it is not possible to change a culture by giving orders.

10 Academics such as Kanter and Peters have previous experience, the time available, are usually behavioural scientists trained in the sociological and psychological aspects and are obviously independent.

Assignment 12a [2 hours]

Write a short essay (no more than 500 words) discussing the following statement.

Workers will only accept changes to their working practices if there is a financial benefit to them.

You should consider theories of motivation in conjunction with your knowledge of communications before attempting this essay.

Assignment 12b [1.5 hours]

Suppose that you have been appointed as personal assistant to the new general manager of a subsidiary of a large, diversified manufacturing company. The subsidiary is essentially a division of the company. It is divided into several departments. It produces a large variety of engineering products ranging from basic components through sub-assemblies to finished products. These are sold to customers outside the group and to other divisions of the group. Many of the basic components and sub-assemblies are produced by a wide range of small, independent firms, often at lower prices and more flexibly. The most profitable part of the business is the sale of finished products.

The new general manager has made a preliminary assessment of the subsidiary's management. Her conclusion is that their efforts are fragmented and unco-ordinated. The introduction of new products is haphazard, many concepts are not pursued through to completion. There is little contact between the staffs of departments as they are located on different sites. Only the sales and accounts staff seem to have contact with customers.

You have been asked to investigate the feasibility of carrying out an organisation development exercise. Write a memorandum to the general manager setting out the aims of such an exercise, what it might be expected to achieve for the company and what the exercise might involve.

Chapter 13

CULTURE IN ORGANISATIONS

Culture and nationality — Influences on culture — Climate

Introduction

All organisations have their own distinctive cultures. But it is too much of a simplification to classify a business's culture as simply being bureaucratic, for example. To do so would be to ignore the variety of sub-cultures that can exist side by side under the public skin of an organisation.

Many forces shape the culture of an organisation. An American firm will be very different from a Japanese one. A charity staffed by volunteers will be unlike a double glazing company. A mechanistic firm with a tall hierarchy will affect the behaviour of its personnel very differently than one with an organic flat structure. Culture is influenced by the organisation's environment and its purpose: compare IBM with Oxfam, an infant school with Oxford University, or the Department of Trade and Industry with Harrods.

Management style and the attitudes of people shape cultures. Walk round the departments of a firm and you will see that each has its own culture. Groups within a department may develop their own cultures. The *climate* of the organisation is more difficult to observe – climate is how people in the organisation perceive the organisation.

Your objectives

After completing this chapter you should:

(a) appreciate the difference between organisational culture and climate;

(b) be able to understand and describe different influences on organisational culture;

(c) understand why various cultures may exist;

(d) appreciate the importance of national differences for organisational culture and the management of firms.

It is common to talk about culture and nationality together – a distinctive American culture as opposed to a Japanese one, for instance. We need to look at this idea very carefully before moving on to the culture of individual organisations.

NOTES

1   CULTURE AND NATIONALITY

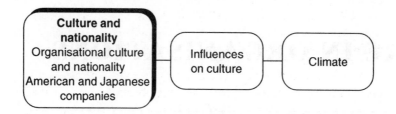

An important factor in your choice of employer is your sympathy with the perceived culture of the organisation. To an important extent the culture of an organisation reflects the characteristics of its society. Your expectations about the way people behave in organisations will be conditioned by national attitudes. The culture of an organisation can be formed by many influences, including the country and the national mores.

Definitions

Organisational culture: the unique character of an organisation, made up of shared beliefs and attitudes, patterns of behaviour and other characteristics that can be observed by outsiders.

Organisational climate: the way that the members of the organisation perceive its structure, rules, beliefs and behaviour.

Mores: customs or conventions regarded as essential to or characteristic of a community.

First we look at organisational culture in the international context.

1.1   Organisational culture and nationality

Organisational culture is strongly influenced by national mores. Behaviour in an American corporation is very different from that in a Japanese company. British firms are different from continental ones. Geert Hofstede studied four dimensions of national culture which measure the differences in people's work-related values. These are:

(a) individualism versus collectivism;

(b) power distance;

(c) uncertainty avoidance;

(d) masculinity versus femininity.

Hofstede defines national culture as

> *...collective mental programming; it is that part of our conditioning that we share with other members of our nation, region, or group but not with members of other nations, regions, or groups.*

> **(Hofstede, G. The cultural relativity of organisational practices and theories. *Journal of International Business Studies*, 1983.)**

He points out that behaviour depends on culture – the British form a queue when they have to wait, the French do not. The common culture manifests itself in government, the legal system, education, industrial relations, organisations and voluntary bodies. The four dimensions can be placed on scales showing differences in national attitudes.

Individualism versus collectivism

Individualism versus collectivism refers to the relation between an individual and his or her fellow individuals. In more individualistic societies everyone is supposed to look after their own self interest and, maybe, their close family. Such a society leaves individuals a large amount of freedom.

At the other end of the scale, in a collectivist society, links between individuals are very tight. People are born into ingroups and are supposed to look after the ingroup's interests. They accept the values and beliefs of the ingroup, and in exchange the ingroup looks after them.

The degree of individualism is related to a country's wealth. There is a high correlation between low income and low individualism. Countries at this end of the scale include Pakistan, Peru and Portugal. At the opposite end are the US, Canada and Denmark. The UK has a higher individualism index than would be expected from per capita GNP, and Sweden a lower one. Germany has higher income and much lower individualism than the UK.

Activity 1 [30 minutes]

Ask ten members of your course or ten colleagues at work 'Who do you think that you have the responsibility to look after: yourself, yourself and your immediate family, your wider family group or your personal community (religious group, village, work group)?'.

Are the results in line with what you would expect in the UK?

Organisations in collectivist societies have to recognise the importance of ingroups. Organisations have to become working ingroups to replace the natural ingroups of the society. Workers' loyalty to the organisation is assured by giving them the same protection and support that they would get from their natural ingroup.

Power distance

Definition

Power distance is concerned with society's reaction to inequality. Some societies allow inequalities in power and wealth to grow, others try to reduce them as much as possible. In organisations the level of power distance is related to the degree of centralisation of authority and the degree of autocratic leadership. This situation continues because it satisfies the needs of both leaders and those without power.

Power distance also relates to how people relate to their superiors and subordinates, where power distance is high, superiors are far less 'accessible' to subordinates than where power distance is low; for example, it would be inconceivable, in a high power distance culture, for bosses and juniors to socialise after work.

Activity 2 [5 minutes]

There has been a recent outcry in the press about the size of salary increases, bonus payments and share options given to the directors of companies, especially those in privatised, monopoly industries. What does this tell you about power distance in the UK?

India has a large power distance and France and Belgium are also fairly high. The UK, US and Australia have a small power distance combined with high individualism. All poor countries are collectivist with large power distances.

Power distance is important for joint ventures and the management of subsidiaries in foreign countries. Different attitudes to leadership and to the location of authority have led to failure for joint ventures. In countries where workers expect to be given orders a different management style is required from the participative approach successful in the UK. It can take a long time to overcome cultural attitudes and to institute team work.

In more individualist countries with large power distance, organisations tend to have a tall hierarchy with clear levels of authority. This suits both managers and workers. Problems tend to be referred up the hierarchy for decisions. Where there is small power distance subordinates expect to participate in decision making and are ready to question management decisions.

Uncertainty avoidance

Uncertainty avoidance is about attitudes to risk. Weak uncertainty avoidance communities:

(a) take risks easily;

(b) are more tolerant of behaviour and opinions different from their own; and

(c) feel relatively secure.

Strong uncertainty avoidance societies:

(a) show higher levels of anxiety and emotionality;

(b) create institutions which try to create security;

(c) have many laws and rules which imply little tolerance of abnormal behaviour and opinions;

(d) have faith in the power of technology and religions that claim absolute truth.

Japan, Latin American and Latin European countries have strong uncertainty avoidance and large power distance. The UK and Sweden combine small power distance and weak uncertainty avoidance. Asian countries have large power distance with medium to weak uncertainty avoidance. This means that UK firms tend towards finding shared solutions to problems and allow more personal initiative. Asian firms often tend to a family model with a patriarchal authority figure who takes the final decision.

For discussion

The student union has invited anyone who wishes to do so to put forward their views at an open forum where they can address the audience and follow it with recruitment to a club. You learn that one intending speaker is a fascist who believes in white supremacy, another is a devil worshipper, a third is a communist who thinks that private property should be confiscated and a fourth is an evangelical who promotes a religion where women may only worship separately from men, cannot own property and are expected to devote themselves to marriage and child bearing. These are in addition to the representatives of the mainstream political parties, gay activists and single-issue groups such as Greenpeace and CND.

Do you think that all these people should be able to put forward their views?

What are your tolerance limits?

Do you think that a business firm could accommodate all these views among its staff?

Masculinity versus femininity

Masculinity versus femininity is concerned with social attitudes to the division of work between the sexes. What does society consider suitable work for women? What jobs should be offered to men?

Activity 3 [5 minutes]

Which country was first to have a woman Prime Minister?

(a) Pakistan

(b) Sri Lanka

(c) Turkey

(d) UK

In the UK during the 1990s there has been a considerable shift in opinion and attitudes. This is shown by the large number of cases brought to the Equal Opportunities Commission by men claiming that they have been rejected for secretarial, domestic and nursing jobs, which employers considered to be women's work. UK organisations cannot assign roles to employees based on gender. Attitudes are different in other countries.

Japan is the most masculine country, having the highest belief that men should take the dominant roles and women should take jobs which are service oriented and caring. Germany, Austria and Switzerland are highly masculine, more moderate are the UK, India and the US, with the Scandinavians being the most feminine. The more feminine the country, the higher is the value placed on preserving the environment, helping others and developing relationships with people.

We now focus on, and contrast, companies from two countries: the US and Japan.

1.2   American and Japanese companies

American companies

America has the highest individualism score of all nations, and is just below average for power distance. The leader controls decisions even though subordinates are permitted to join in the decision making process. Typically the American corporation concentrates decision making at the top. Individual discretion areas are clear and people are held personally responsible for the results of their decisions. Individuals are rewarded for results. The emphasis is on the short term. There is little job security and rapid labour turnover; staff are not loyal to the company. There are many potential sources of conflict in the corporation, not least the fact that plans and decisions are made without involving the lower levels and workers may not agree with them or implement them with enthusiasm.

Managers of American companies are responsible to their shareholders and depend on the market for funds. They are forced to take a short-term view because shareholders and market expect short-term results.

Japanese companies

Japanese firms' culture is a product of their society. The Japanese live in densely concentrated communities in mountainous volcanic earthquake-prone islands, without natural resources – for which they depend on other nations. This makes them collectivist with strong uncertainty avoidance. As a strongly masculine society, they are status conscious and defer to seniority. This is becoming less so, as more Japanese travel – there are now many Japanese students in London – and abandon their parents' workaholic habits.

Decision making is a collective activity (called *ringi*). Before a plan goes to higher management all relevant departments of middle management thoroughly evaluate and, if necessary, modify it before approval. The plan then goes through the same process at every level until it reaches the managing director. The plan can be rejected at any level. When it is finally implemented it is impossible to allocate any individual responsibility. Because of this process, planning is long drawn out, but implementation is speedy and enthusiastic. People feel they are involved and have ownership of the initiative.

Team work is encouraged by this participation and by the system of rewarding the team and not individuals. Promotion to higher status depends on being a good team player. The leader is seen as an enabler, whose role is to assist the group to achieve its objective. Control is by the group rather than by superiors.

Only a small proportion of the Japanese labour force benefits from lifetime employment. Japanese companies employ a large number of temporary workers, mostly female. Small firms do not offer employment protection. However, the core worker in a large corporation enjoys employment protection up to retirement at age 50 or 55 and a salary decided by education, age and length of service, which also determines promotion. Workers are loyal to their firm. Companies take a long view and invest in training. Japanese firms never know what to do with a large number of managers who are surplus to requirements. Despite *manufacturing* productivity, Japanese firms are top-heavy with administrators.

Japanese firms are largely financed by banks. The board of directors is more powerful than the shareholders and can take a long view. Trade unions are company based rather than industry or craft based. Their interests are linked to the success of the company. Current difficulties in the Japanese financial system are loosening these ties.

Activity 4 [10 minutes]

Many American and UK firms are trying to move away from the stereotype in the above example and towards the Japanese model.

List some advantages they hope to gain.

Now we turn to the influences on culture in organisations.

2 INFLUENCES ON CULTURE

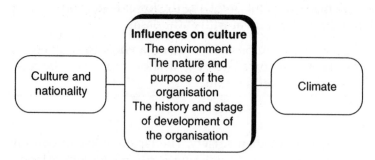

The culture of an organisation is influenced and shaped by:

(a) national mores;

(b) the environment of the organisation;

(c) the nature and purpose of the organisation;

(d) the history and stage of development of the organisation.

(e) the values and beliefs of the management and workers;

(f) the management style;

(g) the structure of the organisation.

We look at values and beliefs, the management style and the structure of the organisation in the next chapter. Here we start by looking at the effects of the environment.

2.1 The environment

The external environment of the organisation has an impact on its internal culture.

EXAMPLES: CHANGES IN THE 'PUBLIC SECTOR' ENVIRONMENT

The change to compulsory competitive tendering has altered the culture of many parts of local government.

Deregulation has changed the attitudes of staff in the telecommunications, gas, electricity and other industries.

Agency status has made previously bureaucratic, inward looking government departments into outward looking, business minded organisations.

The European Union

Membership of the European Community (EC) brought many economic pressures for change, and political change has come with the move to the European Union (EU). For example, although the UK opted out of the Social Chapter of the Maastricht Treaty, larger multinational firms operating in Europe are affected by it. Attitudes in these firms are bound to change. What is regarded as good practice will also spread to other firms.

Government policy

Changes in government policy, often in response to social pressures, affect attitudes in organisations.

EXAMPLE: PENSIONS AND PART-TIME WORKING

Pension provision has been reconsidered since the government made it clear that people should provide for their old age and not depend on the State.

Part-time workers gained the same employment protection and pension rights as full-time employees. This has affected attitudes to employee welfare and part-time staff and changed employee expectations.

Social attitudes

Social attitudes have changed. Between 1971 and 1993 the UK workforce increased from 25.4 million to 28.2 million, and the number in part-time employment rose from 13% to 22%. Around 5 million women work part-time.

Between 1983 and 1993 male full-time employment fell by 1,230,000, and part-time male employees increased by 353,000. During the same period female employment rose by 1,866,000. These changes have altered employee attitudes towards firms and the cultural priorities of workers.

For discussion

In addition to the changes noted above, male self-employment rose by 556,000 and female by 254,000. Female part-time employment increased by 1,049,000 and full-time by 563,000. Trade union membership has fallen significantly.

What effect do you think that these changes are likely to have on the culture of business organisations?

The nature of an organisation, profit making multinational or voluntary charity, and what it does influence its culture.

2.2 The nature and purpose of the organisation

The culture of an advertising agency is very different from that of a car factory or a hospital. The cultures of banks and building societies are also different, although they are broadly in the same industry. A profit making firm providing a service has a different culture from a non-profit voluntary organisation: compare a hotel and a hostel for the homeless.

The time horizon of an organisation also affects its culture. A medical research laboratory looks at a ten year period to develop and test a new drug; the R&D department in a TV firm has three months to redesign the casing of a set.

Remember that culture is the set of commonly held beliefs and attitudes in an organisation. A selling firm will have an action-oriented, short-term approach. Decisions have to be made quickly and are taken by those in authority. Results are what counts as sales mean pay. Compare this with a production-oriented company where quality considerations are paramount. Decisions may still be taken by top management, but they are likely to have passed through committees first. Inter-department co-operation is important. Links with suppliers are cultivated leading to long-term relationships. Design and development may take three years or more, so thinking is longer term.

EXAMPLE: THE NATIONAL HEALTH SERVICE

Change in the Health Service brought the introduction of general management and clinical budgeting. Contracts with fund holding GPs meant a new way of financing. The accounting system and accountability arrangements, including league tables for quality of service, are all part of a continuing effort to change the culture of the service.

The broad aim is more effective direction and control. It requires a shift in the balance of power away from the providers of services to the consumers of these services and the taxpayers who pay for them. It means a major change in corporate culture. There has had to be a radical change in the strongly held beliefs and values of people in the service. Conflicts between consultants and managers have been one result of the shift in the balance of power.

The culture of an organisation is influenced by its history.

2.3 The history and stage of development of the organisation

Culture is influenced by the past. The Co-Op is still influenced by the beliefs of its founders. A family firm will have a distinctive culture strongly dependent on the characteristics of the founding family. When members of the original family remain connected to the firm, it retains the original culture more strongly.

EXAMPLES: HISTORICAL CULTURE

Barclays Bank was formed at the end of the 19th century from several private banks. Top management has always had some representation of these families. Guinness and Pilkington are similar examples.

Forte was a strongly family firm until its take-over in 1996. As it is broken up, its culture will inevitably change.

The Body Shop chain has a culture dependent on its founders, the Roddicks.

Age and culture

A newly founded firm will have a different culture from a long established one. The extent to which age brings change depends partly on the industry. Microsoft retains much of the culture it had when it was founded partly because employees who have become millionaires still turn up for work because they like it.

Discovery- and research-based organisations are likely to retain their culture because of their nature and the type of people who work in them. Newly established firms are less likely to be formal and more likely to encourage initiative. People may be on first names terms regardless of level. They are more likely to 'muck in' and take on any job that needs doing. More levels in the hierarchy and the introduction of professional managers change these attitudes.

Mergers

The number of mergers it has gone through will affect a firm's culture. Baring's bankers found ING's Dutch executives less formal; only one sign of changes in corporate culture that were found to follow ING's take-over. The culture of a multinational such as Ford or Unilever is different from that of a single-country firm.

Activity 5 [5 minutes]

List three ways in which the culture of a newly founded firm may differ from a long established one in the same industry.

The climate of a firm may be very different from its perceived culture.

3   CLIMATE

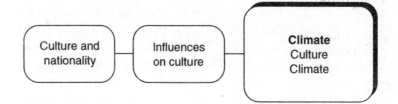

The climate of an organisation is how its members see it. This may be very different to what the outsider perceives as the culture of the organisation.

3.1   Culture

Your perception of the culture of a company is influenced by such factors as the following.

(a) *Attitude to customers* Are staff pleasant, helpful and quick to serve you, or are they more interested in plans for their weekend? Do they use your name, and say 'please' and 'thank-you', or do they just grunt? Is it easy to speak to managers? Can you get through on the phone quickly, or are you left listening to Greensleeves for ages?

(b) *Corporate image* Do staff wear uniforms? Is the logo prominent? Does the brochure show glossy photos of plant and buildings (probably status conscious), or of customers and service (probably customer oriented)? Are buildings smart, clean and well furnished, or are they scruffy? Is literature well designed and helpful, or confusing and irrelevant?

(c) *Actions* Are decisions made quickly, for example on a bank loan or replacing a faulty purchase, or do they have to wait for higher authority? Do you get an apology and recompense for a mistake, or is it covered up? Are deliveries punctual and complete, appointments kept, calls returned and letters answered promptly? Are bills correct and itemised, or frequently wrong?

(d) *Visible structure* Is status easily seen from such things as buildings and office layout, furnishings and fittings, reserved car parking, size and make of company car, secretarial staff, or the way people refer to one another?

From these clues it is easy to build up a picture of an organisation as being formal or informal, caring or uncaring, a status conscious hierarchy or a team working organisation.

Activity 6 [30 minutes]

Using the factors mentioned above, rate your college on a scale of 1 (low) to 5 (high) for each item. For example, reserved parking for all directors and managers would rate 5 for status conscious hierarchy; leaving customers waiting to be served would rate 1 for attitude to customers.

Organisational climate is very much more difficult to perceive than culture is.

3.2   Climate

Climate is concerned with people's attitudes to the organisation. It is really only possible for it to be understood by an insider. It is about how people feel. Examples of what affects corporate climate include the following.

(a) Do people feel that they have control over their work situation? For example, a London commodities broker assigns staff to jobs as required each day; they do not have individual desks or work places and there is no continuity of work or contact with clients or colleagues.

(b) Do people feel that they are treated like valued human beings, or just as impersonal bits of a machine? For example, after eight years service and two promotions in the last three years a credit manager was handed his redundancy notice and pay without warning and told to leave the premises immediately.

(c) What degree of freedom is given to subordinates to show initiative? For example, the purchasing department of a large construction company had strict rules about getting tenders and placing orders. When a young buyer bought a lot of fencing at knock-down prices from a bankrupt sale he was dismissed, even though the fencing was ideal for use on a current contract.

(d) Are subordinates free to talk to senior managers? For example, the managing director of a clothing manufacturer claimed that his door was always open to any member of staff. His secretary ensured that no-one below the rank of department manager ever got through it.

(e) Does the firm have a training and development policy for all its staff? Many firms do not train people because managers think that staff will leave for better jobs. For example, an aerospace firm used to provide training and education for engineers up to degree level, but refused any training or assistance with education for commercial staff.

(f) What is regarded as acceptable behaviour and what is rewarded? Is promotion dependent on 'fitting in' or length of service regardless of ability? Is success for a sales person regarded as the highest possible level of sales regardless of the methods used to make them? For example, when a brilliant young executive was considered for promotion after one year, her department head opposed it on the grounds that she was too young and had too little service. Insurance companies have had to pay millions of pounds in compensation to customers who were wrongly persuaded to switch to personal pensions by commission hungry staff.

You may feel that these examples are unusual or extreme, but they are neither. All too many firms have a corporate climate that leads to:

(a) people being unable to trust management or colleagues;

(b) poor standards of staff behaviour; and

(c) an absence of principles.

For discussion

Why is the corporate climate important for the success of the firm?

Chapter roundup

- Organisational culture is the unique character of an organisation that is made up of shared beliefs and attitudes, patterns of behaviour and other characteristics.

- Organisational climate is the way that the members of the organisation perceive its structure, rules, beliefs and behaviour.

- National mores are important influences on the culture of organisations.

- National differences can be measured using the indicators of individualism versus collectivism, power distance, uncertainty avoidance and masculinity versus femininity. These factors affect the structure of organisations and management and worker behaviour.

- In collectivist societies the successful organisation is one that replaces the natural ingroup.

- Countries with a large power distance tend to produce autocratic management as this is expected by managers and workers.

- Strong uncertainty avoidance gives a preference for formal structures and many rules and regulations.

- Changes in the pattern of employment in the UK have both altered the views of people and responded to changed ideas of what constitutes male and female roles.

- The culture of an organisation is affected by its environment, its nature and purpose and its history and stage of development.

- Climate may be very different from perceived culture. It depends on how the members see the organisation's attitude and behaviour towards them. It can be examined in terms of how people are recognised and rewarded, what control they have over their work and their freedom to use initiative.

Quick Quiz

1 Define organisational culture.

2 Why are national mores relevant to organisational culture?

3 What feature would you expect to find in organisations in a country with large power distance?

4 What features would you expect to find in organisations in a country with strong uncertainty avoidance?

5 Why might a firm from the US experience problems if it sent American managers to run a subsidiary in Pakistan?

6 List three ways in which changes in the environment may affect the culture of an organisation.

7 Would you expect British Aerospace to have the same basic culture as British Airways?

8 List three factors which may affect the culture of a firm over its life span.

9 List three areas where you could look for visible signs of an organisation's culture.

10 What is organisational climate?

11 List three areas which are likely to be important for organisational climate.

Answers to Quick Quiz

1 Organisational culture is the unique character of an organisation made up of shared beliefs and attitudes, patterns of behaviour and other characteristics.

2 National mores affect attitudes, beliefs and behaviour patterns which influence behaviour in organisations.

3 Autocratic leadership.

4 Formal structures and many rules.

5 The managers would expect to lead on the basis that people are motivated by self interest. They would expect staff to contribute to decision making and take initiatives. (Medium power distance and strong individualism). Employees would expect to act as a group, and be looked after by the firm as a group. They would expect to be given orders. (High power distance and strong collectivism)

6 You might have listed: (a) changes in government policy; (b) the law; (c) EU regulations; (d) deregulation and competition; (e) social attitudes; and (f) employee expectations.

7 No, because manufacturing and service industries have different priorities and outlooks.

8 You could have listed any three of the following: (a) the influence of the founders; (b) growth in size and number of departments; (c) employment of experts; (d) mergers and take-overs; and (e) international links.

9 You could have listed any three of: (a) its attitude to customers; (b) image; (c) ways of acting; and (d) visible structure.

10 How people in the organisation perceive its structure, attitudes and behaviour.

11 You could have listed any three of: (a) how people are treated and valued; (b) what determines promotion and rewards; (c) how much control people have over their working environment; (d) freedom to take initiatives; (e) ability to approach superiors; and (f) ethics and standards of behaviour.

Answers to Activities

1 You may find that answers vary with age, ethnic group and marital status, but are likely to tend towards strong individualism.

2 There is small power distance, shown by the unwillingness to accept large differences in income and wealth unrelated to perceived effort.

3 Sri Lanka.

4 Firms hope to gain:

(a) better motivation and employee involvement with the objectives of the firm;

(b) improved work attitudes, which bring benefits such as improved quality;

(c) less conflict;

(d) more team working and employee willingness to accept responsibility.

5 You should have listed: (a) less formality; (b) more flexibility; and (c) greater willingness to take initiatives.

6 Obviously a lot depends on your college, but you are certain to find such indicators as reserved car parking, differences in office accommodation, difficulty in contacting staff on the phone, glossy prospectuses (look out for photos with staff masquerading as students) and remoteness of senior staff.

Assignment 13 [3 hours]

This Assignment continues after Chapter 14. You can tackle it as an individual exercise with a written report, or as a group exercise with presentations and a discussion of findings.

Select an organisation and prepare a report covering the following.

(a) Its nature and purpose and an outline of its history.

(b) The visible signs of its culture.

(c) The national mores which appear to be important influences.

Chapter 14

MANAGEMENT STYLE AND ORGANISATIONAL CULTURE

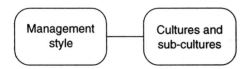

Introduction

Management style depends on the attitudes and beliefs of managers. The way managers see their workers and fellow managers affects the culture of an organisation. The way members of an organisation see their roles and their expectations of what the organisation should provide for them, also shape its culture.

Attitudes, beliefs and expectations at one level within an organisation may be different from those held at another. There may also be differences between units. Several sub-cultures can exist within the same organisation. For example, production staff tend to have different mores and priorities from sales teams; a unionised division of a firm will have a different behaviour pattern from a non-unionised one.

Your objectives

After completing this chapter you should:

(a) be able to outline different management styles;

(b) understand the relationship between management style and organisational culture;

(c) be able to describe organisational cultures;

(d) appreciate the role culture plays in the success of the organisation.

It can be agreed that consideration of management style is the most neglected area of a manager's work. It is not surprising then that few managers succeed in adjusting their style to suit the culture of the organisation and its employees where the culture conflicts with their own personal style.

1   MANAGEMENT STYLE

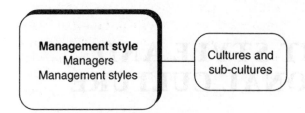

First we look at managers' behaviour

1.1   Managers

The culture of an organisation depends very much on the attitudes and priorities of its managers. The role of managers is to develop in their staff the attitudes and behaviour that will promote efficient performance. This requires that managers stimulate creativity and innovation and enthuse their workers.

Robert Blake and Jane Mouton analysed managerial behaviour in terms of two fundamental ingredients:

(a) concern for production; and

(b) concern for people.

Concern for production versus concern for people

Concern for production involves focusing on the output of goods, research results, invoices completed or service quality. It does not involve specific targets or the results achieved in themselves.

Concern for people focuses on issues such as personal commitment, relationships, workers' self respect and equitable payment.

A manager may show high concern for production and low concern for people, or the opposite, or any combination in between.

The managerial grid

A manager's approach to management can be shown on Blake and Mouton's 'managerial grid'. The ideal manager scores highly on both concern for people and production described as 'Production from integration of task and human requirements.'

The managerial grid can be used to categorise managers into the following.

(a) *Laissez faire* – a manager who shows very low concern for production combined with low concern for people, and who does just enough to stay in the job. This could be someone waiting to retire or who has been passed over for promotion. This manager has abdicated responsibility: staff are left to get on with their work with minimal supervision and direction and therefore tend to be lazy and apathetic.

(b) *Country club* – a manager who scores very low on concern for production but very high on concern for people. These managers want to be liked. They are busy being friendly and trying not to upset people; they are therefore likely to ignore even very good new ideas that might cause trouble. People are encouraged and supported and their mistakes are overlooked. People try to avoid criticisms of each other and production problems are glossed over. This approach can flourish in monopolies and where a unit is protected from competition, perhaps by cost-plus pricing. The working climate may be very pleasant, but the culture is inherently flawed.

(c) *Task centred* – a manager who focuses overwhelmingly on production, expects schedules and targets to be met and expects people to do exactly as they are told. Individual needs are ignored and disagreement is not tolerated. Anything that goes wrong is assumed to be someone's mistake – the culprit must be found and blame placed squarely on them. This approach can achieve high levels of output, at least in the short term. However, the human cost of this approach is high. Subordinates do no more than is asked of them and are indifferent and apathetic. Their creativity is directed towards beating the system. Resentment simmers under the surface and breaks out in union/management confrontations. Both culture and climate are unsatisfactory and unrewarding.

(d) *Dampened pendulum* – a management style which aims for a happy medium. Management pushes hard enough to get acceptable production but yields enough to get acceptable morale. Managers stick to rules and procedures. Going by the book avoids criticism. The approach to problems is to aim at balance and acceptability rather than pursuing appropriate solutions. This style may avoid conflict and ensure survival. It is often a feature of service organisations where it is difficult to measure output.

(e) *Integrator* – a manager who attains high production by getting commitment from the staff. The integrator is a team manager who seeks to integrate people around production. The best solutions to problems are pursued. The goal is the highest attainable level of production, and everyone contributes to this goal. People satisfy their own needs through their accomplishments and from working with others. The manager assumes that workers who know what the stakes are for them will not need direction and control. Staff are treated as capable of planning and controlling their work. Problems are confronted directly and openly and are not treated as personal disputes. Creativity is encouraged. The result is a culture open to ideas which encourages innovation and initiative.

Blake and Mouton believe that managers can learn to be integrators and that both managers and staff should seek that ideal. A manager whose subordinates expect task or country club management should lead them towards the best style.

Activity 1 [10 minutes]

In which of the above categories would you place:

(a) the management of your college;

(b) the management of your department or faculty;

(c) the management of your course?

We can now look at management style in a wider sense.

1.2 Management styles

Management styles can be divided into three broad categories, which can be related to the manager types identified by Blake and Mouton and to national influences on organisational culture.

The styles are as follows.

(a) *Authoritarian*. The leader's word is law. There is little or no discussion or consultation. Decisions are taken and orders are given by the leader, who expects instant obedience. This approach is often successful in sole proprietor firms during an aggressive expansion phase, but frequently fails when the leader is unable to delegate work to specialists to cope with growth. It tends to create an indifferent and resentful workforce with low productivity and poor quality.

The culture and climate are impoverished, innovation and creativity are stifled and there is a climate of fear. The leadership hierarchy is supported by 'yes' men.

(b) *Paternalistic*. This is typical of firms where the founding family still plays a prominent part. It is also the style of Japanese corporations. Management guides the workers by giving advice rather than orders. Workers know that they will be looked after. Workers can be highly motivated and productive as they know that they will share in the results and their loyalty will be repaid. The culture is strongly conformist. Group cohesion ensures that people conform and accept the norms of the group.

(c) *Democratic*. Management retains authority but shares decision making with subordinates. Decisions are taken after discussion and consultation so that subordinates feel involved and committed. There is effective delegation which creates high levels of motivation. The culture is open and participative. Innovation and creativity are encouraged. Individuality is accepted.

For discussion

A recent report on graduate employment stated that a high proportion of newly employed graduates felt that they were not stretched in their jobs and that they were not given the opportunity to make a contribution commensurate with their education and abilities.

To what extent do you think that management style is responsible for this situation? How could it be improved?

Organisation structure is influenced by the nature of management. Authoritarian managements tend towards bureaucratic structures which reinforce the culture of the organisation. Sticking to the rules and procedures and carrying out the allotted task avoids criticism and keeps authoritarian task-centred managements happy. Democratic integrator type managements tend to encourage team working and initiative, which flourish in flat and matrix organisations.

Activity 2   [10 minutes]

Think of three organisations which you know quite well. Include a business, a voluntary organisation such as a club, and another (which could be a quango such as your college). What is the management style of the organisation? Does it relate to the nature and purpose of the organisation?

Theory X and Theory Y

To some extent management style depends on managers' opinions of workers. Douglas McGregor (1906–1964) explored how managers' views can affect their management style by presenting two polarised opinions of people, as follows.

(a) *Theory X* managers assume that most people are lazy, dislike work, are immature and incapable of taking responsibility. They believe that staff need direction and a mixture of carrot and stick to make them perform. Such managers place emphasis on productivity and rewards for performance, while creating controls and rules to ensure that people cannot avoid work.

(b) *Theory Y* managers assume that people have a psychological need to work, want achievement at work, and welcome responsibility. Such managers assume that people seek satisfaction and fulfilment at work. They will exercise self-direction and self-control in the achievement of organisational objectives.

Studies of the effect of implementing Theory X and Y style management have shown that either can be successful or unsuccessful. It is the circumstance in which it is applied that determines its success or failure, not the intrinsic nature of the theory. For example, trying to implement a Theory X based authoritarian management style in a democratic organisation would be likely to fail, because the culture of the organisation would not accept it.

Activity 3 [5 minutes]

You are a manager responsible for the work of three different departments. Would you be able to adopt a management style based on Theory Y?

We have looked at different management styles; now we identify organisational cultures.

2 CULTURES AND SUB-CULTURES

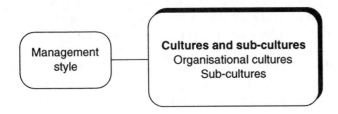

Culture was introduced in Chapter 13 and we looked at Handy's work on organisational structure in Chapter 4. Here we look at how culture relates to management style.

2.1 Organisational cultures

Charles Handy developed the concept of cultures to analyse culture in terms of the way it shapes the behaviour of people working in it. Handy identified four cultural types, as follows.

(a) The *power culture* is usually found in small companies with owner control and in new organisations. There is little formal structure. Key people make decisions. Employees work on the basis of precedents and their own initiative.

(b) The *role culture* is found in bureaucracies with formal, rigid structures and comprehensive rule books. Position in the hierarchy determines decision making ability and initiative is not encouraged. The organisation structure is one of rigid departmentation. Following rules and procedures creates a secure, stable culture.

(c) The *task culture* is a team environment where there is no clear leader. The team is committed to the task. There is a lot of scope for individual input and influence. People are expected to be flexible. It is found particularly in matrix organisations. It is appropriate where flexible response to market changes is important.

(d) The *person culture* is often found in colleges and universities. People try to satisfy their personal ambitions. They use their work as a way to build up personal achievements and successes as a step on the way to promotion or the next job. Lecturers write research articles and books for this purpose. This culture encourages hard work, but the individual's aims may not be the same as the organisation's objectives.

Activity 4 [10 minutes]

Where would each of the three organisations you considered in Activity 2 fit in Handy's types?

As described in Chapter 13, there can be a diversity of cultures in an organisation.

2.2 Sub-cultures

The culture of an organisation is important. It creates a structure for socialising members and sets out guidelines for personal behaviour and relationships. It provides a common core of beliefs and values and legitimises criteria for success and failure.

So long as everyone accepts the broad values of an organisation it can function without major conflict. People have to be in tune with the organisation's objectives. The official view is usually set out in a mission statement, which is written in wide, generally acceptable terms so that everyone in the organisation can identify with it. An organisation's code of conduct must attract the support of its members. For example, the Co-Op Bank has an ethical code which applies to its staff and customers: it includes a ban on doing business with repressive regimes and tobacco firms. Workers in the British American Tobacco Company (BAT) clearly take a different view.

The official culture of an organisation depends on the preferences of its top management. The structure is designed to reinforce the culture. A management which believes in Theory X and has strong uncertainty avoidance and large power distance as characteristics will be likely to establish a tall hierarchy with narrow spans of control and clear rules and procedures. This bureaucratic culture may not suit all parts of the organisation.

The marketing department and the research scientists are likely to develop their own sub-cultures which suit their mores and ways of working. Groups within a department may develop their own cultures. Managers may adopt a dampened pendulum style to avoid conflict, even though the overall style of the firm is task centred.

The relative strengths of influences on culture vary in different parts of the organisation. Sales and marketing are likely to be more affected by the external environment than are accounts and personnel.

The development of sub-cultures becomes dangerous when they reject the cultural values of the organisation as a whole. These unofficial cultures show up when groups act contrary to the beliefs of the rest of the organisation. For example, the Metropolitan Police emphasises sexual and racial equality but is frequently in the news because of sexual and racial harassment of police by police.

An organisation can increase its strength and effectiveness by encouraging the development of different cultures that are appropriate for different activities. Handy defined four types of activity and their appropriate cultures:

(a) routine activities and role culture for assembly production, accounting and pay administration;

(b) guidance activities and power culture for quality standards, budgeting and resource allocation;

(c) development activities and task culture for corporate planning, developing new markets and product innovation;

(d) environmental reaction and power culture for marketing and customer service.

These sub-cultures must work together for the common objective. It would be disastrous if they pursued their own goals or rejected the common beliefs and values of the organisation.

Chapter roundup

- Management styles can be classified using the Blake and Mouton managerial grid. Each creates a culture.
- Culture is influenced by whether the management style is authoritarian, paternalistic or democratic. These also affect organisation structure.
- Culture and climate also depend on managers' opinions of workers, for example on whether management adopts Theory X or Theory Y.
- Cultures can be classified as power, role, task or person.
- The overall culture of an organisation is important because it creates a common core of beliefs, values and behaviour.
- A variety of sub-cultures can exist within an organisation. This can be turned into a strength by matching the culture to the type of activity.

Quick quiz

1 What are the characteristics of a country club manager?
2 What are the characteristics of an integrator?
3 What are the likely effects on the workforce of an authoritarian management style?
4 What is a Theory X manager's view of people?
5 What is a Theory Y manager's view of people?
6 In what type of firm would you expect to find a power culture?
7 What sort of culture would you expect to find in matrix organisations?
8 What sort of culture is suitable for a marketing department?
9 What sort of culture is suitable for an accounts department?

Answers to Quick Quiz

1 Little concern for production and high concern for people, who are encouraged and supported.
2 High concern for both production and people.
3 Indifference, poor motivation and low productivity.
4 They are lazy, immature, incapable of taking responsibility and dislike work.
5 People want to work, achieve and accept responsibility.
6 A sole trader or a newly founded firm with a strong founder.
7 Task.
8 Power.
9 Role.

Answers to Activities

1 Your answer will depend on your college. For example, you may have a task-centred top management, dampened pendulum faculty and laissez faire course leader.
2 Again it depends on the organisations, but clubs can be authoritarian or democratic just like a business, charity or any other organisation

3 No. You would have to adapt your management style to the people in the departments. Some are likely to be Theory X workers.

4 A small business is likely to have a power culture, a large one may have a task culture, a quango may have a role culture, a college a person culture and a voluntary organisation may have any of them – people often seek personal fulfilment through charity work.

Assignment 14 [2.5 hours]

This assignment continues the work you began in Assignment 13.

Add to your analysis of the culture of the organisation by considering its management style and whether all parts of the organisation have the same style. You should consider the following questions.

(a) Does the organisation, or its parts, have an appropriate style for its activities?

(b) Does the culture of the organisation contribute to or inhibit its effectiveness?

(c) Based on the visible signs of the culture, would you have expected the organisation to have the type of management style and culture you have found?

Provide some evidence to support each of your findings.

Now complete your report or presentation for submission.

Chapter 15

GROUPS, TEAMS AND COMMUNICATION

Introduction

Organisations are made up of individuals who form groups. Groups may be official or unofficial. They have their own culture. Individuals who join a group may accept this culture or conceal their disaffection. When a group develops into a team it becomes an effective part of the organisation. The composition of the team is important: a football team cannot have two goalkeepers; a work team cannot function with two leaders. If you have to join a group and your abilities unbalance it, the group may never become an effective team.

Groups have their own behaviour patterns and ways of communicating. These reinforce both the exclusivity of the group and loyalty to it. Sherlock Holmes could tell a person's occupation from a glance at their physical appearance, dress and other belongings. Today's smaller social and work distinctions make it more difficult to pigeon hole people, but there are still clues to be seen: bank and building society staff wear uniforms; scarves and lapel badges distinguish Millwall supporters or members of a Rotary Club; a laptop computer case with a pinstripe suit is a fairly good pointer to an accountant.

Your objectives

After completing this chapter you should:

(a) be able to describe the formation of formal and informal groups;

(b) be able to describe the process by which a group becomes a team;

(c) appreciate the importance of different roles in teams;

(d) appreciate the importance of group and team culture;

(e) understand what makes for effective and ineffective work groups;

(f) understand the dynamics of group communication;

(g) appreciate the difficulty and importance of changing organisation and group culture.

First we look at what is meant by groups and teams.

187

NOTES

1 GROUPS AND TEAMS

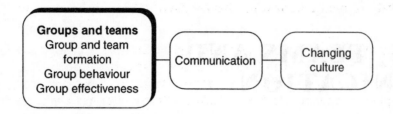

We all belong to groups. They can be social, casual, formal or informal. Social groups include families, friends, clubs, voluntary organisations, religious societies and some work-related groupings of people, such as a regular lunch-time card school. Some groups are work groups, which may be formally established as part of the organisation or informally created by those working together or sharing an interest. Formal groups include committees.

Definitions

Group: a collection of individuals with a common interest and who share a common identity. A group has a leader, a set of social norms and a reason for its existence. It may be informal or formally established and its existence may be permanent or temporary.

Team: a formal group created for a purpose. A team has a leader, an aim and a distinctive culture. It may be formed, for example, to consider the provision of hot drinks in vending machines, to determine corporate strategy, or to win the World Cup.

Activity 1   [10 minutes]

Make a list of all the groups you belong to and mark by each one whether it is formal or informal

Groups may come together spontaneously or be formally established. However, they do not become teams until they have gone through the process of team formation.

1.1 Group and team formation

Organisations create formal groups (also referred to as official groups) automatically as departments and specialisms develop. Groups are also created to perform such tasks as exchanging ideas, sharing information, co-ordinating work and performing tasks that require the collective use of skills. The Board of Directors is a formal group; so are the Health and Safety Committee and the night shift operatives in machine shop four.

Informal (or unofficial) groups form at work because of:

(a) people's needs to socialise;

(b) a need for self-help (for example, a baby sitting circle)

(c) a need for protection and collective action (for example, a union).

The aims of an informal group and the organisation may be different. It is important that organisations recognise the existence of informal groups and try to use them constructively, rather than making what are likely to be futile attempts to suppress them.

A group of people can be appointed to be a team, but a group has to go through the process of becoming a team before it can function as one. The composition of the group will affect its ability to become effective. Simply setting up a team does not make a group of people into a team, nor does it make it effective. Teams have to be formed with care.

Team roles

The most effective groups tend to be no more than a dozen people with members performing each of the following roles.

(a) *Co-ordinator or Chair.* The chair need not be the cleverest, most experienced or best qualified member of the team, but must be someone who works well through other people and is capable of keeping the group focused on its task.

(b) *Shaper.* A member who is full of passion for achieving the objective. The shaper drives the others and may be impatient and domineering.

(c) *Innovator.* An imaginative member who produces original ideas.

(d) *Monitor/evaluator.* An analytical thinker who sees flaws in arguments and perceives practical problems. The monitor/evaluator is objective and often works alone.

(e) *Resource investigator.* A member who has contacts outside the group and who brings in ideas and resources.

(f) *Company worker.* An administrator who can put ideas into practice.

(g) *Team worker.* A supportive member of the group who encourages the others.

(h) *Finisher.* The member who takes on the important but unpopular role of pushing the group to meet deadlines. The finisher is also likely to be the one who checks details and ensures nothing is overlooked.

Activity 2   [20 minutes]

Take some of the groups you identified in Activity 1 and try to name individuals who take on each of the roles described above.

How many of these roles can you identify in your seminar group?

Individuals all have different personalities, traits and preferences. A manager will tend to take on the same preferred role every time. It would be very difficult for someone to act as a finisher if their natural choice was the role of shaper.

R M Belbin, who produced these roles from research reported in 1981, said that the ideal team would consist of one chair or one shaper, one innovator, one monitor/evaluator and one or more of each of the others. A team with two shapers or two innovators would be hampered by conflicts and could be ineffective.

Managers have to select teams from the people they have, and may not be able to create an ideal Belbin team. They should try to analyse individual strengths, especially when replacing members who leave an effective team. The road to disaster is when managers pick people in their own image and end up with an unbalanced group.

Stages in forming a team

Once a group has formed it has to go through certain stages before it becomes an effective team.

(a) *Forming* – where everyone waits for a lead and finds out about the task, rules and other members.

(b) *Storming* – where someone takes the lead, discussion begins, conflicting ideas and opinions are put forward and there is resistance to doing the task.

(c) *Norming* – when conflict is resolved, co-operation begins, roles are established and group norms of behaviour are established.

(d) *Performing* – when teamwork is achieved, roles are accepted, solutions are discussed and agreed, and activities focus on achieving the goals.

Activity 3 [10 minutes]

When your tutorial group was first given a task to complete, how long did it spend on each of stages described above?

Next we look at group behaviour.

1.2 Group behaviour

Groups establish norms or acceptable standards of behaviour. The things which the group has in common and which characterise it are group norms. All members of the group are expected to conform to these. Groups put pressure on members to conform, and those who wish to belong will do so. Failure to conform can lead to conflict with the rest of the group. In extreme cases an individual can be excluded from all desirable groups and forced to seek another job.

Rituals

Groups develop their own rituals, such as meeting in a certain place for coffee breaks, going to the same pub for lunch or meeting after work on Fridays. Individuals may tend to seek acceptance and pretend to conform to such norms as working late, while regularly making excuses to go on time. Similarly, a member may conceal non-adherence to norms by avoiding some aspects of the social activities of the group – having to catch a particular train or getting a lift can be used to avoid after-work drinking sessions.

Where bonus payments are related to group performance there is much stronger pressure on members to conform. Unauthorised breaks and failure to meet targets that affect the performance of the group as a whole are likely to attract strong pressure to conform.

EXAMPLE: GROUP RITUALS IN THE WORKPLACE

An ice cream factory had several lines for filling different flavours of ice cream into tubs, cartons, choc ices and ice lollies. Each filling line had a team, with a leader who allocated jobs – usually in strict rotation so as to avoid boredom. The elite team worked on choc ices. The lowest level in the pecking order was the team responsible for stacking incoming supplies of cartons and loading delivery trucks.

Each team had its special table in the canteen. The ice lolly team brought in cakes they made and shared them. The stackers and loaders took their breaks elsewhere. The choc ice team took their break at a different time from everyone else. Entry to that group was by invitation and seniority. Managers had learned that it was not a good idea to try to allocate new members to choc ices: there would be an astonishing rise in the number of choc ices incorrectly wrapped or partly coated. Teams organised their own informal breaks on a rota basis. Anyone overstaying would lose the next break as the team leader would not relieve them.

The factory paid bonuses to teams that exceeded monthly targets for filling cartons and tubs. There were strict quality controls which included a variation of not more than ½% either side of the declared weight. Quality checks showing unacceptable variations in fill weight led to the conveyor being slowed down and consequent loss of bonuses. Individuals who persistently underfilled in an attempt to earn bonuses were banished to the menial jobs of fetching boxes of empty cartons and removing filled tubs to the cold store. These people would also miss out on rounds of drinks in the Friday pub session.

Activity 4   [10 minutes]

With reference to any group you have been with recently, think of examples of people being pressured to conform to group norms. How was that pressure applied?

Group cohesiveness

Group cohesiveness develops over time as the group moves through the stages to performing. It refers to the ability of a group to stick together. A very cohesive group shows strong loyalty among the members, who stick strongly to the norms of behaviour. A strongly cohesive group can become exclusive, with entry being virtually impossible. Individuals find it much easier to join less cohesive groups and groups in the earlier stages of formation.

Factors which affect the development of group cohesiveness are:

(a) similarity of work;

(b) physical proximity in the work place;

(c) the work flow system and whether or not it gives continuing contact;

(d) the structure of tasks – whether individualised or group;

(e) group size – smaller groups are more cohesive;

(f) threats from outside – where a group sees other groups as the enemy;

(g) prospects of rewards;

(h) leadership style of the manager;

(i) common social factors, such as race, social status and cultural origins.

Activity 5 [10 minutes]

How important are the above factors in the groups to which you belong?

Next we look at the factors that affect the effectiveness of groups, and the features of effective and ineffective groups.

1.3 Group effectiveness

The personalities of group members and the traits they bring to the group play an important part in deciding its effectiveness. As we have seen, two shapers or two innovators would lead to confusion. Personal goals also affect effectiveness. It is easy for groups, especially informal ones, to decide that a low level of productivity is the norm. Groups can be motivated to improve their performance. This requires:

(a) a clearly defined task;

(b) effective leadership;

(c) small group size;

(d) skills and abilities matched to the task;

(e) proximity at work, for example an open plan office;

(f) rewards that are regarded as fair by the group.

Factors for identifying effective work groups

A number of factors are involved in identifying effective and ineffective work groups. Some are quantifiable and others are qualitative.

Effective work group	*Ineffective work group*
Quantifiable factors	
(a) Low rate of labour turnover	(a) High rate of labour turnover
(b) Low accident rate	(b) High accident rate
(c) Low absenteeism	(c) High absenteeism
(d) High output and productivity	(d) Low output and productivity
(e) Good quality of output	(e) Poor quality of output
(f) Individual targets are achieved	(f) Individual targets are not achieved
(g) There are few stoppages and interruptions to work	(g) Time is lost owing to disagreements between supervisor and subordinates
Qualitative factors	
(a) There is a high commitment to the achievement of targets and organisational goals	(a) There is no understanding of organisational goals or the role of the group
(b) There is a clear understanding of the group's work	(b) There is a low commitment to targets
(c) There is a clear understanding of the role of each person within the group	(c) There is confusion and uncertainty about the role of each person within the group
(d) There is a free and open communication between members of the group and trust between members	(d) There is mistrust between group members and suspicion of the group's leader
(e) There is idea sharing	(e) There is little idea sharing
(f) The group is good at generating new ideas	(f) The group does not generate any good new ideas

(g) Group members try to help each other out by offering constructive criticisms and suggestions

(h) There is group problem solving which gets to the root causes of the work problem

(i) There is an active interest in work decisions

(j) Group members seek a united consensus of opinion

(k) The members of the group want to develop their abilities in their work

(l) The group is sufficiently motivated to be able to carry on working in the absence of its leader

(g) Group members make negative and hostile criticisms of each other's work

(h) Work problems are dealt with superficially, with attention paid to the symptoms but not the cause

(i) Decisions about work are accepted passively

(j) Group members hold strongly opposed views

(k) Group members find work boring and do it reluctantly

(l) The group needs its leader there to get work done

For discussion

Select a group you are involved in, for example a seminar or tutorial group, and analyse its effectiveness in terms of the features it shows from the above list. How valid are these factors in deciding whether or not a group is effective?

Relationships with other groups

A group's effectiveness is also affected by its relationships with other groups. Contact with other groups can bring power struggles, personal conflict between leaders, territorial disputes and distrust of motives. Relations in the work place often seem to parallel gang warfare in Los Angeles, where each group will go to any lengths to protect its turf.

Effectiveness can be improved and constructive competition encouraged by:

(a) rewarding groups on the basis of their contribution to the organisation as a whole and their efforts to collaborate, rather than rewarding only individual group performance;

(b) encouraging staff to move across group boundaries so that understanding and co-operation are improved;

(c) avoiding putting groups into situations where one must emerge a winner and another a loser;

(d) encouraging communication between groups through committees, discussion groups, joint planning meetings and so on.

Next we look at the important topic of group communication.

2   COMMUNICATION

We have seen how individuals come together to form groups, and how groups go through the stages of becoming teams. The formal groups in an organisation – departments, levels of management and project teams – have their official, formal channels of communication and specific ways of communicating. Informal groups develop their own channels and language.

EXAMPLE: INFORMAL GROUPS

A large international banking group has an unknown number of informal groups who maintain contact through e-mail messages written in their individual 'languages'. Nicknames for people and places keep information from outsiders.

Organisations develop their special signals which ensure recognition by other members and, in some cases, by the general public. The 'old school tie' says 'I belong to the Old Academicians'. Even if the wearer has never returned to the school or taken part in any activities of the former pupils, the tie communicates membership of an exclusive group. Members of LIFFE (London International Financial Futures Exchange) wear their strikingly coloured jackets to show which firms they represent. There are less visible ways of communicating membership of groups and organisations: greetings and references to events and people all establish membership.

Communication in groups is important for the organisation. There must be effective communication within the group for it to function efficiently. Groups have to communicate with each other effectively to ensure that information travels through the organisation and that correct action is taken.

We look next at group communication, why it is efficient and what may cause it to break down.

2.1 Group communication

Do not assume that communication within groups is always effective or that the size of the group is the only factor that has an impact on the effectiveness of communications. Communication networks, as described in earlier chapters, show us the pattern of communications within the group, but it is the combination of the following that determines the outcome of internal communications:

(a) the make up of the group;

(b) the task it is intended to carry out;

(c) the size of the group;

(d) the communication network employed.

Activity 6 [15 minutes]

A group has formed to plan your college ball. Within the ten members of this group there are two very strong personalities with very different tastes in music.

Referring back to Belbin's work on group membership, identify which roles these two individuals will fulfil, and highlight any potential conflicts or barriers to effective decision making that might result. Note down also, any factors that you consider would act as noise, and which would thus impair communication.

We have seen that to work effectively in a group we need to have a balance of roles and thus of personalities. Too many chiefs and not enough Indians creates a top-heavy group that is effective at commencing the task but is unlikely to carry it through to a conclusion.

Imbalance of group structure is most clearly seen by looking at the patterns of communications. A network that is clearly seen within a group will change without prompting if any one member of the group is replaced by another who cannot fulfil the same role. For example, if there are two central 'kingpins' within a star configuration, it is no longer a star. The network becomes distorted and communications are disrupted.

The task a group is formed to undertake can determine the way the group is structured and the network it employs. For example, simple problems can be addressed best by a small group using the star configuration, whereas complex problems can be dealt with better by a slightly larger group using all channel communication. (Note that a complex problem does not necessarily need a proportionately larger group than a single one. In fact if a group increases in size there is a point beyond which communication no longer improves; it may even be impaired by the sheer size of the group, as the potential for noise and redundancy increases.)

The most common form of noise affecting the effectiveness of communication within groups is the lack of a basic skill: the ability to listen. Whether the communication is carried out verbally, in written form or visually, it is very common for individuals to skim the information and start preparing a response whilst they are still receiving it. This is not conducive to effective communication. If you take nothing more from this text, you should understand that the greatest improvement you can make to your communication skills is to concentrate on listening!

Activity 7   **[30 minutes]**

Next time you are sitting with your colleagues in the college canteen, make a conscious effort to listen to all that is being said without joining in the conversation. Analyse what is said and ask yourself the following questions.

(a) Does what is being said match the body language being used?

(b) What information are you gaining from what is being left unsaid?

An area of group dynamics that improves the effectiveness of communications is the sense of belonging. The need to belong is innate to all of us, to some degree. A sense of belonging engenders feelings of loyalty which makes us more likely to share information within the group, as opposed to outside it. Couple this with the sense of a common goal, and you have a powerful motivating force for effective communication.

The organisation that wants to change must do more than alter its structure and create effective teams: it must change its culture

3   CHANGING CULTURE

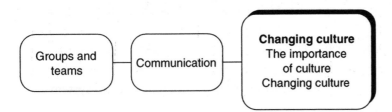

3.1   The importance of culture

Much of this book has been about changing organisations. Environment, workers, technology and management thinking all create pressure for change. Management, workers, structure and culture all resist change.

The competitive environment has changed, and if firms do not alter their culture and create appropriate flexible structures they will go out of business. Technology has created new markets, new ways of doing business and new methods of organisation. Firms that do not respond to these opportunities will fail.

We have seen the factors which create the need for change. They can be summarised as:

(a) increasing competition in a global market;

(b) changes in the environment

   (i) deregulation and less government intervention;

   (ii) demographic and social change and increasing expectations of consumers and workers;

(c) technological change, especially in IT, production methods and the speed of developing new products.

Change in any one of these could be enough to cause a firm to alter its structure and organisation. A company could face change in all of them at once. Unless it is flexible enough to cope with a turbulent environment, it will fail to seize opportunities or compete successfully.

There are many examples of successful companies failing to realise the opportunities brought by change. Some have responded to change by restructuring, but have failed because they did not change the embedded culture of the organisation or key groups within it.

Burns and Stalker showed how traditional Scottish firms failed to introduce electronics work. Groups (departments) had stable career structures and engaged in power struggles with other groups for resources to protect their interests. The formal system was bypassed by groups who went to the top for decisions. There was an official organisation and an unofficial parallel set of relationships between the chief executive and dozens of subordinates. The result was to overload the boss and create paralysis in the organisation.

There are three responses to change when the organisation does not change itself:

(a) the *ambiguous figure system* described above;

(b) the *mechanistic jungle*, where the organisation responds by creating more bits of bureaucracy, such as liaison officers, or a contract department, which depend for their existence on the perpetuation of the problems;

(c) the *superpersonal system*, where committees are created which form new groups competing for loyalties with the traditional departments. Departments have the advantage that they control the career structure and hold the group norms as people with similar characteristics work together.

Activity 8 [15 minutes]

A college is a good example of a superpersonal system. The committee structure is supposed to co-ordinate the departments, but the committees actually have little or no control over them.

List the committees in your college and identify any that can take resource decisions.

Essentially an organisation consists of three interlocking relationship systems:

(a) the formal authority system;

(b) the career system of individuals who compete for advancement and who evaluate everything in terms of their prospects; and

(c) the political system of departments and groups which compete for power.

None of these welcome radical change, which upsets their calculations and takes away their advantages.

Trying to change the structure may avoid the ineffective responses discussed above. The firm may create matrix-style project teams and enter into co-operative alliances with suppliers and customers. It may be successful for a time, but unless its culture changes there will be no genuinely new approach that generates lasting success.

Culture is partly influenced by the environment. The more insulated from environmental change a group is, the less impact there will be on the group culture. Culture develops out of the history and internal environment of the organisation. Unless there is some dramatic change, the culture of many groups will change only slowly, if at all.

Different aspects of culture affect the possibility of changing it.

(a) *Level*: this may be:

    (i) basic assumptions, which are bound up with national culture;

    (ii) historically embedded attitudes and values of the organisation; or

    (iii) the manifestations of corporate culture.

(b) The *political element*, where power groups, such as a management level or a department, try to protect the organisation's embedded culture because it is bound up with their power and influence.

(c) The existence of *sub-cultures*, which causes different reactions to change from different groups within the overall culture.

EXAMPLE: THE BBC

The BBC, in 1996, was reorganised from a collection of departments dealing with the different TV and radio programmes into two departments: one for production and one for delivery of programmes. This was a major change, made by John Birt, the Director General, in an attempt to alter radically the bureaucratic culture of the organisation. It was met by a predictable outcry as each power group rallied its friends in the media to put out stories about how the change would end the ethos of the BBC as a public service and destroy individual parts such as the World Service. Change was inevitable given the growing competition from commercial TV and radio, the soon to open terrestrial Channel Five and restrictions on financing through the licence fee. Whether the reorganisation will change the culture of the BBC remains to be seen.

Next we look at changing culture.

3.2 Changing culture

Remember that the culture of an organisation is a vital element in its past success. It is important to all the members. Changing it is a dangerous undertaking, however necessary it may be. There are basically two approaches to change:

(a) incremental, and

(b) earthquake (or transformational).

Changing culture means changing values and beliefs. People who feel threatened by the process are likely to turn to the old hierarchical structure for protection. They try to reinforce the old ways. This is always a potential reaction to the earthquake approach. The sudden change is the result of a new chief executive, a merger or a crisis. Any of these may be the result of a period of decline. The organisation which aspires to be successful should try to anticipate the need for change.

Incremental change gives time for each step to be appraised before the next is taken. The management can go through the process of unfreezing attitudes, experimenting with new attitudes and refreezing desirable attitudes. This can be done in different groups at different times and at varying paces. For example, the firm could start with those departments, like marketing and sales, which react most with the environment. Changing attitudes to customers and quality of service depends on getting people to accept the new vision. Once their attitudes have unfrozen, behaviour can be changed. When acceptable new attitudes and behaviour are in place, refreezing keeps them there.

The steps in the process are as follows.

(a) Get people to face up to their unsatisfactory norms and question their embedded culture.

(b) Develop new, desirable attitudes and behaviour.

(c) Reinforce the new culture with rewards and opportunities.

Here are the steps in the process of changing corporate culture.

(a) Develop a mission statement, and discuss and refine it until it is generally agreed.

(b) Develop a succinct statement of core values.

(c) Develop detailed standards of behaviour consistent with the mission and core values.

(d) Communicate the mission, values and standards to everyone in the organisation and ensure that they are incorporated into induction and training programmes.

(e) Provide role models from top management down through the hierarchy.

(f) Reinforce the new culture through the reward and promotion systems, recruitment procedures and symbols such as the corporate image.

(g) Evaluate the extent of cultural change by monitoring changes in beliefs, attitudes and behaviour and by measuring results

It is important to emphasise the break with the past. Changing the name, corporate logo, uniform and even the location all contribute to the new start.

This process is not likely to be easy. The deeper the level of culture to be changed, the more difficult it will be. Basic assumptions are the most difficult to change. Behavioural aspects such as using customers' names and answering the phone before the fourth ring are the easiest. The more cultures and sub-cultures there are the longer the process will take, and the more difficult it is likely to be. Top down processes are likely to gain short-term acceptance but not change assumptions. A participative approach where people are involved in the process and contribute to it is likely to bring lasting change but is very time consuming.

For discussion

Assume that your college is told that from next session it will receive no government funding and will have to operate on a fully commercial basis. From your knowledge of its culture, how would you expect different departments and groups to react? How difficult would it be to change the culture of the college?

Chapter roundup

- A group is a collection of individuals with a common interest and who share a common identity.
- A team is a formal group created for a purpose.
- Effective teams require the right mix of people in the correct roles.
- The stages of forming a team are: forming, storming, norming and performing.
- Groups establish behavioural norms to which members are expected to conform
- Pressure is put on members to conform to group norms. Some may join in willingly and eagerly; some individuals may pretend to conform; others may end up excluded from all groups.
- Group cohesiveness develops over time as members accept group norms and develop mutual loyalties.
- Groups may be effective or ineffective. Their effectiveness can be analysed by reference to qualitative and quantitative factors.
- The efficiency of internal group communications depends on the size and composition of the group as well as the communication network.
- Noise affects the efficiency of group communication, in particular failure to listen.
- Changing an organisation must involve more than a change to its structure: the culture of the organisation and of the groups in it must be changed also.
- The organisation should implement a programme of cultural change. The deeper the level of culture and the more groups there are, the more difficult and time consuming the process will be.

Quick quiz

1. What is the difference between a group and a team?
2. Give three reasons why people form informal groups at work.
3. What are the essential roles in a team to make it effective?
4. What happens during the storming stage of team formation?
5. How would you know that a team was performing?
6. What are group norms?
7. List five factors affecting group cohesiveness.
8. List three quantitative measures that could be used to identify an effective work group.
9. Is the communication network the determinant of efficient communication within a group?
10. What is the greatest cause of noise in group communication?
11. What is a superpersonal system?
12. What are the three systems that coexist in an organisation?
13. What are the three stages of changing attitudes?
14. What is likely to be the best approach to changing culture?

Answers to Quick Quiz

1 A group is a collection of individuals who share certain norms. A team is a formal group formed for a purpose.

2 (a) To socialise, (b) for self help, (c) for protection and collective action,

3 One chair or one shaper, one innovator, one monitor/evaluator and one or more of each of resource investigator, company worker, team worker and finisher.

4 Despite resistance to doing the task, someone takes the lead, discussion begins and conflicting ideas and opinions are proposed.

5 Teamwork is achieved, roles are accepted, solutions are discussed and agreed and activities focus on achieving the goals.

6 The characteristics and acceptable standards of behaviour to which members are expected to conform.

7 You should have listed five of the following: (a) similarity of work, (b) physical proximity, (c) the work flow system, (d) the structure of tasks, (e) group size, (f) threats from outside, (g) prospects of rewards, (h) leadership style and (i) common social factors.

8 You should have listed three of the following: (a) low rates of labour turnover, (b) low rates of accidents, (c) low rates of absenteeism, (d) high output, (e) high productivity, (f) high quality, (g) targets are achieved, (h) few stoppages.

9 No; efficient communication depends on other factors also, for example size of the group and noise.

10 Failure to listen.

11 The creation of committees as a response to change when the organisation itself does not change.

12 (a) Formal authority, (b) career and (c) political.

13 (a) Unfreezing, (b) experimenting and (c) refreezing.

14 A participative one.

Answers to Activities

1 You might have listed many groups, for example: your tutorial group (formal), a hockey team (formal), your friends at the weekly disco (informal) and your regular coffee break crowd (informal).

2 You will be lucky if your seminar group contains each role. You may have a shaper, an innovator and a team worker. You do not want more than one of each of the first two.

3 You may have spent most time on forming and storming – it depends on how many of the group had done group work before. Some seminar groups never seem to get past forming and have to be reorganised.

4 You may be unfortunate enough to work where the norm is to stay late even if there is no real work to do. In this situation people who leave on time are regarded as slackers, so there is an unspoken threat of dismissal.

5 In work groups the two most important factors are often group size and the leadership style of the manager.

6 You are right if you said that both individuals are shapers. They are both dynamic and passionate about their own beliefs. Both wish to be the dominant force within the group. This could cause the group to split into factions, each vying with the other for the central role. The inward loyalty created toward the part of the group an individual feels a sense of belonging with may inhibit communication between the two parties, thus acting as noise, one of the most powerful barriers to communication.

7 If you found this Activity difficult because you could not resist the temptation to join in, then you have found an area of weakness that you should work on. You must

concentrate on listening and inwardly digesting information. If you do so, you will improve your listening skills, and you will find that this brings benefits to your personal development.

8 The only committee likely to have any resource allocating powers is the Academic Board, but only in the sense that it approves course development. Faculties and departments control financial, material and human resources. Resource allocation is the prerogative of the executive.

Assignment 15   No time limit

This assignment does not involve a formal written output, but is something that you can do all the time. We all live through each day in a series of groups; analyse the groups you see and take part in by considering the following.

(a) In social and informal groups try to establish who plays each role as chair, innovator and so on. Who has the ideas about where to go on Saturday night? How does the group communicate – does it have its own language and symbols?

(b) In work groups think about why the group was established; try to identify the stages of formation, the roles of members and the features which show whether or not the group is efficient. Practice listening.

(c) A good exercise in analysing groups is to observe the behaviour of political parties. They are formal groups. They tend to communicate in their own 'in' language and you will find that leading politicians are so busy speaking to their members that they fail to communicate to the general electorate. The parties have a problem common to all groups: there are too many would-be chairs, shapers and innovators.

ANSWERS TO ASSIGNMENTS

NOTES

Answer to Assignment 1

Your completed table should be as follows:

Comparison of business organisations

Features	Sole trader	Partnership	Private company	Public company	Mutual society
Creation	Informal	Informal or deed	Register	Register	Register
Legal status	Personal	Personal	Separate	Separate	Separate
Liability	Unlimited	Unlimited (except Ltd partner)	Limited	Limited	Limited
Publicity Audit Reporting of results	No	No	Yes	Yes	Yes
	No	No	Yes	Yes	Yes
Ownership	Self	Partners	Shareholders	Shareholders	Members
Control	Self	Partners	Shareholders	Shareholders	Members
Management	Self	Partners	Board	Board	Board
Transfer of membership	Sale	None	Sell shares	Sell shares	No
Duration	Temporary	Temporary	Permanent	Permanent	Permanent
Ownership of assets	Self	Partners	Ordinary shareholders	Ordinary shareholders	Members

Answer to Assignment 2

As an example of the kind of things you should have covered, a professional body is a company limited by guarantee, owned by its members, managed by a council and run day-to-day by the chief executive and the staff. It is established to provide services to members, organised in regional branches with branch committees, financed by subscriptions. Policy is decided by the AGM at which the council is elected. It provides courses and examinations through its Education Department.

Answer to Assignment 3

An example is Jones Brothers Department Store

It is organised in sales departments and support departments such as accounts and warehouse.

1. The mission is to be the best department store in town providing high quality goods and services to our customers.
2. Products are household goods and furniture, clothes, gardening goods, electrical and kitchen goods, hairdressing and haberdashery.
3. The market is the area around the town.
4. Purchase from original manufacturers and contract making of clothing.
5. The retail park ten miles away.

Answer to Assignment 4

Jones Brothers

(a) Objectives: to make a return on capital of 20% before tax and to increase turnover by 5%.

(b) Structure as above, managed by the Board and the Managing Director to whom the Department Heads and Buyers report.

(c) Culture is paternalistic as it is a family firm; there is an emphasis on customer service and a certain resistance to change.

(d) The structure is traditional as expected from the culture.

(e) Span of control is narrow with a tall hierarchy through Department Heads, Section Buyers, First Hands down to floor staff.

(f) Yes as information passes quickly up and down the hierarchy. No in terms of lateral communication.

(g) Yes as it adjusts its stock and advertising, layout and marketing to the area.

The firm achieves its objectives helped by the way in which departments are empowered to manage their own sales mix.

Answer to Assignment 5

Jones Brothers would not benefit from cross-discipline teams in the context of bringing together sales, accounts and warehouse staff, but would benefit from more cross-department experience by sales staff so that there could be greater flexibility in staffing.

Answer to Assignment 6

Here is an example of the kind of things you could have included:

The morning routine at the school I attended involved the whole school trooping into the assembly hall and sitting on the floor. This was a somewhat degrading experience for those of us who were older. We then sat through the Headmaster's deep and meaningful lesson for the day, usually including the message that we were young adults and should behave as such. He towered over us from the stage, wearing his once pristine, but now decidedly tatty, academic robes.

The messages were all wrong. We should behave like adults, and yet we were sitting on the floor like six year olds, looking at the headmaster's nasal hair. Even his use of his robes emphasised the point that we were subordinate, not equals (and probably never would be).

Then something changed. The school gained a new headmaster. No longer were the sixth form expected to attend morning assembly. Instead they met in their (newly provided) common room for a 30 minute meeting with their year tutor. This was a chance to discuss issues of concern, current affairs and even, on occasion, sex, drugs and rock 'n' roll. We changed too. We began to feel that the school was 'ours', not just somewhere we went. We began to develop a conscience about the way things were done, telling off first years for dropping litter, and generally becoming more responsible.

It became evident that some ways of communicating with us were more effective than others; anything that was aimed at forcing compliance was met with resistance, approaches that sought our co-operation were received with interest and discussion.

This should give you a flavour of they differing ways in which rituals can have an effect. By making the pupils feel inferior the old headmaster caused a reaction that prevented the pupils from hearing his message properly. The change of ritual signalled a change of attitude towards the pupils, indicated that the culture was different and created a positive atmosphere in which communication could take place.

Answer to Assignment 7

Check your report against the following guidance:

The *Terms of reference* are given in the questions:

(a) identify communication problems;

(b) make recommendations for the future.

Your *Introduction* should not retell the story, but should outline the salient points: the size and nature of the organisation, the individuals, and the circumstances.

In the *Main body* of your report, you should highlight any problems, such as:

(a) the owner of Gibbs Motors listens to rumours and ignores his own experience

(b) there is an over reliance on verbal communication

(c) there is a reluctance on the part of the owner to enter into written communication with his supplier

(d) the owner of Gibbs Motors does not encourage feedback from suppliers or staff.

(You may also identify other problems.)

You may have decided that some of these problems are symptoms of a deeper problem. You should draw all this together into your *Conclusion*.

In your *Recommendations* you should have included the need to:

(a) identify appropriate media for the message;

(b) use written communications where records are needed;

(c) encourage and listen to feedback;

(d) ensure that the message actually reaches its intended recipient.

Your recommendations should be detailed and focused on the case. They *must* be backed up by reasoned argument.

Answer to Assignment 8

There are two ways to approach this problem. You can present the changes as a *fait accompli* or as a tentative suggestion. If you can create a feeling amongst the staff that they have some say in the decision you are more likely to minimise potential problems. Your first task is to decide what information you require. Will they even consider nights? How often would it be acceptable for them to rotate onto nights? Are there individuals with special circumstances?

It is possible that this move by management will create new jobs and signal greater job security for those already employed. If this is the case, your questionnaire could start with such positive news. For example:

'Due to increasing demand for our product we are now in a position to expand and create XX new jobs. In order to do this and rationalise our operations we are considering the possibility of increasing the present two-shift pattern to a three-shift pattern. We would appreciate the views of our staff as to if and how this could be introduced to the benefit of us all.'

Put yourself in the position of the employee whose working life is likely to be disrupted. Make a list of the positive and negative aspects to this change. For example:

Positive: Extra money for night work, several days off together after this shift.

Negative: Disruption to family and social life; single parents will find difficulty in finding over night child care.

When you have done this, try to phrase the questions in such a way as to highlight the positive and minimise the negative. For example:

'If you were to work a night shift as part of your working pattern, which of these options would you prefer:

(a) two night shifts followed by two days off (e.g. work Monday, Tuesday and have Wednesday, Thursday off. Back to work 7 am on Friday).

(b) five night shifts followed by four and one half days off (e.g. work Monday to Friday, off Saturday to Wednesday. Back to work 3 pm Wednesday).'

You could also add:

'If you have an alternative suggestion which still ensures that the hours per fortnight are correct, please explain below.'

The important points to remember when doing this assignment are:

(a) know what information you require;

(b) in this circumstance you will also be giving information, so ensure that it is accurate but worded in a positive way;

(c) either/or answers are less open to misinterpretation; use them wherever possible;

(d) engender a feeling of participation by requesting suggestions. Resentment and indignation will act as noise, and impair receipt of the information you are giving as well as affecting the answers you will receive.

Answer to Assignment 9

What information do you require?

You would first need to establish that the region in question is actually performing below targets by comparing the real and projected figures.

You would then need to decide if the targets are achievable.

The next information would be a breakdown across the region to find out if it is the whole region or an individual which is below target levels.

Based on this information you would then move in one of two directions: investigating reasons internally or externally to the organisation. The kinds of things you may want to know may be the following.

Externally

- Has there been an upsurge in unemployment in the region causing disposable income to be reduced and thus consumer spending?
- Has there been an increase in local competition?
- Has there been adverse local publicity?

Internally

- Has the individual or regional manager had problems outside work which have had an impact on performance (e.g. bereavement or illness)?
- Have systems changed within the organisation which reduce the time available for sales people to spend with the customer?

The answers to these questions can be gained from employees at all levels in the organisation. For example, the sales data will already be on file at the main office, local employees are the best people to ask about local developments.

It would be all too easy to rush around and discuss the situation with everyone and anyone, but your time would be better spent planning what you want to know, deciding who may have that information, and then communicating with those individuals.

The responses to most of the questions you will need to ask may well need clarification, and so verbal communication may be the best medium. It is possible that an investigation of this nature could be construed by the employees as a 'witch hunt' – to avoid this face-to-face verbal communication will give an opportunity for non-verbal communication to reinforce your concern and support for the team, rather than giving the impression that you are looking for someone to blame.

For the collection of figures from your main office a written medium could be used, although the use of technology may speed up the process.

Do not forget that throughout your investigation you will also have to remain in regular communication with your Board of Directors. You may also have to deal with the media, if news in your downturn in sales becomes public knowledge. Failure to do this may have an adverse effect on your share price.

In a situation like this you will need free access to any member of the sales team and thus any network other than an all channel one would hinder the process.

Answer to Assignment 10

Your answer should address the following issues.

As an organisation, what is our objective when dealing with this situation? Our objective is to protect our corporate image. We have a good reputation at present and how we deal with this situation may impact on future sales. We need to be seen as responsible and trustworthy.

Based on this objective we have no alternative other than to break the news of this potential problem before the media does. What approach should we take? The alternatives are:

(a) tell the press that there is scare mongering going on and the product is safe

(b) tell the press that a potential problem has been found in the US but that it is due to the method of manufacture and does not apply in the UK

(c) tell the press that a potential problem has been found – we do not believe that the drug is related to the deaths but patients should visit their doctors to discuss the situation

(d) tell the press that due to a potential problem the drug is to be withdrawn until further investigations can clarify if there is a problem.

Having decided on one of the above courses of action, we then need to ask: who needs to know, and what do they need to know? Your list should be divided into two sections, within the organisation and external to the organisation, and may include the following.

Internally

All employees. This could be done through meetings with unions, works councils and quality circles or by letter to each individual.

Externally

Legal bodies such as the licensing authority and government department. This may be done verbally backed up by written communication. All facts which are known will be needed including technical data.

The general public. This can be done through the various news media (press advertisements, editorial, news conferences). The message should contain information which a patient will need to know, i.e. how the news affects them.

Doctors who prescribe the drug will need detailed information in order to be able to advise their patients. This must be done in writing to reduce the risk of ambiguity.

All the channels of communication used should be of a formal nature. In a situation as potentially serious as this you cannot risk inaccurate information being passed on. It is not possible to prevent this altogether but it can be minimised.

If the organisation were to disregard the threat to their future corporate image they might decide to keep their heads down and hope that the story would never break. This could be considered an irresponsible and risky strategy for both the patients and the organisation.

Answer to Assignment 11

Your report should draw attention to the areas of potential conflict in terms of military wars and trade wars. The outbreak of trade wars, for example, could seriously disrupt supplies of key components. Political change in China, Taiwan and elsewhere could have dramatic effects. The specific market is turbulent also. There is fierce competition and bankruptcies are not uncommon. Escom's German parent went into receivership in 1996 bringing the closure of its UK subsidiary. You should consider which type of structure could respond most flexibly to change in both the general and specific environments given that rapid technical development and sudden political and market changes are both features of the industry.

Answer to Assignment 12a

You should have included the following points in your essay:

(a) The statement makes the assumption that money is the only means to motivate the worker. You should refute this by the use of motivation theories such as Maslow and Hertzberg. (See Core Module 3, Chapter 4.)

(b) The statement also assumes that there is no commitment on the part of the worker to the success of the organisation. You should refer to McGregor's theory X and Y. (See Core Module 3, Chapter 2, Section 3.4 and Chapter 15 of this book.)

(c) You should highlight the ways in which the needs and objectives of the individual can be aligned with those of the organisation by effective communications.

Answer to Assignment 12b

You should cover the aims of OD programmes and the process from preliminary planning to completion and evaluation, the role of the change agent and the three main areas of action programmes in OD – programmes to change behaviour, to improve problem solving and to make structures effective.

These should be explained in terms of the situation in the case study.

Answer to Assignment 13

Using a college as an example you would explain its nature as an educational institution run as a quango with the objective of providing education and training, you could quote the mission statement.

The visible signs of culture include such things as reserved car parking, the state of buildings and rooms, the way staff and students are accommodated and the publications and information. There are plenty of other indicators like the refectory provision, especially in the evenings. You may want to concentrate on one faculty.

National mores include the respect or otherwise for education, attitudes to study or earning, beliefs like the idea that professional staff do not strike and so on.

Answer to Assignment 14

The management style of a college is likely to vary from task – top management – to country club – in certain sections and departments. You should be looking for evidence of management style. The culture of a college may or may not help achieve its objectives, it depends on what the objectives are. Objectives may include research publication but the culture is strongly oriented to teaching. You should be careful to define the objectives and explain the culture. You may be able to make comparisons between departments.

GLOSSARY

All channel configurations all members of a group can freely communicate with other members.

Bureaucracy a form of organisation where tasks and duties are allocated to clearly defined positions in a hierarchy of authority which operates on the basis of rules and regulations to secure uniformity of action.

Chain configuration with this network the situation is much the same as with the circle configuration, with individuals only communicating with their immediate chain neighbours.

Circle configuration in this configuration the group has no defined leader. All members communicate with their immediate neighbours only.

Communication channel a route along which communication may travel.

Compulsory competitive tendering a process that has been forced onto public sector organisations by central government. It entails the obligation to ask for tenders to carry out specific activities on behalf of the organisation. This process has to be repeated at regular intervals (yearly or three yearly, typically).

Corporate identity the way in which an organisation presents itself to those outside by the use of such things as logo, livery etc.

Corporate image the way in which an organisation is perceived by those outside it.

Culture the shared values and beliefs of the members of an organisation. It encompasses codes of behaviour, levels of personal interaction and binds the members together to form a cohesive group.

De-layering the removal of one or more layers of middle management, accompanied by the devolving of responsibility and authority further down the organisation structure.

Debentures these are stocks, not shares, and represent a loan to the company. They are not part of the share capital. Debenture holders are creditors of the business and receive a fixed rate of interest. They take no part in running the company.

Deferred shares also known as founders' shares, these shares exist in some companies. The maximum rate of dividend on ordinary shares is fixed and any remaining profits after paying them and the preference dividend goes to the holders of deferred shares. This provides for the original founders of the company to benefit from its success even after they have transferred control to a wider shareholding. They sometimes also have a vote if there is a takeover bid.

Downsizing the term used to describe the contraction of an organisation so that it concentrates on its core activities.

Economies of scale economies that arise within a firm as output increases and average total cost falls. The economies arise from technical factors (such as employing larger, more efficient machines) and from such managerial factors as specialisation, bulk-buying and mass marketing.

Empowerment – employees are all given the right to take decisions relevant to their sphere of work which would previously have been taken by supervisors; teams are often empowered.

Feedback a response to communication which lets the message sender know that the message has been received and understood (or not, as the case may be).

Group a collection of individuals with a common interest and who share a common identity. A group has a leader, a set of social norms and a reason for its existence. It may be informal or formally established and its existence may be permanent or temporary.

Mission statement a statement that sets out an organisation's purpose in society in general terms describing what it exists to achieve.

Mores customs or conventions regarded as essential to, or characteristic of, a community.

Noise a term used to describe any external influence that interferes with or degrades effective communication (including, but not restricted to, audible sound).

Ordinary shares shares that receive a dividend determined by the Board of Directors according to the size of the profits. These shares are the equity and the holders own the company.

Organisation a clearly definable group of people who act together to achieve a common goal or set of objectives.

Organisation development a strategy for improving organisational effectiveness by changing the beliefs, values and structure of organisations through collaboration between an external consultant and the management of the organisation.

Organisational climate the way that the members of the organisation perceive its structure, rules, beliefs and behaviour.

Organisational culture the unique character of an organisation, made up of shared beliefs and attitudes, patterns of behaviour and other characteristics that can be observed by outsiders.

Outsourcing the term used to describe the process of employing outside contractors to perform tasks which, although not core activities of the organisation, were formerly performed in house. Examples can be cleaning, security, legal work and occupational health. Outsourcing should not be confused with outworking.

Outworking the term used to describe a formerly office based function being carried out primarily from the home of the job-holder. This form of working has become popular in the financial services and data processing industries. The effects on the organisation are (a) to reduce overheads on expensive office accommodation and (b) to access the pool of (predominantly) female labour who have childcare commitments that prevent them from taking office-based work. Outworking should not be confused with outsourcing.

Power distance is concerned with society's reaction to inequality. Some societies allow inequalities in power and wealth to grow, others try to reduce them as much as possible. In organisations the level of power distance is related to the degree of centralisation of authority and the degree of autocratic leadership. This situation continues because it satisfies the needs of both leaders and those without power.

Preference shares shares that receive a fixed rate of dividend before any other class of shareholder is paid anything. Some preference shares have the benefit of being 'cumulative', which means that any unpaid dividends are carried forward until there is enough profit to cover them.

Price/earnings ratio the P/E figure is the ratio of the price of the share on the market to the earnings per share and is a handy way of comparing the worth of holdings in different businesses.

Private sector that sector of the economy comprising all activities that are not government owned. Business organisations in the private sector that exist to make a profit include sole traders, partnerships, mutual societies and private and public companies.

Public sector that sector of the economy that includes all central and local government and public corporations that are government owned.

QUANGOs quasi-autonomous non-government organisations.

Redundancy the term used to describe superfluous or irrelevant information contained within a message.

Rituals repeated patterns of behaviour that have a symbolic meaning. In life we consider religious and historical ceremonies to be rituals. Within organisations, rituals can be the office Christmas party, or the way that information is passed on to various individuals within the organisation.

Shop floor level all those at the lower end of the scalar chain, not only those in the manufacturing industries.

Span of control the number of subordinates working to a superior. For example, if there are five workers reporting to a manager, the span of control is five.

Star configuration also known as the 'wheel' configuration, the star is the most centralised of the communication networks. It includes a 'link' person through whom all communication must travel. The 'satellite' individuals communicate only with the 'link' person (or department) and not with each other.

Strategic alliance – an arrangement with another organisation to co-operate in some way (for example, in jointly developing a new product).

Synergy the phenomenon by which the combination of two units produces more than the separate parts added together. Synergy arises from a merger when the new firm can shed costs and increase profits by cutting out duplication of activities, for example one of the sales forces.

Team a formal group created for a purpose. A team has a leader, an aim and a distinctive culture. It may be formed, for example, to consider the provision of hot drinks in vending machines, to determine corporate strategy, or to win the World Cup.

Y configuration in this network there is a key person at the linkage of the three arms of communication, but this does not result in clear leadership of the kind found in the star configuration.

INDEX

213

REVIEW FORM

NAME ....

COLLEGE ....

We would be grateful to receive any comments you may have on this book. You may like to use the headings below as guidelines. Tear out this page and send it to our Freepost address:

Clare Donnelly, BPP Publishing Ltd, FREEPOST, London W12 8BR

Topic coverage:

Summary diagrams, signposts, definitions, chapter roundups, and quizzes.

Activities, discussion topics and assignments.

Errors (please specify, and refer to a page number):

Other:

FIRST 50 SO

YOU SHOULD PLAY ON THE OCARINA

ISBN 978-1-5400-7002-9

Visit Hal Leonard Online at
www.halleonard.com

Contact Us:
Hal Leonard
7777 West Bluemound Road
Milwaukee, WI 53213
Email: info@halleonard.com

In Europe, contact:
Hal Leonard Europe Limited
42 Wigmore Street
Marylebone, London, W1U 2RN
Email: info@halleonardeurope.com

In Australia, contact:
Hal Leonard Australia Pty. Ltd.
4 Lentara Court
Cheltenham, Victoria, 3192 Australia
Email: info@halleonard.com.au

CONTENTS

ALL OF ME

OCARINA

Words and Music by JOHN STEPHENS
and TOBY GAD

1.
1st time D.C.
2nd time Fine

2.

D.S. al Fine
(take 1st ending)

ALL YOU NEED IS LOVE

OCARINA

Words and Music by JOHN LENNON
and PAUL McCARTNEY

AMAZING GRACE

OCARINA

Traditional American Melody

ARIRANG

OCARINA

Korean Folksong

Andante espressivo

HAMABE NO UTA

Words and Music by
TAMEZO NARITA

Andantino (♩. = 60)

BEST SONG EVER

Ocarina

Words and Music by EDWARD DREWETT,
WAYNE HECTOR, JULIAN BUNETTA
and JOHN RYAN

CARNIVAL OF VENICE

OCARINA

By JULIUS BENEDICT

CASTLE ON A CLOUD
from LES MISÉRABLES

Music by CLAUDE-MICHEL SCHÖNBERG
Lyrics by ALAIN BOUBLIL, JEAN-MARC NATEL
and HERBERT KRETZMER

OCARINA

CHOCOBO'S THEME
from FINAL FANTASY XII

OCARINA

By NOBUO UEMATSU

CIRCLE OF LIFE

from THE LION KING

OCARINA

Music by ELTON JOHN
Lyrics by TIM RICE

Moderately (with an African beat)

EVERMORE
from BEAUTY AND THE BEAST

OCARINA

Music by ALAN MENKEN
Lyrics by TIM RICE

Sturdy Ballad

FLY ME TO THE MOON
(In Other Words)

OCARINA

Words and Music by
BART HOWARD

FIGHT SONG

OCARINA

Words and Music by RACHEL PLATTEN
and DAVE BASSETT

17

THE FOOL ON THE HILL

OCARINA

Words and Music by JOHN LENNON
and PAUL McCARTNEY

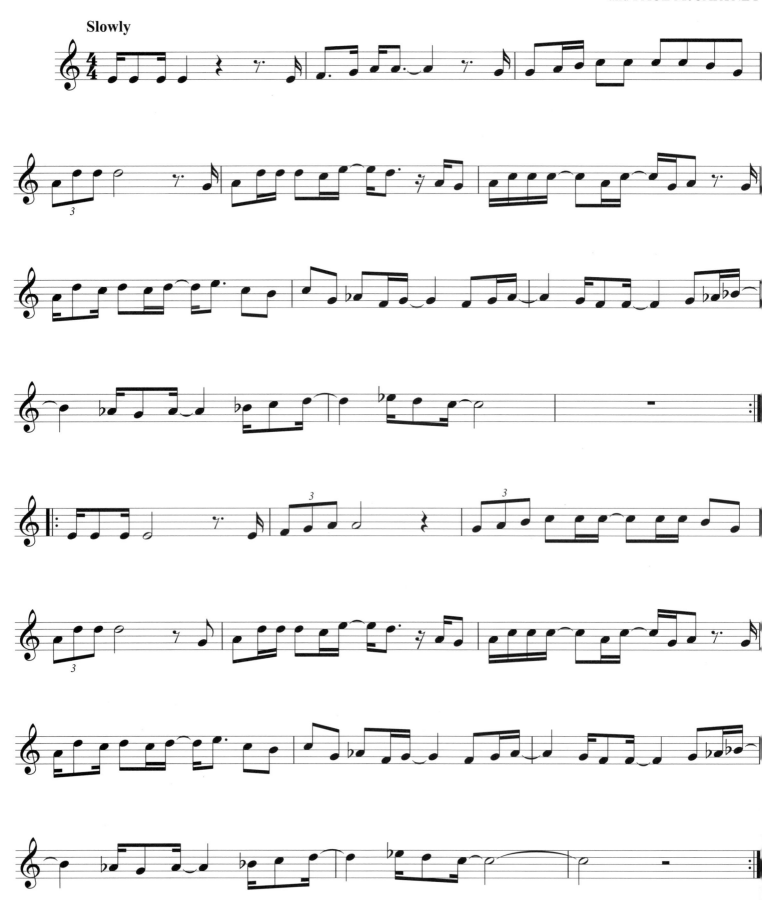

FOREST OF LOVE

OCARINA

Music by SOJIRO

GABRIEL'S OBOE
from the Motion Picture THE MISSION

OCARINA

Words and Music by
ENNIO MORRICONE

GOD BLESS AMERICA®

OCARINA

Words and Music by
IRVING BERLIN

Moderately

THE GODFATHER
(Love Theme)
from the Paramount Picture THE GODFATHER

OCARINA

By NINO ROTA

HALLELUJAH

OCARINA

Words and Music by
LEONARD COHEN

Moderately slow, in 2

SAKURA
(Cherry Blossoms)

Traditional Japanese Folksong

Gently

THE GOOD, THE BAD AND THE UGLY
(Main Title)
from THE GOOD, THE BAD AND THE UGLY

OCARINA

By ENNIO MORRICONE

HAPPY
from DESPICABLE ME 2

OCARINA

Words and Music by
PHARRELL WILLIAMS

HELLO

OCARINA

Words and Music by
LIONEL RICHIE

Slow Ballad

HELLO, DOLLY!

from HELLO, DOLLY!

OCARINA

Music and Lyric by
JERRY HERMAN

HOW DEEP IS YOUR LOVE

from the Motion Picture SATURDAY NIGHT FEVER

OCARINA

Words and Music by BARRY GIBB,
ROBIN GIBB and MAURICE GIBB

I WILL ALWAYS LOVE YOU

OCARINA

Words and Music by
DOLLY PARTON

ITSUMO NANDODEMO
(Always With Me)

OCARINA

Music by YOUMI KIMURA
Lyrics by WAKAKO KAKU

JUST GIVE ME A REASON

OCARINA

Words and Music by ALECIA MOORE,
JEFF BHASKER and NATE RUESS

JUST THE WAY YOU ARE

OCARINA

Words and Music by BRUNO MARS,
ARI LEVINE, PHILIP LAWRENCE,
KHARI CAIN and KHALIL WALTON

Moderately

LET IT BE

OCARINA

Words and Music by JOHN LENNON
and PAUL McCARTNEY

MAS QUE NADA

OCARINA

Words and Music by
JORGE BEN

LET IT GO
from FROZEN

OCARINA

Music and Lyrics by KRISTEN ANDERSON-LOPEZ
and ROBERT LOPEZ

Slowly, in 2

MY HEART WILL GO ON
(Love Theme from 'Titanic')
from the Paramount and Twentieth Century Fox Motion Picture TITANIC

Music by JAMES HORNER
Lyric by WILL JENNINGS

OCARINA

PURE IMAGINATION
from WILLY WONKA AND THE CHOCOLATE FACTORY

Words and Music by LESLIE BRICUSSE
and ANTHONY NEWLEY

OCARINA

NIGHT TRAIN

OCARINA

Words by OSCAR WASHINGTON
and LEWIS C. SIMPKIN
Music by JIMMY FORREST

Slow Blues

43

ROAR

OCARINA

Words and Music by KATY PERRY,
MAX MARTIN, DR. LUKE,
BONNIE McKEE and HENRY WALTER

ROLLING IN THE DEEP

OCARINA

Words and Music by ADELE ADKIN
and PAUL EPWORTH

SATIN DOLL

OCARINA

By DUKE ELLINGTON

SCARBOROUGH FAIR/CANTICLE

OCARINA

Arrangement and Original Counter Melody b
PAUL SIMON and ARTHUR GARFUNKEI

SEE YOU AGAIN

from FURIOUS 7

Ocarina

Words and Music by CAMERON THOMAZ,
CHARLIE PUTH, JUSTIN FRANKS
ANDREW CEDAR, DANN HUME,
JOSH HARDY and PHOEBE COCKBURN

SHAKE IT OFF

OCARINA

Words and Music by TAYLOR SWIFT
MAX MARTIN and SHELLBACK

STAND BY ME

Ocarina

Words and Music by JERRY LEIBER,
MIKE STOLLER and BEN E. KING

Moderately, with a beat

THE STAR-SPANGLED BANNER

OCARINA

Words by FRANCIS SCOTT KEY
Music by JOHN STAFFORD SMITH

STAY WITH ME

Words and Music by SAM SMITH,
JAMES NAPIER, WILLIAM EDWARD PHILLIPS,
TOM PETTY and JEFF LYNNE

Carina

STOMPIN' AT THE SAVOY

OCARINA

By BENNY GOODMAN
EDGAR SAMPSON and CHICK WEBB

Bright Swing

SUMMERTIME

from PORGY AND BESS®

CARINA

Music and Lyrics by GEORGE GERSHWIN,
DuBOSE and DOROTHY HEYWARD
and IRA GERSHWIN

TAKE ME HOME, COUNTRY ROADS

OCARINA

Words and Music by JOHN DENVER
BILL DANOFF and TAFFY NIVERT

UPTOWN FUNK

OCARINA

Words and Music by MARK RONSON
BRUNO MARS, PHILIP LAWRENCE, JEFF BHASKER, DEVON GALLASPY
NICHOLAUS WILLIAMS, LONNIE SIMMONS, RONNIE WILSON
CHARLES WILSON, RUDOLPH TAYLOR and ROBERT WILSON

A WHOLE NEW WORLD

from ALADDIN

OCARINA

Music by ALAN MENKEN
Lyrics by TIM RICE

YESTERDAY

OCARINA

Words and Music by JOHN LENNON
and PAUL McCARTNEY

Slowly

MORE GREAT OCARINA PUBLICATIONS

Christmas Carols for Ocarina
Arranged for 10, 11 & 12-Hole Ocarinas
30 favorite carols of the holiday season: Angels We Have Heard on High • Away in a Manger • Coventry Carol • Deck the Hall • God Rest Ye Merry, Gentlemen • It Came upon the Midnight Clear • Jingle Bells • Joy to the World • O Come, All Ye Faithful • O Holy Night • Silent Night • Up on the Housetop • We Wish You a Merry Christmas • and more.

00277990 ....$9.99

Christmas Favorites for Ocarina
Arranged for 10, 11 & 12-Hole Ocarinas
Play 23 holiday classics in arrangements tailored to this unique wind instrument: Blue Christmas • Christmas Time Is Here • Do You Hear What I Hear • Frosty the Snow Man • Have Yourself a Merry Little Christmas • The Little Drummer Boy • The Most Wonderful Time of the Year • Rockin' Around the Christmas Tree • Silver Bells • White Christmas • Winter Wonderland • and more.

00277989 ....$9.99

Disney Songs for Ocarina
Arranged for 10, 11 & 12-Hole Ocarinas
30 Disney favorites, including: Be Our Guest • Can You Feel the Love Tonight • Colors of the Wind • Do You Want to Build a Snowman? • Evermore • He's a Pirate • How Far I'll Go • Kiss the Girl • Lava • Mickey Mouse March • Seize the Day • That's How You Know • When You Wish Upon a Star • A Whole New World • You've Got a Friend in Me • Zip-A-Dee-Doo-Dah • and more..

00275998 ....$9.99

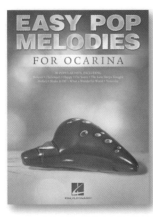

Easy Pop Melodies for Ocarina
Arranged for 10, 11 & 12-Hole Ocarinas
30 popular hits: Believer • City of Stars • Every Breath You Take • Hallelujah • Happy • I'm Yours • The Lion Sleeps Tonight • My Heart Will Go on (Love Theme from *Titanic*) • Perfect • Rolling in the Deep • Shake It Off • Some Nights • The Sound of Silence • Stay with Me • Sweet Caroline • Uptown Girl • What a Wonderful World • Yesterday • You've Got a Friend • and more.

00275999 ....$9.99

Folk Songs for Ocarina
Arranged for 10, 11 & 12-Hole Ocarinas
41 well-known songs: Alouette • Aura Lee • The Banana Boat Song • Follow the Drinki Gourd • Frere Jacques (Are You Sleeping?) Hava Nagila (Let's Be Happy) • Home on th Range • Hush, Little Baby • Joshua (Fit th Battle of Jericho) • Kumbaya • La Cucarach • Loch Lomond • My Bonnie Lies over th Ocean • My Old Kentucky Home • My Wil Irish Rose • Oh! Susanna • Scarboroug Fair • Shenandoah • Swing Low, Sweet Chariot • This Little Light of Min • Twinkle, Twinkle Little Star • Volga Boatman Song • When Johnny Come Marching Home • The Yellow Rose of Texas • and more.

00276000..$9.9

Hal Leonard Ocarina Method
by Cris Gale
The Hal Leonard Ocarina Method is comprehensive, easy-to-use beginner's guide designed for anyone just learning to play th ocarina. Inside you'll find loads of technique tips and fun songs to learn and play. Th accompanying online video, featuring auth Cris Gale, provides further instruction a well as demonstrations of the music in th book. Topics covered include: a history of th ocarina • types of ocarinas • breathing and articulation • note names an key signatures • meter signatures and rhythmic notation • fingering charts many classic folksongs • and more.

00146676 Book/Online Video...................................$14.9

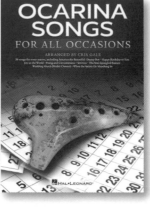

Ocarina Songs for All Occasions
Arranged for 10, 11 & 12-Hole Ocarinas
arr. Cris Gale
30 songs for every season: America, th Beautiful • Auld Lang Syne • Danny Bo • Hail to the Chief • Happy Birthday You • Joy to the World • The Old Rugge Cross • Pomp and Circumstance • Seviva • The Star-Spangled Banner • Weddin March (Bridal Chorus) • When the Saints G Marching In • and more.

00323196..$9.9

WWW.HALLEONARD.COM